HTML 4 For Dummies®

W9-BNR-762

Global Structure

`<!DOCTYPE>`	Document type
`<ADDRESS> ... </ADDRESS>`	Address
`<BODY> ... </BODY>`	Body
`<DIV> ... </DIV>`	Logical divisions
`<H1> ... </H1>`	Level 1 head
`<H2> ... </H2>`	Level 2 head
`<H3> ... </H3>`	Level 3 head
`<H4> ... </H4>`	Level 4 head
`<H5> ... </H5>`	Level 5 head
`<H6> ... </H6>`	Level 6 head
`<HEAD> ... </HEAD>`	Head
`<HTML> ... </HTML>`	HTML document
`<META>`	Meta information
`<SPAN> ... </SPAN>`	Span
`<TITLE> ... </TITLE>`	Document title
`<!-- ... -->`	Comment

Tables

`<CAPTION> ... </CAPTION>`	Table caption
`<COL>`	Columns
`<COLGROUP>`	Column group properties
`<TABLE> ... </TABLE>`	Table
`<TBODY> ... </TBODY>`	Table body
`<TD> ... </TD>`	Table cell
`<TFOOT> ... </TFOOT>`	Table footer
`<TH> ... </TH>`	Table head
`<THEAD> ... </THEAD>`	Table head
`<TR> ... </TR>`	Table row

Language Definition

`<BDO> ... </BDO>`	Bi-directional algorithm

Text Tags

`<ABBR> ... </ABBR>`	Abbreviation
`<BLOCKQUOTE> ... </BLOCKQUOTE>`	Blockquote
` `	Line break
`<CITE> ... </CITE>`	Short citation
`<CODE> ... </CODE>`	Code
`<DEL> ... </DEL>`	Deleted section
`<DFN> ... </DFN>`	Defined term
`<EM> ... </EM>`	Emphasis
`<INS> ... </INS>`	Inserted section
`<KBD> ... </KBD>`	Keyboard text
`<P> ... </P>`	Paragraph
`<PRE> ... </PRE>`	Preformatted text
`<Q> ... </Q>`	Short quotation
`<SAMP> ... </SAMP>`	Sample text
`<STRONG> ... </STRONG>`	Strong emphasis
`<SUB> ... </SUB>`	Subscript
`<SUP> ... </SUP>`	Superscript
`<VAR> ... </VAR>`	Variable text

Lists

`<DD>`	Definition description
`<DIR> ... </DIR>`	Directory list
`<DL> ... </DL>`	Definition list
`<DT>`	Definition term
`<LI>`	List item
`<MENU> ... </MENU>`	Menu list
`<OL> ... </OL>`	Ordered list
`<UL> ... </UL>`	Unordered list

...For Dummies: #1 Computer Book Series for Beginners

HTML 4 For Dummies®

Cheat Sheet

Links

`<A> ... </A>`	Anchor
`<BASE> ... </BASE>`	Relative addressing base
`<LINK> ... </LINK>`	Link

Inclusions

`<APPLET> ... </APPLET>`	Applet
`<AREA>`	Image map hot spot
`<IMG>`	Inline image
`<MAP> ... </MAP>`	Image map
`<OBJECT> ... </OBJECT>`	Object embedding
`<PARAM>`	Object parameter

Style Sheet Tags

`<STYLE> ... </STYLE>`	Inline style information

Presentation Controls

`<B> ... </B>`	Boldface
`<BASEFONT>`	Base font
`<BIG> ... </BIG>`	Big text
`<CENTER> ... </CENTER>`	Center
`<FONT> ... </FONT>`	Font appearance
`<HR>`	Horizontal rule
`<I> ... </I>`	Italic
`<S> ... </S>`	Strike through
`<SMALL> ... </SMALL>`	Small text
`<STRIKE> ... </STRIKE>`	Strike through
`<TT> ... </TT>`	Teletype text
`<U> ... </U>`	Underlined text

Frames

`<FRAME>`	Frame definition
`<FRAMESET> ... </FRAMESET>`	Frame group definition
`<IFRAME> ... </IFRAME>`	Inline frame
`<NOFRAMES> ... </NOFRAMES>`	Frame alternative

Forms

`<BUTTON> ... </BUTTON>`	Form button
`<FIELDSET>`	Set of fields
`<FORM> ... </FORM>`	User input form
`<INPUT>`	Input object
`<ISINDEX>`	Single line input
`<LABEL> ... </LABEL>`	Control label
`<LEGEND> ... </LEGEND>`	Fieldset caption
`<OPTION>`	Selectable item
`<SELECT> ... </SELECT>`	Select input list
`<TEXTAREA> ... </TEXTAREA>`	Text input area

Scripts

`<NOSCRIPT> ... </NOSCRIPT>`	No script
`<SCRIPT> ... </SCRIPT>`	Inline script

...For Dummies: #1 Computer Book Series for Beginners

HTML 4 FOR DUMMIES®

by Ed Tittel and Stephen N. James

IDG Books Worldwide, Inc.
An International Data Group Company

Foster City, CA ♦ Chicago, IL ♦ Indianapolis, IN ♦ Southlake, TX

HTML 4 For Dummies®

Published by
IDG Books Worldwide, Inc.
An International Data Group Company
919 E. Hillsdale Blvd.
Suite 400
Foster City, CA 94404
www.idgbooks.com (IDG Books Worldwide Web site)
www.dummies.com (Dummies Press Web site)

Library of Congress Catalog Card No.: 98-70136

ISBN: 0-7645-0331-6

Printed in the United States of America

10 9 8 7 6 5 4 3 2 1

1O/RQ/QS/ZY/IN

Distributed in the United States by IDG Books Worldwide, Inc.

Distributed by Macmillan Canada for Canada; by Transworld Publishers Limited in the United Kingdom; by IDG Norge Books for Norway; by IDG Sweden Books for Sweden; by Woodslane Pty. Ltd. for Australia; by Woodslane Enterprises Ltd. for New Zealand; by Longman Singapore Publishers Ltd. for Singapore, Malaysia, Thailand, and Indonesia; by Simron Pty. Ltd. for South Africa; by Toppan Company Ltd. for Japan; by Distribuidora Cuspide for Argentina; by Livraria Cultura for Brazil; by Ediciencia S.A. for Ecuador; by Addison-Wesley Publishing Company for Korea; by Ediciones ZETA S.C.R. Ltda. for Peru; by WS Computer Publishing Corporation, Inc., for the Philippines; by Unalis Corporation for Taiwan; by Contemporanea de Ediciones for Venezuela; by Computer Book & Magazine Store for Puerto Rico; by Express Computer Distributors for the Caribbean and West Indies. Authorized Sales Agent: Anthony Rudkin Associates for the Middle East and North Africa.

For general information on IDG Books Worldwide's books in the U.S., please call our Consumer Customer Service department at 800-762-2974. For reseller information, including discounts and premium sales, please call our Reseller Customer Service department at 800-434-3422.

For information on where to purchase IDG Books Worldwide's books outside the U.S., please contact our International Sales department at 650-655-3200 or fax 650-655-3295.

For information on foreign language translations, please contact our Foreign & Subsidiary Rights department at 650-655-3021 or fax 650-655-3281.

For sales inquiries and special prices for bulk quantities, please contact our Sales department at 650-655-3200 or write to the address above.

For information on using IDG Books Worldwide's books in the classroom or for ordering examination copies, please contact our Educational Sales department at 800-434-2086 or fax 817-251-8174.

For press review copies, author interviews, or other publicity information, please contact our Public Relations department at 650-655-3000 or fax 650-655-3299.

For authorization to photocopy items for corporate, personal, or educational use, please contact Copyright Clearance Center, 222 Rosewood Drive, Danvers, MA 01923, or fax 978-750-4470.

About the Authors

Ed Tittel is the coauthor of numerous books about computing and the World Wide Web, including *The CGI Bible* (with Mark Gaither, Mike Erwin, and Sebastian Hassinger) and *The Hip Pocket Guide to HTML* (with James Michael Stewart and Natanya Pitts, who also contributed substantially to this book, even though their names do not appear on its cover). These days, Ed aims his efforts at Internet programming-related topics, both as a writer and a member of the NetWorld + Interop program committee.

Ed has been a regular contributor to the trade press since 1987 and has written over 300 articles for a variety of publications, including *Computerworld, Infoworld, Windows NT Magazine, IIS Solutions,* and *NetGuide.* He also works for several online 'zines, including *Interop Online.*

Ed enjoys working at home, where his real job is perfecting his "universal tonic" — homemade chicken stock. When he's not pounding the keyboard, he's either out playing pool, burning calories, or using that stock in his kitchen to create culinary compositions for friends and family.

Contact Ed at etittel@lanw.com or visit his Web site at www.lanw.com.

Stephen Nelson James is also the coauthor (with Ed Tittel) of the best-selling *MORE HTML For Dummies,* 2nd Edition, and of *ISDN Networking Essentials* and *PC Telephony for Home and Small Office.* Steve has also authored numerous computer-related magazine articles, software user's manuals, and WWW pages. He is a former environmental biologist and ex-president/CEO of FYI, Inc., a software development company. When he's not writing or surfing the Net, you can find Steve out on the roads in the hills around Austin doing what he really loves best: riding his bicycle!

Contact Steve at snjames@wetlands.com.

ABOUT IDG BOOKS WORLDWIDE

Welcome to the world of IDG Books Worldwide.

IDG Books Worldwide, Inc., is a subsidiary of International Data Group, the world's largest publisher of computer-related information and the leading global provider of information services on information technology. IDG was founded more than 25 years ago and now employs more than 8,500 people worldwide. IDG publishes more than 275 computer publications in over 75 countries (see listing below). More than 60 million people read one or more IDG publications each month.

Launched in 1990, IDG Books Worldwide is today the #1 publisher of best-selling computer books in the United States. We are proud to have received eight awards from the Computer Press Association in recognition of editorial excellence and three from *Computer Currents'* First Annual Readers' Choice Awards. Our best-selling *...For Dummies*® series has more than 30 million copies in print with translations in 30 languages. IDG Books Worldwide, through a joint venture with IDG's Hi-Tech Beijing, became the first U.S. publisher to publish a computer book in the People's Republic of China. In record time, IDG Books Worldwide has become the first choice for millions of readers around the world who want to learn how to better manage their businesses.

Our mission is simple: Every one of our books is designed to bring extra value and skill-building instructions to the reader. Our books are written by experts who understand and care about our readers. The knowledge base of our editorial staff comes from years of experience in publishing, education, and journalism — experience we use to produce books for the '90s. In short, we care about books, so we attract the best people. We devote special attention to details such as audience, interior design, use of icons, and illustrations. And because we use an efficient process of authoring, editing, and desktop publishing our books electronically, we can spend more time ensuring superior content and spend less time on the technicalities of making books.

You can count on our commitment to deliver high-quality books at competitive prices on topics you want to read about. At IDG Books Worldwide, we continue in the IDG tradition of delivering quality for more than 25 years. You'll find no better book on a subject than one from IDG Books Worldwide.

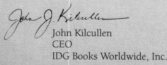

John Kilcullen
CEO
IDG Books Worldwide, Inc.

Steven Berkowitz
President and Publisher
IDG Books Worldwide, Inc.

Eighth Annual
Computer Press
Awards ≥1992

Ninth Annual
Computer Press
Awards ≥1993

Tenth Annual
Computer Press
Awards ≥1994

Eleventh Annual
Computer Press
Awards ≥1995

Author's Acknowledgments

Our biggest thanks go to our readers, who made the first, second, and third editions of this book such a success. Their feedback continues to improve our fourth edition! We have way too many folks to thank, so we'd like to begin by thanking everybody who helped us whom we don't mention by name. Actually, we couldn't have done it without you, even if we don't name you here! Thanks for your help, information, and encouragement. Please keep your e-mail coming!

Ed Tittel: I must share my thanks with many different constituencies. I'll begin with friends and family — thanks to Mom, Dad, Kat, Mike, Helen, Yvonne, Alex, and the "Florida Mafia." Second, a talented crew of technical people helped me over a variety of humps, large and small. I would like to specifically mention Mark Gaither, Dan Connolly, and David Strom. You guys are the greatest! Third, there's a whole crowd of other folks whose information has helped me over the years, especially the originators of the Web — most notably Tim Berners-Lee, Bert Bos, Håkon Lie, and the rest of the W3C team. I'd also like to thank the geniuses, sung and unsung, at NCSA, Netscape, Microsoft, and anyplace else whose Web collections I visited, for helping pull the many strands of this book together. I'd also like to thank Steve James for sticking with me from the first edition to the fourth!

Steven Nelson James: As always, a heartfelt thank you to Ed Tittel for his leadership and direction. My eternal gratitude to my family, Trisha, Kelly, and Chris for their understanding and support. And finally, a very sincere thank you to all of you who have purchased the prior editions of *HTML For Dummies,* thereby making this edition possible. Please continue to keep our e-mail filled with your great comments and suggestions.

Together, we want to thank the editorial staff at IDG Books Worldwide, especially Ted Cains, our copy editor; Robert Wallace, one of the mellowest and most professional project editors we've ever worked with (of course, our early submission of these materials made it easy for him to be calm); Ellen Camm, our latest — and greatest — acquisitions editor; Diane Steele, who let us keep this "strange torpedo" moving; and the other editorial and production folks, including Darren Meiss and Regina Snyder.

Please feel free to contact either of us, care of IDG Books Worldwide, 919 E. Hillsdale Blvd., Suite 400, Foster City, CA 94404. Ed's e-mail is etittel@lanw.com; Steve's is snjames@wetlands.com.

Publisher's Acknowledgments

We're proud of this book; please register your comments through our IDG Books Worldwide Online Registration Form located at: http://my2cents.dummies.com.

Some of the people who helped bring this book to market include the following:

Acquisitions, Development, and Editorial

Project Editor: Robert H. Wallace

Acquisitions Editor: Ellen Camm

Media Development Manager: Joyce Pepple

Permissions Editor: Heather Heath Dismore

Copy Editor: Ted Cains

Technical Editor: Kevin Spencer

Editorial Manager: Colleen Rainsberger

Editorial Assistant: Darren Meiss

Production

Project Coordinator: Regina Snyder

Layout and Graphics: Lou Boudreau, Angela F. Hunckler, Brent Savage, Todd Klemme, Janet Seib, Deirdre Smith, Ian Smith, Michael A. Sullivan

Proofreaders: Arielle Carole Mennelle, Christine Berman, Rachel Garvey, Nancy Price, Rebecca Senninger, Janet M. Withers

Indexer: Sharon Hilgenberg

Special Help

Joell Smith, Associate Technical Editor; Access Information Group; Stephanie Koutek, Proof Editor

General and Administrative

IDG Books Worldwide, Inc.: John Kilcullen, CEO; Steven Berkowitz, President and Publisher

IDG Books Technology Publishing: Brenda McLaughlin, Senior Vice President and Group Publisher

Dummies Technology Press and Dummies Editorial: Diane Graves Steele, Vice President and Associate Publisher; Mary Bednarek, Acquisitions and Product Development Director; Kristin A. Cocks, Editorial Director

Dummies Trade Press: Kathleen A. Welton, Vice President and Publisher; Kevin Thornton, Acquisitions Manager

IDG Books Production for Dummies Press: Beth Jenkins Roberts, Production Director; Cindy L. Phipps, Manager of Project Coordination, Production Proofreading, and Indexing; Kathie S. Schutte, Supervisor of Page Layout; Shelley Lea, Supervisor of Graphics and Design; Debbie J. Gates, Production Systems Specialist; Robert Springer, Supervisor of Proofreading; Debbie Stailey, Special Projects Coordinator; Tony Augsburger, Supervisor of Reprints and Bluelines; Leslie Popplewell, Media Archive Coordinator

Dummies Packaging and Book Design: Patti Crane, Packaging Specialist; Kavish + Kavish, Cover Design

◆

The publisher would like to give special thanks to Patrick J. McGovern, without whom this book would not have been possible.

◆

Contents at a Glance

Cartoons at a Glance

By Rich Tennant

page 59

page 319

page 7

page 213

page 341

Fax: 978-546-7747 • E-mail: the5wave@tiac.net

Table of Contents

Chapter 7: Introducing the Unrepresentable: HTML Entities 179

Chapter 8: Building Basic HTML Documents 193

Part III: Advanced HTML 213

Chapter 9: Using HTML Tables Effectively 215

Introduction

. . . .

*W*elcome to the wild, wacky, and wonderful possibilities inherent in the World Wide Web. In this book, we introduce you to the mysteries of the HyperText Markup Language used to build Web pages, and initiate you into the select, but growing, community of Web authors.

If you've tried to build your own Web pages before but found it too forbidding, now you can relax. If you can dial a telephone or find your keys in the morning, you too can become an HTML author. (No kidding!)

When we wrote this book, we took a straightforward approach to telling you about authoring documents for the World Wide Web. We tried to keep the amount of technobabble to a minimum, and stuck with plain English as much as possible. Besides plain talk about hypertext, HTML, and the Web, we include lots of sample programs and tag-by-tag instructions for building your very own Web pages.

We also include with this book a peachy CD that contains each and every HTML example in usable form and a number of other interesting widgets for your own documents. We also include 12 extra chapters of materials on that CD, which discuss lots of important topics that we simply couldn't fit between the covers of the book. Finally, the CD also includes the magnificent and bedazzling source materials for the *HTML 4 For Dummies* Web pages, which you might find a source of inspiration and raw material for your own use!

About This Book

Think of this book as a friendly, approachable guide to HTML and to building readable, attractive pages for the World Wide Web. Although HTML isn't hard to learn, it can be hard to remember all the details needed to create interesting Web pages. Some sample topics you find in this book include the following:

- Exploring the origins and history of the World Wide Web
- Designing and building Web pages
- Uploading and publishing Web pages for the world to see
- Creating interesting page layouts
- Testing and debugging your Web pages

Although you might think that building Web pages requires years of training and advanced aesthetic capabilities, we must point out that this just ain't so. If you can tell somebody how to drive from their house to yours, you can certainly build a Web document that does what you want it to. The purpose of this book isn't to turn you into a rocket scientist; it's to show you all the design and technical elements you need to build a good-looking, readable Web page, and give you the know-how and confidence to do it!

How to Use This Book

This book tells you what the World Wide Web is all about and how it works. Then, it tells you what's involved in designing and building effective Web documents to bring your important ideas and information to the whole world — if that's what you want to do.

All HTML code appears in monospaced type like this:

```
<HEAD><TITLE>What's in a Title?</TITLE></HEAD>...
```

When you type in HTML tags or other related information, be sure to copy the information exactly as you see it between the angle brackets (< and >) because that's part of the magic that makes HTML work. Other than that, you find out how to marshal and manage the content that makes your pages special, and we tell you exactly what you need to do to mix the elements of HTML with your own work.

Due to the margins in this book, some long lines of HTML markup, or designations of World Wide Web sites (called URLs, for Uniform Resource Locators), may wrap to the next line. On your computer though, these wrapped lines appear as a single line of HTML, or as a single URL, so don't insert a hard return when you see one of these wrapped lines. Each instance of wrapped code is noted as follows:

```
http://www.infomagic.austin.com/nexus/plexus/lexus/praxis/
                 this_is_a_deliberately_long.html
```

HTML doesn't care if you type tag text in uppercase, lowercase, or both (except for character entities, which must be typed exactly as indicated in Chapter 7 of this book). To make your own work look like ours as much as possible, enter all HTML tag text in uppercase only.

Assume = Makes an A** Out of U and Me

They say that making assumptions makes a fool out of the person who makes them and the person who is subject to those assumptions. Even so, we make a few assumptions about you, our gentle reader:

- ✔ You can turn your computer on and off.
- ✔ You know how to use a mouse and a keyboard.
- ✔ You want to build your own Web pages for fun, for profit, or because it's part of your job.

In addition, we assume you already have a working connection to the Internet, and one of the many fine Web browsers available by hook, by crook, or by download from that same Internet. You don't need to be a master logician or a wizard in the arcane arts of programming, nor do you need a Ph.D. in computer science. You don't even need a detailed sense of what's going on in the innards of your computer to deal with the material in this book.

If you can write a sentence and know the difference between a heading and a paragraph, you can build and publish your own documents on the World Wide Web. If you have an imagination and the ability to communicate what's important to you, you've already mastered the key ingredients necessary to build useful, attractive Web pages. The rest is details, and we help you with those!

How This Book Is Organized

This book contains five major parts. Most parts contains four or more chapters, and each chapter contains several modular sections. Any time you need help or information, pick up the book and start anywhere you like, or use the Table of Contents and Index to locate specific topics or key words.

Here is a breakdown of the parts and what you find in each one.

Part I: Building Better Web Pages

This part sets the stage and includes an overview of and introduction to the World Wide Web, its history, and the software that people use to mine its treasures. It also explains how the Web works, including the HyperText Markup Language to which this book is devoted, and the server-side software and services that deliver information to end-users.

HTML documents, also called Web pages, are the fundamental units of information organization and delivery on the Web. Here, you also discover what HTML is about and how hypertext can enrich ordinary text. Next, you take a walk on the Web side and build your very first HTML document. You also work through a primer on basic Web page layout and design, to jump-start construction of your own HTML documents and Web sites.

Part II: A Tour of the HTML Basics

HTML mixes ordinary text with special strings of characters, called markup, that instruct browsers how to display HTML documents. In this part of the book, you find out about markup in general and HTML in particular. This includes logical groupings for HTML tags, a complete dictionary of HTML tags, and an equally detailed discussion of HTML character entities. Then, we build a basic HTML page by the numbers to help you understand that process thoroughly and completely. By the time you finish Part II, you should have a good overall idea of what HTML is, what it can do, and how you can use it yourself.

Part III: Advanced HTML

Part III takes all the elements covered in Part II and puts them together to help you build commercial-grade HTML documents. This includes working with HTML tables, building complex pages, developing on-screen forms to solicit information and feedback, working with HTML style sheets, and creating clickable image maps to let graphics guide your user's on-screen navigation. After that you tackle how to create clear navigation aids in your pages and go through the steps involved in going live with a Web site.

Part IV: The Part of Tens

In the concluding part of the book, we sum up and distill the very essence of what you now know. Here, you have a chance to review the top do's and don'ts for HTML markup, to rethink your views on document design, and to catch and kill any potential bugs and errors in your pages before anybody else sees them. Finally, you end your adventure by revisiting your Web server situation, as you reconsider whether your pages should reside on an Internet service provider's Web server or you should build a Web server of your very own.

Part V: Appendix

The last part of this book contains an appendix that details what's on the *HTML 4 For Dummies* CD-ROM. As noted in the Appendix, the materials on the CD-ROM are organized into 12 separate modules and introduce materials that wouldn't fit into the book. The first three extras clue you in to additional capabilities of HTML and Web servers: Extra 1 covers HTML frames and how to use them in your Web pages; Extra 2 talks about the Common Gateway Interface (CGI) and other techniques you can use to create interactive Web pages or tie server programs into your Web world; Extra 3 introduces Dynamic HTML, which lets you do much of what CGI supports on a Web server on the client side of a Web connection instead.

Extra 4 covers the ins and outs of testing and debugging your Web pages, as you face down your all-too-human frailty and errors so that your users don't have to do this onerous task for you. You emerge from this extra with an understanding of alpha- and beta-testing protocols. Then, in Extra 5, you tackle the subject of soliciting user feedback, which can help to keep your materials fresh and interesting and your Web site in your users' best possible graces.

We devote Extras 6 through 10 to authoring, validation, site-management, and other software tools that can help you automate much of the work involved in designing, building, and maintaining a Web site. Extra 6 kicks off with an overview and explanation of the kinds of tools out there and how you might use them on your site. Extras 7 through 9 cover specific Web-oriented tools that UNIX, Macintosh, and Windows (in that order) users find most appealing. Then, Extra 10 caps off this information with the details on our own particular favorites from this set of tools, with a discussion of how and why we use the particular tools that we do.

Extra 11 covers ten ways to help you decide whether you should mount your own presence on the Web directly or host your Web site at an Internet service provider's location instead. Here, the idea is to uncover the financial and technical factors that may lead you to do this work yourself on your own premises, or to do it somewhere else on a third-party's Web server.

Extra 12 concludes the CD-ROM extension to the book with a glossary of technical terms from all the textual materials associated with *HTML 4 For Dummies,* including the chapters in the book and the extras on the CD.

By the time you make it through all the materials in the book and on the CD, you should be pretty well-equipped to build your own Web documents, and perhaps even ready to roll your own Web site!

Icons Used in This Book

This icon signals technical details that are informative and interesting, but not critical to writing HTML. Skip these if you want (but please, come back and read them later).

This icon flags useful information that makes HTML markup, Web page design, or other important stuff even less complicated than you feared it might be.

This icon points out information you shouldn't pass by — don't overlook these gentle reminders (the life you save could be your own).

Be cautious when you see this icon. It warns you of things you shouldn't do; the bomb is meant to emphasize that the consequences of ignoring these bits of wisdom can be severe.

When you see this spiderweb symbol, it flags the presence of Web-based resources that you can go out and investigate further. You can also find all these references on the Jump Pages on the CD that comes with this book!

This icon tells you that some additional related information is elsewhere in this book.

Text marked with this icon contains information about something that's on this book's CD-ROM.

Where to Go from Here

This is the part where you pick a direction and hit the road! *HTML 4 For Dummies* is a lot like the parable of the seven blind men and the elephant: It almost doesn't matter where you start out, you'll look at lots of different stuff as you prepare yourself to build your own Web pages. Who cares if anybody else thinks you're just goofing around — we know you're getting ready to have the time of your life.

Enjoy!

Part I
Building Better Web Pages

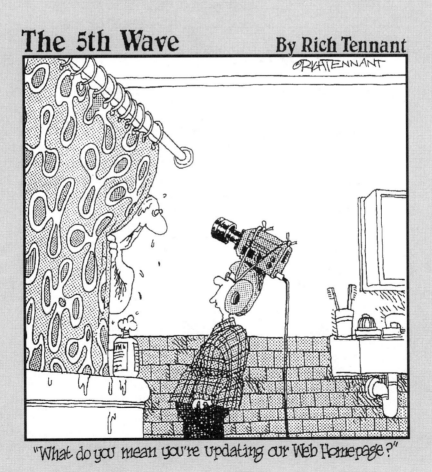

The 5th Wave   By Rich Tennant

"What do you mean you're updating our Web Homepage?"

In this part . . .

This part includes an introduction to the World Wide Web, explaining its history and the software that people use to mine its treasures. We also cover how the Web works, including the HyperTextMarkup Language to which this book is devoted, and the server-side software and services that deliver information to end-users. We show you what HTML is about and how hypertext can enrich ordinary text. Then you find out how to design and build your very first HTML document.

Chapter 1

The Web's THE Place to Be!

- -

In This Chapter

▶ Defining the World Wide Web

▶ Examining other Internet search tools

▶ Making the most of the Web — browsers and search tools

▶ Examining Web background and terminology

▶ Looking at exploding Web growth

▶ Interpreting Web pages

▶ Accessing the Web

- -

*T*o understand HTML, you must first understand the needs that it serves and the world in which it works. HTML *(HyperText Markup Language)* is a plain-text language that uses simple tags to support one of the most exciting information environments ever built: The World Wide Web (Web, WWW, or W3, for short). The Web represents a major step toward making all kinds of information accessible to average folks like you and me.

From Small Things, Big Things Sometimes Come

Tim Berners-Lee and his colleagues at the European Laboratory for Particle Physics (CERN) in Geneva, Switzerland, had no idea what they were starting when they hacked together a way for physicists to share research results with each other. Nevertheless, they started a strange and wonderful phenomenon that has taken the whole Internet by storm. Originally, they wanted to build an online system that enabled ordinary users to share data, without having to master arcane commands or esoteric interfaces. By 1992, users outside CERN were creating Web pages, too. This led to powerful, graphical browsers for a broad range of desktop computers and workstations. By 1993, the Web had become the most popular and powerful Internet tool of all. Today, the Web rules supreme!

To use the Web, you need a way to access the Internet, a Web browser, and a place to start. After that, you can scan the information that shows up on your screen and follow chains of information for the rest of your life (without ever again having to come up for air).

But wait a minute! Before you get lost in the Web's infinite strands, you may want to consider a few more details about how the Web works. (But we won't stop you from trying out the Web — just check in here when you come back!)

What is the Web, and where is it strung?

By now, you probably have a vague idea that the Web consists of a vast, amorphous blob of text, image, audio, and video data that is scattered across networks and computers worldwide. Hence the name, World Wide Web.

And now, a word from our sponsor . . .

According to Tim Berners-Lee, one of the Web's chief architects (and a founding father in its original development), "The World Wide Web is conceived as a seamless world in which ALL information, from any source, can be accessed in a consistent and simple way." (This quote is taken from a Web page entitled *W3 Concepts* by Berners-Lee that is, alas, no longer publicly available.) By working with HTML, you can not only roam this seamless world, you can even contribute to the Web's growth and proliferation!

What's in the words?

As you read through this book, you may encounter some words of Web jargon you don't recognize. You may also encounter a fair number of acronyms, like HTTP, that don't make a lot of sense to you, either. Don't worry — this is pretty normal when tackling a new subject in the computer world, where gibberish is the norm, and acronyms proliferate like mushrooms! The good news is we've included a glossary on the CD-ROM that contains definitions for many terms you may not know, and for all the acronyms we could find herein. Therefore, if you see a word you don't know, check the glossary on the CD-ROM: You may find enlightenment there! If not, drop us an e-mail and make us explain the word to you; maybe we don't know what it means, either. . . . But if we do, the word will show up in the next edition, guaranteed!

Before the Web: Other Internet Navigation Tools

To understand the extraordinary impact of W3, you may want to look at previous Internet navigation tools. These other tools require considerably more user expertise than Web browsers do. While you take this trip down memory lane, please keep the following in mind: Although Web browsers can replace older Internet navigation tools, browsers can work with these tools as well. Through HTML links, browsers call on other services to locate and retrieve files, messages, and other goodies from the vast Internet storehouse of data.

FTP (no, it's not about flowers — that's FTD!)

FTP *(File Transfer Protocol)* is a cross-platform tool for transferring files to and from computers anywhere on the Internet. *Cross-platform* means that you can use a Macintosh or a PC to grab files from a UNIX or Windows NT box. Figure 1-1 shows a graphical FTP menu; notice the PC file system is on the left (what's on your machine) and the remote file system is on the right (what's on the FTP server).

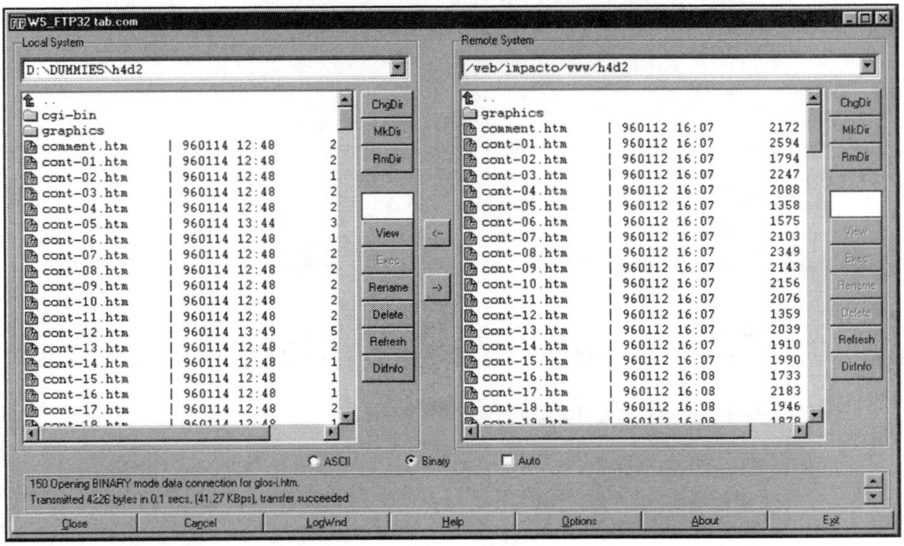

Figure 1-1:
A graphical
view of FTP.

By navigating the directories shown, you can copy files between these two systems, as your access rights allow. In English, "navigating the directories" means finding the directories where the files you want reside; and "access rights" refer to your ability to do things (like copy, delete, or update) to files on the FTP server. News Flash! You can access and transfer FTP files directly from your Web browser, because it knows how to do the job.

Burrowing around in Gopherspace

Gopher was created by a team of dedicated programmers at the University of Minnesota, home of "The Golden Gophers" athletic teams. More than a totemic animal, Gopher is a good tool for browsing files on the Internet. Gopher servers are extensively interlinked, much like the Web. In addition, all Gopher interaction occurs through a consistent menu interface that makes all systems look alike, as in Figure 1-2. You can search any Gopher server by keyword or filename, so that you have considerable flexibility when finding your way around. As with FTP, a Web browser can access gopher resources, too.

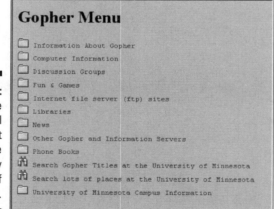

Figure 1-2:
The primeval Gopher at the University of Minnesota.

The beauty of mailing lists and electronic mail

A little-known bit of trivia is that you can find much information on the Internet through e-mail and tools like FTP and Gopher. By stating a request to the right e-mail servers — thereby accessing mail service programs such as *listserv* and *majordomo* — users with sufficient savvy can get to just about anything on the Internet without touching anything but their keyboards. And — you guessed it — you can access e-mail in most modern Web browsers, too!

Usenet

Usenet is a worldwide message system in which anyone can read and post articles (see Figure 1-3). Usenet organizes articles into *newsgroups* named by topic and focus. These newsgroups have varying degrees of internal organization — from strict moderation to freeform conversation. In some cases, you can approach Usenet with a specific question and come away with an answer immediately, but other queries may go unanswered for weeks. Persistence, coupled with an appreciation for Usenet's workings and the rules of proper Internet behavior (sometimes called *netiquette*), are your keys to success. Most up-to-date Web browsers let you access newsgroups.

To find out more about the Internet, take a trip to your local bookstore, where you'll find no shortage of Internet-related titles. (We counted well over 100 on our last visit!) You should pay particular attention to John R. Levine, Carol Baroudi, and Margaret Levine Young's *The Internet For Dummies,* 5th Edition (1998) and Levine and Young's *More Internet For Dummies,* 3rd Edition (1997), both from IDG Books Worldwide, Inc.

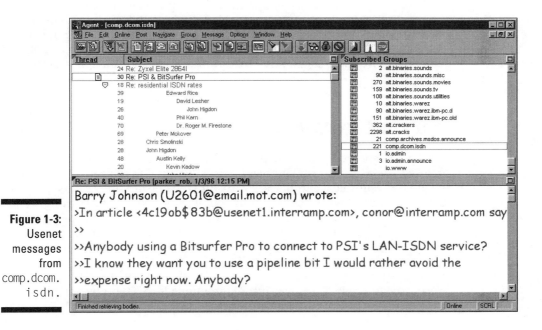

Figure 1-3:
Usenet
messages
from
comp.dcom.
isdn.

Why Is the Web a "Big Deal"?

We hope that you can come up with answers to this question on your own by now. But we'll run this one down, just to be sure: The World Wide Web represents a major development in information access on the Internet, covering an astonishing amount of ground. The Web also makes finding your way around huge collections of data easy and intuitive, while hiding most of the ugly details involved. Any one of these reasons makes the Web important and useful; all together, they make the Web a genuine step forward in the way we use and share information in our daily lives.

Of Browsers and Search Tools

For most ordinary users, their Web access software — called a Web browser or client — is the most important piece of Internet software they use. Today, you can find many browsers for PCs running Windows, a more limited selection for DOS-only machines, and several options for Macintosh, UNIX, and most other kinds of computers. All graphical Web browsers share a common, point-and-click approach to interacting with information. Even character-based browsers, like Lynx, make it easy to pick and follow links by selecting appropriate highlighted text. Here's a quick look at some of the players.

Internet Explorer

You get a version of Internet Explorer (IE), Microsoft's entry into the Web browser arena, as part of Windows 95 or Windows NT. You can also obtain the most recent release from the Microsoft Web site at `www.microsoft.com`. IE is "number two with a bullet" in the popularity sweepstakes among Web browsers (behind the Netscape browsers), and its stats just keep improving. IE's extensions include some proprietary, but powerful, programming extensions, and its inclusion with the best-selling desktop and server operating systems around (that is, Windows 95 and Windows NT) means that IE is a force to be reckoned with. As you'll see throughout this book, IE exerts considerable force over future directions for Web browser features and functions.

Lynx

Lynx is a text-only Web browser. That is, it can neither display nor deliver graphical or multimedia elements (although Lynx can display graphics using an external file viewer on appropriate systems). Even so, Lynx provides useful Web access for users on so-called *dumb terminals* (computers with no

processing capabilities that rely on a central computer), because Lynx
supports keyboard navigation and boldface display of hypertext links
(which is how the program got its name: Lynx = links. Get it?). The somewhat drab, but nonetheless effective, Lynx user interface appears in
Figure 1-4.

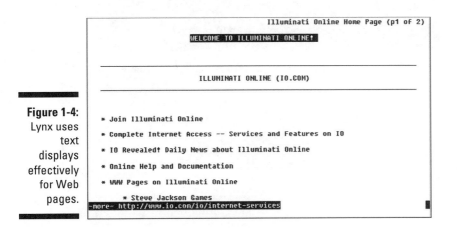

Figure 1-4:
Lynx uses
text
displays
effectively
for Web
pages.

Mosaic

Mosaic is a graphical Web browser developed by a team of programmers at
the National Center for Supercomputing Applications (NCSA). One of
Mosaic's original programmers, Marc Andreesen, left NCSA to form his own
Internet service company — Netscape. Mosaic was the first *full-featured*
graphical browser and has spawned many clones. While facing stiff competition from Netscape and Microsoft, Mosaic continues to hold its own against
these other browsers. You can find many flavors of Mosaic today, including
versions for X Windows (primarily for UNIX), Microsoft Windows, and the
Macintosh.

Netscape Navigator

Netscape Navigator remains the Internet's most popular Web browser,
offering clear evidence of its developers' wisdom and experience and
including numerous advanced capabilities. Navigator's list of features,
advancements, and add-ons boggles the mind — with additions made almost
daily. Available both as shareware and in commercial form, Navigator
provides one of the best and most popular Web interfaces that we've
encountered anywhere. The black-and-white shot of Netscape's home page
shown in Figure 1-5 can't capture all of Navigator's capabilities, but it's not
too bad!

Figure 1-5:
Even today,
Netscape
browsers
are still
used by
over 70
percent of
Web
surfers.

Uniform Resources on the Web

The World Wide Web's most significant feature is the ability to shield and even protect users from the unfriendly UNIX-derived environment on the Internet. With the Web, you can locate information simply: Web resources have special names — called URLs or *Uniform Resource Locators* — that describe the protocols needed to access a resource and point to each resource's Internet location.

URLs hold the keys to the Web

If you examine any URL closely, it looks something like this:

```
http://www.w3.org:8080/hypertext/WWW/Addressing/Addressing.html#spot
|—1—|———2——— |—3—|————————4———————— |———5———— |—6—|
```

This URL has six parts that work as follows:

1. **Protocol/data source:** For network resources, this part is usually the name of the protocol used to access the data that resides on the other end of the link. The syntax for this part of the name is as follows:

    • **ftp://** points to a file accessible through the File Transfer Protocol.

- **gopher://** points to a file system index accessible through the Gopher protocol.

- **http://** points to a hypertext document (typically, an HTML file) accessible through the Hypertext Transfer Protocol.

- **mailto:** links to an application through which you can compose an e-mail message to send to a predefined address.

- **news://** points to a Usenet newsgroup and uses the Network News Transfer Protocol (NNTP) to access information.

- **telnet://** links to a remote log-in on another Internet computer, typically to select from a predefined menu.

- **WAIS://** points to a Wide-Area Information Server on the Internet and provides access to a system of indexed databases.

- **file://** indicates that the file is local and not on a public Web page (that is, not available outside your directory). Use this syntax for local data (typically, HTML files from your desktop machine's hard disks or other drives), but note that syntax varies from browser to browser. If you're desperate for more information about accessing local files, see the sidebar "URL syntax and punctuation for local file access."

2. **Domain name:** The domain name for the Web server in which the desired Web page or other resource resides.

3. **Port address:** In most cases, the default port address for http is *:80* (and you can omit it), but you may see URLs with other numbers. When present, this number identifies a process address for a Web session. In general, if a number appears in the URL, you should include it.

4. **Directory path:** The page's location in the Web server's file system.

5. **Object name:** The actual name of the HTML file for the desired Web page or the name of any other resource that you require.

6. **Spot:** Sometimes, getting users to the HTML file isn't enough: You want to drop them at a particular location *within* the file. By preceding the name of an HTML *anchor* with a pound sign (#) and tacking it onto a URL, you direct the browser to jump right to a specific location. This is handy for large documents, where readers might otherwise need to scroll a long way to get to the information they need.

URL syntax and punctuation for local file access

When trying to access local files, look for a menu selection in your browser that lets you search your local file system (like "Open File" or "Open Local File"). If that doesn't work, we've had pretty good results with the following approach:

```
file:///<drive ID>|<directory
spec>/<filename>
```

Notice the three forward slashes after the colon. After the drive ID (which would be a letter for DOS or the volume name for Macintosh, NetWare, and so on), use a vertical bar character (|) in place of a colon. Then when specifying the directory path (spec), use forward slashes (/) to separate directory levels. Follow the path with the exact name of the file, and you should be able to access it with your browser.

If the preceding strategy doesn't work for you, look in your browser's Help file for enlightenment: Often, the solution is just a few screens away. Search for a phrase such as "Open file" or "Open local file," and you should get the information you need.

Make those URL keys fit

All in all, the most important thing to remember about URLs is to enter them *exactly as they're written,* because they don't work if they're not exactly right. When you use a Web browser, cutting and pasting URLs into a hotlist, bookmark, or text file is better than typing them out, because you reduce the possibility of error. You can also use the Add Bookmark or Add To Favorites features in Navigator and Explorer, respectively, when you come across a site you want to visit again.

For more information on URLs, consult this one:

```
www.w3.org/hypertext/WWW/Addressing/Addressing.html
```

This resource describes the details for URL syntax and supported protocols, and it points to specifications and other documents on the subject. A word to the wise: The W3C site gets a lot of traffic, so you may get timed out trying to connect. (In English, *timed out* means you wait forever, and then your browser tells you it can't retrieve the page!) We've had good luck getting there during off hours, like 3 a.m. Eastern Standard Time.

TIP

Extensions: `.htm` or `.html`?

As you develop your Web site and start creating links to your own HTML documents and to other sites, you'll find that ordinarily you use the `.html` extension when you key in a document's URL or when you create an HTML document. Some Web servers require all four characters in the file extension to recognize the `.html` extension in your Web document link. If the page resides on a server using DOS, the server ignores the fourth letter (the `l`).

Make sure that you change (to `.html`) the extensions of the `.htm` files that you upload from a DOS or Windows computer to a UNIX server (or make sure the server recognizes files that end in `.htm` as valid HTML files). In addition, simple Macintosh text editors (like SimpleText) don't place default `.htm` or `.html` extensions after a file name. So, Mac webmasters, keep a watchful eye on your extensions to maintain compatibility with PCs.

Danger! Explosive Growth

The word *exploding* conjures an image of something that's unsafe to crawl into, but exploding describes just how fast the Web is growing. Even though its introduction (in 1991) makes it one of the newest Internet applications around, the Web has already become the most popular Internet application of all. According to numerous sources, the Internet enjoys an annual growth rate of over 500 percent (or it increases 5 times each year, if you like smaller numbers)!

Wherever you get your statistics about W3, you find a unanimous opinion that Web usage is growing dramatically and user ranks are swelling robustly. The only real question then becomes, "How can I possibly find what I really need out there on the Web?" For Web publishers, this question translates into, "How can I let people know where my pages are?"

The following URL provides pointers to the references we consulted to compile our statistics. It's a list of pointers (also called *hotlist* in Web-speak) to sites ranging from the Library of Congress to collections of Web information and Internet resources:

```
lcweb.loc.gov/global/internet/inet-stats.html
```

A Scintillating Survey of the Web, Worldwide

At this point, you should have some idea about the Web's origins; now take a quick look at some of the many treasures that W3 offers.

Jumping-off points galore

Every browser comes with a predefined home page; many offer excellent starting points for exploration. Three browsers in particular — Netscape Navigator, Microsoft Internet Explorer, and NCSA Mosaic — offer outstanding home pages with "Starting Points," topic indexes, and search engines to help you locate items of interest. However, the Web is a mystical thing — whose circumference encompasses the world, and whose center is everywhere — so no "perfect starting point" really exists.

Search pages, anyone?

You can find a variety of search pages on the Web. These pages provide links to background applications, called *search engines,* that examine loads of data repositories on the Internet and, based on keywords that you supply, can return URLs matching the topics that you want.

The major search pages are nicely represented in a number of places, but we find the Yahoo! "Searching the Web" page most useful. The URL for this page is

```
www.yahoo.com/Computers_and_Internet/Internet/
            World_Wide_Web/Searching_the_Web/
```

Try it on for size; pick a search engine and try a search with a term of interest. (For best results, pick a specific term like *coriander,* instead of a general term like *spices.*)

As you travel the Web, pay attention to page layouts and to the use of indexes, graphics, and hotlists. You can glean a great deal from these examples, both good and bad. You can also select View Source in your browser to see the HTML that represents each page!

Under the Hood: How the Web Works

Now that you know what the Web is, where it came from, and what a big deal it has become, you can start to grapple with how it actually works. Despite the volume of connected information and the different ways of presenting and delivering that information, the Web works through a single basic set of mechanisms.

The Web is more than just the browser that you use on your desktop. The hidden structure of the Web is just as important as the utility you use to access it. The Web has two labor-handling sides: storage/retrieval and display/input. A Web *server* (located elsewhere on the network) typically handles the storage and retrieval part. The browser on your desktop (sometimes called a *client*) handles the display of information and recognition of input, when appropriate.

In the grand scheme of the computer world, this approach to handling information delivery is called *client/server computing*. Client/server has become an industry buzzword; nevertheless, the approach does confer some appreciable benefits:

✔ Because this approach divides the processing load, clients concentrate on providing the best possible user interface. Also, the client's location on your desktop simplifies showing cool graphical displays and powerful visual controls.

✔ Likewise, servers concentrate on maximizing their ability to handle lots of requests; this lets Web servers handle tens of thousands to millions of resource requests per day with ease.

✔ Another benefit of client/server derives from the location where servers store the information that clients use: Residence on a server makes information easy to share, permits better control, and lets information providers decide how much power and capability to provide.

✔ By keeping dollars and data concentrated in one place — at the server — a client/server approach helps maximize server performance (where it does the greatest good for the most users). A server environment also helps protect data through backups, rigorous controls over data access, and accurate logging of request statistics.

In short, clients handle user interaction, and servers provide rapid retrieval and delivery of information. Client/server capabilities are well-realized on the World Wide Web, which features powerful, graphical clients (browsers) and fast, powerful servers. By working together, these elements contribute to the Web's burgeoning popularity.

Networking Takes Protocols

In diplomatic circles, a protocol is a set of rules that keeps professionals — friends and enemies alike — from making fools of each other (or themselves). For networks, methods of bulletproof communication are equally necessary and appreciated. Thus, you shouldn't be surprised to learn that the rules and formats that govern the methods by which computers communicate over a network are also called *protocols*.

How Webs talk: The HyperText Transfer Protocol (HTTP)

HTTP is an Internet protocol for a specific application — the World Wide Web. It provides a way for Web clients and servers to communicate, primarily through the exchange of messages from clients (like "Give me this" or "Get me that") and servers (like "Here's the page you asked for" or "Huh? I can't find what you want").

To fully understand HTTP, you need to fully understand TCP/IP. A longish sort of acronym, *TCP/IP* stands for Transmission Control Protocol/Internet Protocol, which is the name given to the full set of protocols used on the Internet. But to begin writing good Web documents, you don't need to know much about either topic. Nevertheless, we have included a list of reference materials for you masochists out there.

Acronymophobes, beware!

One thing you have to realize, if you want to become a real webmaster, is that when you climb onto the Web, you join the Internet community. If there's ever been an unabashed bastion for acronyms — those multiletter combinations that nerds use to refer to things like personal computers (PCs); disk-operating system (DOS); random access memory (RAM); or compact disc, read-only-memory (CD-ROM) — it's the Internet crowd.

Because we're talking about Web lore, the term *webmaster* is a ubiquitous name for a person who holds the Web protocols on

high — a veteran of the Web trenches, who lives, eats, and breathes the Web. You may become good enough to be called a webmaster — someday!

So, if your most fiendish nightmare is of drowning in a bowl of alphabet soup, maybe you'd better rethink your Web-oriented efforts! Because networking in general, and the Internet in particular, is a field that revels in acronyms. And when you discuss Internet protocols, you find no better gathering spot for bizarre and obscure alphanumeric combinations.

TECHNICAL STUFF

Welcome to the Nebulous Zone . . .

In the Nebulous Zone, different kinds of computers freely exchange information with one another, and mere implementations bow to the demands of an all-encompassing standard. TCP/IP is a world unto itself: More bits use TCP/IP in a day on today's Internet than are required to store every piece of printed material known to humankind before 1950.

TCP/IP is so complicated and involved that covering TCP/IP in any depth is way beyond the scope of this book. Therefore, we'd like to give you some choice references:

✔ The Internet is the subject of at least two other ...*For Dummies* books: *The Internet For Dummies*, 5th Edition (1998) by John R. Levine, Carol Baroudi, and Margaret Levine Young; and *More Internet For Dummies,* 3rd Edition (1997) by Levine and Young. Both books are good places for beginners to start investigating the basics of TCP/IP.

✔ *TCP/IP For Dummies* by Marshall Wilensky and Candace Leiden (IDG Books Worldwide, Inc., 1995) is a great place to continue your TCP/IP investigations. In addition to covering the topic in wonderfully amusing detail, the book provides a hard-to-beat, but gentle, introduction to TCP/IP.

✔ O'Reilly & Associates covers TCP/IP with a Nutshell handbook for UNIX system administrators, *TCP/IP Network Administration*, by Craig Hunt.

✔ A truly definitive look at TCP/IP comes from Douglas E. Comer, author of *Internetworking with TCP/IP*, a three-volume set (Prentice-Hall 1996, 2nd Ed., 1991, 1993; Volumes 2 and 3 were authored with David L. Stevens). Comer's books are often regarded as the best general references on TCP/IP.

✔ The ultimate authority on TCP/IP comes from a standards body called the Internet Architecture Board (IAB). Within the IAB, the Internet Engineering Task Force (IETF) drafts and maintains Internet standards of all kinds, including those for protocols, in the form of numbered documents called *Requests for Comment* (RFCs). Table 1-1 has more information on RFCs.

For a listing of all current protocol-related RFCs, consult RFC 2200 "Internet Official Protocol Standards," which is available in at least three ways. (If 2200 is no longer current, it'll tell you it's been obsoleted by a new document, and you can follow a link to the new reigning standard.)

If you take the time to examine the RFC collection, you'll be going straight to the horse's mouth, where TCP/IP and related matters are concerned!

Table 1-1	Three Methods for Examining RFCs
Service	*Method*
e-mail	Send e-mail to `mailserv@ds.internic.net` and type **file/ftp/rfc/rfc2200.txt** in the message body.
FTP	Anonymous FTP to `ds.internet.net` (password = your e-mail address); look in directory **RFC/** for the file named RFC2200.TXT.
Web	`www.cis.ohio-state.edu/htbin/rfc/rfc2200.html` for the contents of RFC 2200.
	`www.cis.ohio-state.edu/hypertext/information/rfc.html` has general RFC information.

The straight dope on HTTP

Protocols that link clients and servers together must handle requests and responses. Consequently, you'll not be surprised to know that information exchanges on the Web happen in four parts, all classed as specific message types for HTTP.

✔ **Connection:** The client tries to connect to a specific Web server (your browser may display a status message like `Connecting to HTTP Server`). If the client can't connect, the attempt usually times out and the browser displays a `Connection timed out` message.

✔ **Request:** The client asks for a Web resource. The request includes the protocol to use the name of the object to find, and information about how the server should respond to the client.

✔ **Response:** Now, it's the server's turn. If the server can deliver the requested object, it responds with a delivery in the requested form. If it can't deliver, the server sends an error message explaining why not.

✔ **Close:** After the server transfers information to respond to a request, the connection between client and server is closed. You can easily reopen a connection with another request — for example, by clicking on a link in the current object — that jumps you back to reestablish the connection.

After it transfers a requested object, HTTP has done its job. Then, the browser must interpret and display what the server delivered, and another strand in the Web unfurls.

HTML: HyperText Markup Language

After the Web server returns the response to a Web request, the browser takes over to interpret and display the information.

HTML is a *markup language* that describes the structure of a Web document's content plus some behavioral characteristics. All Web browsers can understand and interpret this language. HTML is itself defined using a more complex markup language known as the *Standard Generalized Markup Language* (SGML — that's as much as you need to know about SGML to write Web documents).

HTML is a way of representing text and linking text to other kinds of re-sources — including sound, graphics, multimedia, and other types of files — that allows the concurrent display of different kinds of data and lets different resources augment and reinforce one another.

As delivered by a Web server, HTML is nothing more than a plain-vanilla text file. This file includes two kinds of text:

- ✔ **The content:** Text or information for display or playback on the client's screen, speakers, and so on.
- ✔ **The markup:** Text or information to control the display or to point to other information items in need of display or playback.

Also, a browser must convert a third kind of data — encoded files — and hand them off to the right kind of helper application if needed. This hand-off may involve a graphics program for an icon or image, a sound player program to handle audio, a video player program for a video file, or any other program necessary to reproduce a particular kind of information. Increasingly, however, such extensions find their way into Web browsers and are supported directly within the same general program.

HTML files include both control information (tags) and content (text), which together describe the appearance and contents of Web pages. HTML also provides mechanisms to tie in other Internet protocols and services on the Web — like FTP, Gopher, Usenet, e-mail, WAIS, telnet, and HTTP — so Web pages can deliver many kinds of resources.

Accessing the Web

A crucial ingredient in gaining access to the Web — the one that lives up to the "World Wide" in its name — is an attachment to the Internet. In fact, the biggest constraint on your enjoyment of the Web is likely to be the size of the pipe that connects you to the Internet (and it to you). The term *pipe* refers to how much data the connection between you and the Web server can accommodate; like a water pipe, the bigger the connection between you and your server, the faster things can move. Because waiting for screens to complete is a big drag, the faster the data goes, the better you'll like it!

Here are the two basic ways to establish Internet link-ups:

- ✔ Over the telephone system and into another computer or network that's connected to the Internet.
- ✔ Over a network and onto the Internet (or onto another computer that's properly connected).

Contact your ISP (Internet service provider) to get detailed information on how to maximize your speed and access to the Web.

Chapter 2

Getting Hyper

. . . .

In This Chapter

▶ Understanding basic HTML concepts

▶ Linking up the strands in the Web

▶ Looking for hypertext examples

▶ Getting past hypertext — to hypermedia

▶ Going for the graphics

▶ Dealing with multimedia display/playback

▶ Bringing multiple media together on the Web

. . . .

The real secret behind the HyperText Markup Language is that there is no secret: Everything's out in the open with HTML, just waiting for the right interpretation. The beauty of HTML is its simple content — it's just a stream of plain characters, which makes virtually any text editor a potential HTML generator. The challenge of using HTML is working within its boundaries. That is, HTML relies on the order in which characters occur and the way that they're used to produce the right results.

Even though Web browsers can be forgiving (when you use *some* browsers to view documents with *certain* omitted or misstated elements), the best way to use HTML is to understand and work within its structure. Because your readers can use so many different browsers, the only way to get consistent Web page appearance and behavior is to know the rules for creating HTML documents and to use them to your readers' advantage!

This chapter presents the fundamental ideas behind HTML and introduces the concepts and operation of hypertext. Along the way, we hope that you begin to appreciate some of the basic principles behind building well-structured, readable Web pages.

HTML Basics

HTML's name reflects the two key concepts that make it work (and that make the World Wide Web such an incredible phenomenon):

- ✓ **Hypertext:** A way of creating multimedia documents; also a method for providing links within and between documents.

- ✓ **Markup language:** A method for embedding special tags that describe the structure as well as the behavior of a document (not a way of discussing a preschooler's efforts with crayons on the wall!).

The simplicity and power of HTML markup lets anyone create Web documents for private or public use. The power of hypertext, with its built-in support for multimedia and document links, creates the incredible breadth and reach of the Web. Making Web documents is so easy and straightforward that anyone can do it — as long as you play by the rules.

Of Links and Sausages

HTML supports links within the same document, but also to completely different data elements elsewhere on the Web. Both types of links work the same way: Put the correct HTML tags around text or graphics to create an *active* (linked) area; when readers visit your Web site and click on the active area, the link transports them to another spot within the same file, to another document in the same Web site, or off to some other Web site. Figure 2-1 shows a *hotlist* that includes links to several resources on HTML. Each of these links connects to a valuable source of information on the Web.

Methods used to denote links vary from one browser to the next, but all browsers give some kind of visual clue that you've selected an active area on the screen. You may see text underlined in a bright color, a font change to boldface, or a graphic outlined in a contrasting color. You may see image maps in which your only visual cues are a changing set of coordinates (in the browser's status line) that correspond to the location of your cursor on screen. Using this kind of link is like playing an adventure game: You're not always sure where you're going or what you'll find after you get there!

Jumping around inside documents

One variety of link connects points within the same document; these are called *internal anchors*. Webmasters often use this kind of link to move readers from a table of contents (at the top of an HTML file) to related

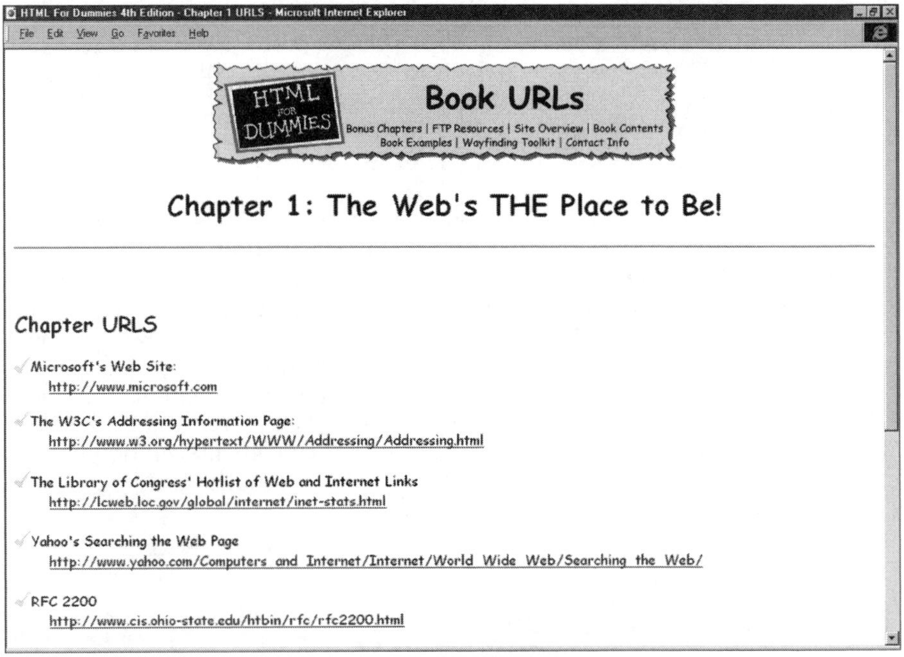

Figure 2-1:
A simple
HTML link
example.

sections throughout a document. Also, you can use this method to jump directly to the start of the document from its end — this beats the heck out of scrolling up through a long file!

Jumping around is a key advantage of hypertext — namely, the ability to circumvent the linear nature of paper documents and to provide rapid, obvious ways to navigate within (or among) documents. Sure, you can do the same thing with the table of contents or the index of a paper book by looking up what you want and flipping the pages yourself. But hypertext automates this task for you, so that you can effortlessly jump around inside and between documents by creating links that are a snap (or actually, a click) to use.

Jumping across documents (and services)

By using a combination of links and Uniform Resource Locators (URLs) on your pages, HTML can link your page to other Web pages, no matter where they reside on the Web. Because URLs can reference a variety of protocols and services on the Internet (not just other HTML files), you can link through telnet, WAIS, Gopher, FTP, USENET newsgroups, or even e-mail.

The same hypertext technology that lets you jump around inside a document also lets you reach any other resource available through the Web, so long as you know its exact URL (address). HTML's simple text-tagging technique erases the difference between here and there. With a single click of the mouse or selection of the right text field, you are there, or the information is here. . . . Anyway, you get it.

The Web as we know it today springs from the work of individual Web weavers who include links to other documents from their Web sites. That is, individual documents may constitute the contents of the Web, but the links among those documents reveal the Web's true nature. Hyperlinks make up the strands in the Web that tie people, ideas, and locations together.

Whenever you reference a URL in an HTML document, cut and paste that URL from a browser address window if at all possible. You save time on typing — some URLs can get pretty long — and even better, you get the reference right. For an additional check, test the URL with a browser to make sure that it's still valid after you copy it.

You've Used Hypertext, Without Knowing It

At this point, you may be saying something like, "What is this hypertext stuff?" Although hypertext may seem strange and exotic, you're probably much more familiar with it than you think. Your own desktop computer undoubtedly contains several hypertext applications that you use regularly.

For example, if you use Microsoft Windows, every time you run the Windows Help utility, you use a hypertext application. In addition, Figure 2-2 shows a screen that covers some of Microsoft Word for Windows' technical support options. Notice the three buttons on the upper portion of the screen shot: "Help Topics," "Back," and "Options." These buttons work like the navigation tools for a Web browser; they let you return to where you've been (Back), or examine the range of available links within a document (Help Topics and Options). The underlined phrases (such as <u>taskbar</u>) are links to text within the help system. They work much like the HTML links via your browser. In fact, Microsoft is in the process of switching its Help system over to use HTML directly!

Macintosh users can identify HyperCard or SuperCard as hypertext; they will also recognize our references to application Help utilities. Others will have to take our word for it and not assume that these are games of chance! Here again, hypertext applications have concepts in common with the Web, including some kind of home page, various navigation tools (shaped arrows and specific commands), multimedia data, and plenty of links to select.

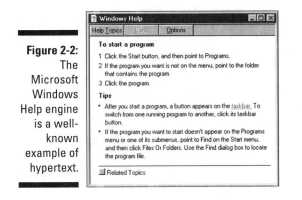

Figure 2-2:
The
Microsoft
Windows
Help engine
is a well-
known
example of
hypertext.

Likewise, UNIX users familiar with FrameMaker or other multimedia authoring tools can find common ground with the Web's hypertext capabilities. Yet again, the concepts of a home page, document navigation and linkage, and integrated multimedia help to realize the notion of hypertext and how it operates.

The difference between the preceding examples and the Web is in the kinds of links they support: Only the Web can jump across the Internet and follow links to other Web documents and servers. Enabling this ability gives HTML its unique value and, of course, makes the Web so popular.

Beyond Text Is Multimedia

If you include non-text files (like sound, graphics, and video) in Web pages, you must employ a certain amount of alchemy. Shipping Web information in a format called *MIME* (Multipurpose Internet Mail Extensions) makes it possible for a Web server to deliver multiple forms of data to your browser in a single transfer. Actually, MIME is a technique designed to bundle attachments within individual e-mail files. The following paragraphs tell a little more about how this works.

After a MIME file with attachments shows up at your workstation, additional processing begins immediately. The text portion of the message file arrives first. It contains a text-only HTML page description that lets the browser get right to work building and displaying the text portions of the page. Because the text arrives first, you may see placeholders or icons for graphics when you first see a Web page. Eventually, graphics or other forms of data will replace these placeholders as their related attachments arrive.

While a user views a Web page, the browser receives attachments in the background. As they arrive, the browser identifies these attachments by file type or by description information contained within an attachment tag (as specified by the MIME format or its associated Internet Media Type). After the browser identifies a file, it can handle playback or display. Table 2-1 shows a list of common file types used on the Web, including expansions for the inevitable acronyms that such files often invoke.

Table 2-1   Common Sound, Graphics, and Motion-Video Formats on the Web

Extension	Format	Explanation
Sound Formats		
.RA	RealAudio	Used with RealAudio Web Server and RealAudio Player add-on for browsers.
.SBI	Sound Blaster Instrument	Used for a single instrument with Sound Blaster cards (multi-instrument: .IBK).
.SND, .AU	8KHz mulaw	Voice-grade sound format used on workstations (such as Sun, NeXT, HP9000, and so on).
.WAV	Microsoft Waveform	Sound format used in Windows for event notification.
Still-Video (Graphics) Formats		
.GIF	Graphics Interchange Format	Compressed graphics format commonly used on CompuServe; easy to render multiplatform. Can be interleaved (displayed gradually) or not, depending on how image is created.
.JPEG, .JPG	Joint Photographic Experts Group	Highly compressed format for still images, widely used for multi-platform graphics.
.PDF	Portable Document Format	Adobe's format for multiplatform document access through its Acrobat software.
.PS	PostScript	Adobe's type description language, used to deliver complex documents over the Internet.

Extension	Format	Explanation
Motion-Video Formats		
.AVI	Audio Video Interleaved	Microsoft Video for Windows standard format; found on many CD-ROMs.
.DVI	Digital Video Interactive	Another motion-video format, also found on CD-ROMs.
.FLI	Flick	Autodesk Animator motion-video format.
.MOV	QuickTime	Apple's motion-video and audio format; originated on the Macintosh, but also available for Windows.
.DCR	Director	A "shocked" (animated) version of a Macromedia Director multimedia file.
.MPEG, .MPG	Motion Picture Experts Group	Full-motion video standard using frame format similar to .JPEG with variable compression capabilities.

Many Web sites contain large amounts of information on file formats and programs; here are two of the best that we turned up by searching on the string "common Internet file formats" at www.excite.com:

When other kinds of files need special handling (beyond the scope of most browsers), the browser hands off these files to other applications for playback or display. Such *helper* or *plug-in* applications have the built-in smarts to handle the formats and the processing needed to deliver on demand the contents of specialized file.

The process normally works something like this:

1. The browser builds a page display that includes an active region (underlined or outlined in some way) to indicate the attachment of a sound, video, or animation playback.

2. If the user selects the active region (the link), the browser calls on another application or plug-in to handle playback or display.

3. The helper or plug-in takes over and plays back or displays the file.

4. After the helper completes display or playback, the browser reasserts control, and the user can continue on.

A standard part of browser configuration supplies the names and locations of helper programs, or configures specially tailored add-ons called plug-ins, to assist the browser when such data arrives. If the browser can't find a helper application or plug-in, it simply won't respond to an attempt to display or play back the requested information. For plug-ins, however, most browsers can recognize what they're missing, and some (like Navigator or IE) will ask you if you want to add the missing plug-in to your current configuration.

For example, RealAudio is a common sound player plug-in for Web browsers, primarily for PCs running some flavor of Windows. As part of the configuration that occurs when you install a plug-in, associations between particular file types (like the .SBI and .WAV file extensions common on the PC) and the plug-in may be automatically established. Once this association is created, the browser automatically invokes the plug-in when it encounters files with those extensions. This causes the sounds to play (which, we assume, is a good thing!).

For comprehensive listings of PC, Mac, and UNIX plug-in or helper applications, and links to their sources, start your search at one of the following URLs:

```
browserwatch.iworld.com/
tucows.myriad.net/acc95.html
wwwhost.cc.utexas.edu/learn/use/helper.html
```

You should also check out both the Netscape and Microsoft sites for information about the latest plug-ins. (For example, Netscape has a link to a set of pages labeled "Plug-ins" in the "Software Download" section of its home page at home.netscape.com.)

Some useful helper applications for Windows include (visit
`www.shareware.com` for download locations):

- ✔ **For still graphics:** Lview is a good, small graphics viewer that can
  handle .GIF, .PCX, and .JPEG files. It also supports interesting image
  editing capabilities.

- ✔ **For video:** You want to use QuickTime for Windows (for QuickTime
  movies) or MPEGplay for .MPEG video files.

- ✔ **For PostScript viewing:** Ghostview for Windows works with a program
  called Ghostscript that allows users to view or print PostScript files
  from any source, including the Web. Because so many documents on
  the Internet have the PostScript format, we find these to be useful
  programs.

All in all, a good set of plug-ins or helper applications can make your
browser even more effective at bringing the wonders of the Web to your
desktop. With the right additions, your browser can play back or render just
about anything you run into!

The value of visuals

Without a doubt, graphics add impact and interest to Web pages, but that
extra punch comes at a price. You can get carried away by the appeal of
pictures and overdo using them on your Web page. (Overdoing applies as
much to those small images you use for buttons and on-screen controls, as
it does to large images that dress up a Web page.)

Therefore, when you use graphics, remember these two things:

- ✔ Not everybody that reads your page can see the graphics. Readers may
  not see graphics because they use a character-mode browser (that
  can't display them) or because they switch off their graphics displays
  (a common option on most Web browsers to conserve *bandwidth,* or
  their ability to move data, and to improve response time).

- ✔ Graphics files — even compressed ones — can sometimes be quite
  large, often ten or more times bigger than the HTML files to which they
  belong. Moving graphics takes time and consumes bandwidth. Also, it
  penalizes users with slower modems far more than it penalizes those
  attached directly to the Internet.

Sometimes graphics are essential — for example, when using a diagram or
illustration to explain your material. At other times, impact is important —
such as on a home page where you make a first impression. Under these
circumstances, using graphics is perfectly appropriate, but be sensitive to
the different capabilities and bandwidths of your readers.

Think of the following rules of thumb for using graphics effectively in your Web pages. (As you examine the work of others, see what happens to your attitude when you find that they have violated some or all these rules.)

- ✔ Keep your graphics small and uncomplicated whenever possible. This reduces file sizes and keeps transfer times down.

- ✔ Keep file sizes smaller by using compressed formats (like .GIF and .JPEG) whenever you can.

- ✔ Create a small version (called a *thumbnail*) of a graphic to include on your Web page (an easy way to do this is by sizing your image on screen, and then taking a screen shot when you display it in the proper dimensions; usually 100x100 pixels or so). If you must use larger, more complex graphics, link thumbnails to full-sized versions of the graphics. This spares casual readers the impact of downloading large versions every time they access your page (and keeps Internet use under better control, making you a better *netizen*!).

- ✔ Keep the number of graphic elements on a page to a minimum. Practically speaking, this means at most a half dozen graphic items per page, where most items are compact, icon-like navigation controls and others are content-specific graphics. Here again, you want to limit page complexity and to speed transfer times.

Sometimes, the temptation to violate these rules can be nearly overwhelming. If you must break the rules, be sure to run your results past some disinterested third parties. (You can learn more about testing techniques in the Extras section on the CD-ROM that accompanies this book.) Watch them read your pages if you can. Listen carefully to their feedback to see whether you've merely bent these rules or smashed them to smithereens!

Also, remembering that not everyone who accesses your pages can see your graphics should help keep you humble. For readers who don't have graphical browsers, or who turn graphics off, try to think of ways to enhance their reading experience without graphics.

Mavens of multimedia

The rules for graphics go *double* for other forms of multimedia. If graphics files are large when compared to HTML text files, then sound and video files are HUGE. They are time-dependent; therefore, the longer they play, the bigger they are, and the longer the browser takes to download them to your computer. Although they're appealing and definitely increase the interest level for some topics, sound and video files are not germane to many topics on the Web. Use them sparingly or not at all, unless your Web site is an Internet radio show or movie theater.

With the advent of the smaller, faster display and interactivity tools for the Web (such as Java, VRML, and Shockwave), the Web employs more and more multimedia applications. Java *applets* work with Navigator, IE, and other browsers to allow quick display of animated graphics and other special effects. VRML (Virtual Reality Modeling Language) is similar to HTML but provides 3D viewing capabilities. Shockwave is the name of the Macromedia plug-in that allows Director movies to appear inside Web pages. Explaining these tools goes beyond the scope of this book, but you can look forward to using them in your Web pages, once you master the basics of HTML. If you want more information about these tools, check out these URLs:

- ✔ **Java — Sun Microsystems:** www.javasoft.com or java.sun.com
- ✔ **VRML:** www.vrml.org/
- ✔ **Shockwave and Director — Macromedia:** www.macromedia.com

Once again, the trick is to make large files available through links instead of including them on pages that everyone must download. Label these active regions with the size of the associated file, so that people know what they're in for if they choose to download the material. (For example: `Warning! This points to a 40K sound byte of a barking seal.`)

Bringing It All Together with the Web

Step back from multimedia hyperspace and back to the cyberspace world of your future Web page. Now that you understand the basic concepts behind the Web and HTML and have met (briefly) some tools of the trade, you should read the following paragraph carefully. It embodies the essence of all successful Web pages.

The three most important factors in building good Web pages are content, content, and content (Get the idea?). If content is well-organized, engaging, and contains links to interesting places, your Web site can become a potent tool for education and communication. If your Web site is all flash, sharing it can be an exercise in sheer frustration (and humiliation for the webmaster . . . that's you!). Therefore, if you put your energy into providing high-quality content and link your readers to other high-quality, content-filled pages, your Web site will be a howling success. If you don't, your site will become the electronic equivalent of a ghost town!

In the next chapter, you discover what's involved in using — and building — documents for the Web. Step into our parlor for a look at what's in (and on) a Web page.

Chapter 3

What's in a Page?

*T*he trick to understanding HTML lies in knowing how to separate the two components of the HTML file: the *content* and the *controls*. (Controls are also known as *tags* or *markup*.) You can present the majority of *content* in a plain text (ASCII) file with no tagging whatsoever.

If you look at an HTML source file, you see *markup* in the file that doesn't show up when your browser displays the page. Markup consists of the characters that show up within the HTML bracket markers (< and >) and control how characters appear on screen. If you're puzzled, don't worry — we have plenty of examples throughout the book.

The really interesting parts of HTML are the combinations of markup and content, such as the commands used to entitle pages or control textual guideposts — headers, graphics, lists of elements, and so on. Before you can read, write, and understand HTML, you must be able to mentally separate the structure of a document from its controls.

Building good Web pages requires that you understand the distinction between content and controls, and use each of them to their best effect. In this chapter, you begin to appreciate the components of a Web page, and you find out how to assemble these pieces to create readable Web documents.

It's All in the Layout

The human eye and brain are marvelous instruments, capable of scanning incredible amounts of material and zeroing in on the things that are most important to the reader. As a Web-page designer, your mission (should you choose to accept it) is to aid the reader in locating a page's salient features quickly and efficiently. Nothing communicates this concern — or your lack of it — more quickly than a document's layout.

Layout is the overall arrangement of the elements in a document. Layout isn't concerned with the placement of individual text elements on a page. Instead, layout involves the number of elements, how you arrange them, and how much white space surrounds them.

The layout of a document — whether a Web page, a letter to your sister, or an advertisement in a magazine — is a crucial part of communicating with users. For materials in which reader interest is mandatory, layout may not appear to be of concern (this may explain why tax forms look boring). For documents in which interest must be generated, layout is nearly as important as the information that such documents deliver.

Think of all the boring textbooks that you've slogged (slept?) through, with pages and pages of text and the occasional graphic crammed between two half-page paragraphs. By comparison, think of a magazine or television advertisement that you've seen recently. The people who designed the advertising grabbed your interest by creating eye-catching images, using appealing language, and delivering arresting combinations of elements.

When it comes to building Web pages, your job can be as challenging as the one faced by advertising designers. You shouldn't assume that your material is of such great interest to the world that your Web pages can stress content at the expense of layout. You're up against millions of other sites on the WWW. Even if your site's content is completely unique, you encourage users to visit more often and to link your site to theirs by making your layout as inviting as possible.

Because attention to layout adds to the accessibility of any document, you do your users a service by building a good layout. At the same time that you make your page more pleasant to read, you deliver its content quickly and effectively, which is everyone's goal in the information age.

What Are You Trying to Say?

As markup languages go, HTML is simple and easy to learn. Unfortunately, this fact creates a nearly overwhelming temptation to rush out and build Web pages right away. In fact, you're probably wondering when we're going to get around to putting HTML tags on text here, aren't you? (Cheer up! We get to that in Chapter 4.)

Whether you're an individual who's trying to share information with others, or an organization seeking to advertise its products and services, the impetus to publish online ASAP is powerful. Nevertheless, we advise you to step back and do a little analysis and design work, instead of trying to build "killer Web pages" on the fly.

Who's listening?

Knowing your audience is critical to building Web pages that people can use. If you don't know who's going to visit your Web site, and why they should want to, you're just putting together a *vanity page* that a few Web surfers may visit once. We all know that vanity pages comprise the majority of the personal pages on the Web; but if you have a real reason for building your Web site, you want to know what it is and how to emphasize it to potential users.

More importantly, you must base your Web document design on certain assumptions about your audience. While this is true for both advertisements and for encyclopedias, the focus on form and excitement is a little more intense and urgent for ads than for encyclopedias. You could do worse than to create the initial interest and impact of an advertisement, but you want to go further than most ads and deliver the depth of content that your audience most likely wants, even if that content isn't encyclopedic in nature.

How can you get to know your audience? Think of it as a form of hunting: Identify your target group and then start hanging around their haunts, whether in cyberspace or in the real world. Watch and listen to them. When you recognize their interests, you can target their needs and duly consider the factors that can hook them into your content. You must deliver solid, usable information to your target group so that they come back for more and spread the word about what you have to offer.

Design springs from content — and intent

Web pages built around long documents with complex ideas take more forethought and are more difficult to design. That's a big surprise . . . NOT. Short, single-concept documents are not necessarily easy to make into good Web pages. No matter how long, short, complex, or simple your content, you need to follow this basic principle: Design springs from content, as form follows function. Also, remember the audience that you intend to reach and then emphasize the high points that your research shows interests your potential users.

Create an outline before you start writing (or creating HTML, for that matter). An outline helps you organize your information and determines the order of topics and your needs for graphics, sound, or other multimedia information. Finally, the outline also provides a blueprint as you construct the document that realizes its contents.

By identifying topics and major elements in your document, you highlight relationships between those components (and possibly between its components and other information sources on the Web). Therefore, outlining content plays a key role when establishing links and presenting your users with visual clues on how to read and navigate your document.

A matter of intent

The intent behind a document — to inform, educate, persuade, or question — also plays a major role in your design.

- ✔ If your goal is to inform, reduce the number of eye-catching displays and try to direct your users' vision to the highlights of the information your document contains.

- ✔ If your goal is to persuade or sell, try to hook users' attention with compelling visuals and riveting testimonials; then follow through with important details.

- ✔ If your goal is to question something, raise the issues early and provide pointers to additional discussion and related information afterward.

In each case, the goal behind a document strongly conditions its execution and delivery. That's why understanding your intent is so important.

Establish key messages

At the beginning of your document design process, you must answer the question at the head of this section — "What are you trying to say?" Approach this task by outlining key ideas or messages that you seek to convey and put the most important ones first. Then follow each main idea with any relevant information to make your case, prove your point, or otherwise substantiate what you say.

If you follow this exercise carefully, much of the content will emerge gracefully from your outline. Important relationships among various elements of your document (and other documents) will also reveal themselves as you work through the outlining process.

Think about superstructure and information flow

Superstructure refers to the formal mechanics of how you communicate a document's organization and navigation. It includes elements such as

- ✔ a table of contents
- ✔ a set of common controls
- ✔ an index
- ✔ a glossary of technical terms

In short, the superstructure is the wrapping that you wind around your content so that users can find their way to the information they want, and that helps them understand what they read or view. For any given document, you may not need every element of superstructure, but for most documents — especially longer ones — some elements of superstructure help, and others are absolutely essential.

- ✔ **The TOC (table of contents):** From a lifetime of exposure to printed materials, we expect a table of contents at the beginning of a document to lay out its topics and coverage. The beauty of hypertext is that you can build links that take users directly from any entry in the TOC to the corresponding information in the document. Thus, the TOC becomes not just an organizational map for your document but a convenient navigation tool.

- ✔ **Common controls for all screens:** To promote readability and familiarity within your Web site, include common controls in each individual document. Common controls can be a set of clickable icons (or text links for users with nongraphical browsers) that your visitors use to page backward or forward, to jump back to the TOC, or to return to your Home Page. If you include a search tool for keywords in the document, make the tool accessible from any document. Whatever you do, establish a common look and feel for your pages; then your users can navigate more easily. Consistency may be "the last refuge for the unimaginative," but it does promote familiarity and ease of use!

- ✔ **Index or search engine?:** Helping users locate key words or individual topics helps them get the best use from your content. Another great thing about hypertext is that an old-fashioned index may be unnecessary. Because your content is online and accessible to the computer, you can often replace an index with a built-in search engine for your Web pages.

Chapter 14 covers search engines, including tools to index your documents online.

✔ **A glossary helps manage specialized terms and language:** If you cover a subject that's full of jargon, technical terms, or other forms of arcane gibberish (beloved of experts and feared by newcomers), include a glossary with your Web pages. Fortunately, HTML includes a text style specifically built for defining terms, which, in turn, helps you to construct a glossary whenever you need one. You still have to come up with the definitions yourself — unless you can find a Web site with a glossary that you can link to your page. Ahh, the beauty of the Web!

Grab the audience's attention . . .

If you've ever watched a movie at a theater equipped with a THX sound system, you're probably familiar with the phrase "The audience is listening." It comes up at the conclusion of the THX demonstration, which usually happens immediately before the feature presentation.

The THX demonstration consists of a simple "THX" graphic that fills the entire screen. A loud, sustained orchestral chord, overlaid with a powerful pipe-organ note, accompanies the graphic. The musical effect starts quietly, builds to a peak over 20 seconds, and then fades away on a low pedal-tone that you swear moves the entire theater. The sensation is similar to standing at the end of the runway while a jet fighter comes toward you and takes off over your head at 200+ mph. It definitely (and almost deafeningly) gets your attention. Having raised the audience nearly out of its seats, the demonstration concludes with the modest phrase: "The audience is listening."

Even though we don't recommend this audio effect for most Web pages, we do encourage you to grab your users' attention when they first glimpse your page. Nothing does this as effectively as a tasteful image coupled with a brief, compelling introduction. Include information that tells why your page is important, what it contains, and how to get around. Get your users interested, get them oriented, and then they'll be hooked!

They're after the goods . . . don't get in the way!

After grabbing your users' attention, help them find your real content. Make your superstructure visible, but don't let it get in the way. If you include pointers that direct users to the details, make them obvious and easy to distinguish from the rest of a page. Overly complex designs, layouts, or flow of information hamper easy access to the content.

This advice translates into some important rules, particularly for introductory materials. Keep your welcome (home) page simple and elegant. Use short, direct sentences. Keep your focus on the topic(s) at hand. Use the superstructure to emphasize your content. For a complex Web site, include a link to an "About this site" page for those who want to understand the site's structure and function.

What should they remember?

It's well known that people exposed to new materials generally remember ten percent of the concepts — at best. When designing Web documents, keep asking yourself, "What 10 percent do I want my users to remember?" This question helps you focus on the important ideas so that you can direct the audience to them and reinforce those ideas throughout your Web pages.

Also true, if somewhat sad, is that most users remember a limited amount of detail as well. Remembering ten percent of concepts doesn't translate into remembering 10 percent of the overall content: Would you remember ten out of a hundred pages in a document that you'd never seen before? This sometimes means presenting less information than you might otherwise be inclined to convey so that you can concentrate on what's really important. Therefore, save yourself time and trouble, and focus on the important stuff right from the outset!

Also, don't be too ambitious: Strongly related concepts linger in memory far better than loosely linked or unrelated ones. As with so much else in life, maintaining your focus is the key to successful communication.

Meet the Elements of Page Design

Okay, the previous sections introduce you to some important design concepts for building Web pages. At this point, you should be ready to meet the elements that make up an HTML document. These elements may sound familiar, because many are integral parts of any well-written document. Others may be less familiar, perhaps because of the terminology or because the concepts — like hypertext links — don't equate with normal printed materials.

Nevertheless, the following building blocks make up Web pages. After we give you a tour of these basic elements, we discuss related information flows and design elements.

Tagging text

Including tags along with text is what separates HTML from any ordinary ASCII file. In HTML, tags are enclosed within angle brackets: For example, a document head is indicated by a `<HEAD>` tag. Most HTML tags travel in pairs, so that `<HEAD>` actually marks the beginning of a document head and a corresponding `</HEAD>` marks its end.

Some tags include particular values, called *attributes*, that help describe a pointer or a reference to an external data element. Other attributes label information to be communicated back to a Web server; still others add to the physical description of a display object (for example, the alignment or dimensions of a graphical element).

Attributes provide sources and destinations for links within and across documents: These attributes (called *link anchors* or *anchors,* for short) describe the relationship between two named locations in the Web, whether in the same or different documents.

A linked location is indicated by a document reference (for access to other documents), a location reference (for a point inside the same document), or a combination of the two (for a point inside another document). For more information on such links, please read about `<BASE>`, `<A>` (anchor), and `<LINK>` tags in Chapter 6.

Many HTML tags require that certain attributes be specified; others can take on optional attributes and values; still others never acquire attributes. You find out what's what as you discover the elements of document design presented in this book.

Titles and labels

Every HTML document needs a title to identify it to users. Titles have three other important aspects as well:

- ✔ Titles appear in hotlists, which makes them a navigation or selection tool for users who use them.
- ✔ Titles let robots (automated Web site searchers) grab a brief description of any HTML document; this makes entries within search databases more accurate and useful.
- ✔ Titles help you manage your documents, especially when they're complex and voluminous.

Whenever you display a Web document, the title shows up in the window's title bar. Figure 3-1 shows the window for an HTML Style Guide with the title, "Style Guide for online hypertext," prominently displayed.

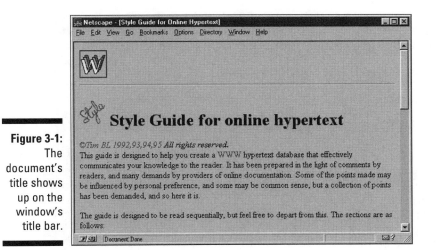

Figure 3-1:
The
document's
title shows
up on the
window's
title bar.

Labels aren't required but they act as a good document-organizing tool. Labels help to identify sections or topic areas in a document and provide better navigation for users, especially when you use them for links. As you see in Parts II and III of this book, if you use the NAME attribute inside an anchor, you can direct an HTML link to a named section in a document, as well as to the head of a document. Anchors also signal to other browsers, "To point to me, reference me by my anchor's NAME attribute."

```
<A NAME="Mexican Dove">Linda Paloma</A>
```

If some author, or even the original author, wants to link to the Linda Paloma area of the current document, all they need to do is create an HTML link definition by using the anchor's NAME (in this case, "Mexican Dove").

Text and hypertext links

Anyone writing HTML has only one kind of link available — a unidirectional association between a source and a target. But one kind of link has four uses:

- ✔ **Intradocument linking** provides a way to move from one location to another inside the same document.

- ✔ **Interdocument linking** provides a way to move from one document to another document.

- ✔ **Linking to an *agent* program** that acts on behalf of the Web server provides a way for an HTML document to handle a query or provide a service (such as information gathering).

- ✔ **Linking to a nontext object** provides a way to access graphics, sounds, video, or some other form of multimedia.

Interestingly enough, links inside HTML files to other types of data — like sound, graphics, motion video, and so on — enable HTML's hypertext aspects. Along with these external links, HTML's inter- and intradocument links create the connections that compose the Web. No matter how they're used, links define the Web's look and feel.

Overcoming two-dimensional thinking

Although hypertext is new and exciting, you may find it difficult to overcome the legacy of thousands of years of linear text. In other words, even though document designers can do nifty and creative things with linking and hypermedia, they have to fight a nearly overwhelming tendency to make their documents read like books. You must exploit the hypertext capabilities of HTML displays and links in appealing and useful ways, or your Web pages won't live up to their potential or the expectations of your users.

In the sections that follow, you have a chance to examine some common organizational techniques for building Web documents; you also encounter documents that can exist only on the Web.

Stringing pages together the old-fashioned way

Some pages demand to be read in sequence: for example, a narrative that builds on previous elements. For such material, string pages together as shown in Figure 3-2. If you have a document of five pages or more — if you believe Tim Berners-Lee in his *Hypertext Online Style Guide* — you should chain them together sequentially anyway.

Figure 3-2:
Chain
pages
together
to read
them in
sequence.

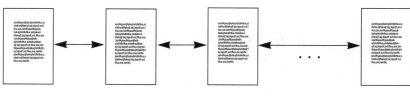

The nice thing about hypertext is that you can chain pages together forward and backward; then you can easily "turn" pages either way. Don't be afraid to include other appropriate links in this basic structure (such as links to other HTML documents, a glossary, or other points inside your document).

Hierarchies are easy to model in HTML

If you construct documents from an outline, a hierarchical approach to links should immediately make sense. Most outlines start with major ideas and divisions that you refine and elaborate to wind up with all the details of a complete work. Figure 3-3 shows a four-level document hierarchy that organizes an entire set of documents (perhaps even a whole Web site).

HTML itself has no limits on the levels of hierarchies you can build; the only limit is your own (and your audience's) ability to handle complexity. For both your sakes, keep yours from getting too big or too deep.

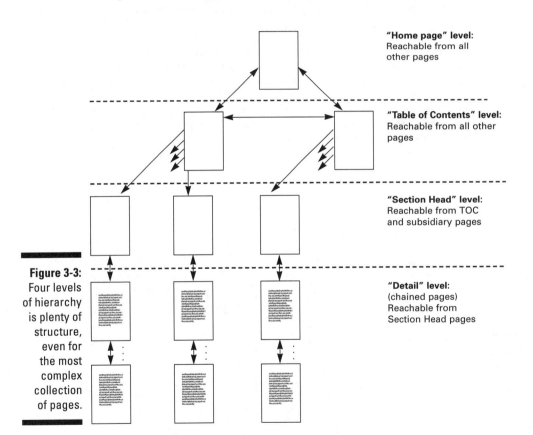

"Home page" level:
Reachable from all
other pages

"Table of Contents" level:
Reachable from all other
pages

"Section Head" level:
Reachable from TOC
and subsidiary pages

"Detail" level:
(chained pages)
Reachable from
Section Head pages

Figure 3-3:
Four levels
of hierarchy
is plenty of
structure,
even for
the most
complex
collection
of pages.

Multiple tracks for multiple audiences

It isn't unusual to build a document that includes different kinds of information to meet the needs of different audiences. By using HTML, you can easily interlink basic introductory documents (like a tutorial or technical overview) with in-depth reference materials. That way, your home page can point beginners to a tutorial and lead them through an overview before assaulting them with the down-and-dirty details of your "real" content.

This kind of organization, depicted in Figure 3-4, lets you notify experienced users how to bypass introductory materials and access your in-depth content directly. Such an approach lets you design for multiple audiences without lots of extra work.

The organization in Figure 3-4 differs somewhat from that depicted in Figures 3-2 and 3-3. It emphasizes links between related documents more than the flow of pages within those documents. In fact, the kind of document pictured in Figure 3-4 would probably combine elements from both a linear and a hierarchical structure in its page flows. Users would read the tutorial from front to back (or at least a chapter at a time), but they would consult the reference section by topic (and only rarely read all the way through).

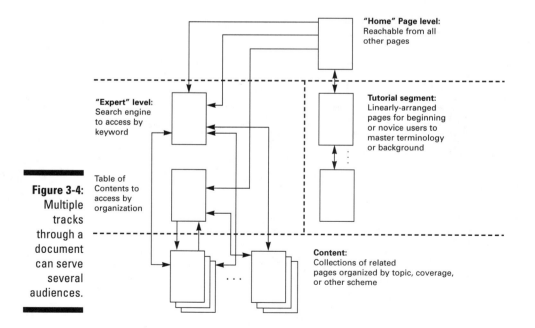

Figure 3-4: Multiple tracks through a document can serve several audiences.

"Home" Page level: Reachable from all other pages

"Expert" level: Search engine to access by keyword

Tutorial segment: Linearly-arranged pages for beginning or novice users to master terminology or background

Table of Contents to access by organization

Content: Collections of related pages organized by topic, coverage, or other scheme

A bona-fide Web wonder: The "hotlist" or "jump page"

Some of the best resources we've located on the Web consist of nothing more than lists of annotated references to other documents. These lists usually relate to one or more specific topics. You can see this kind of document structure in Figure 3-5, which shows a single page that points to multiple pages in various locations. In this example, the picture fails to do justice to the concept. For a better illustration, you need to look at a real Web page. Consequently, we advise you to check out the URL listed below — it's quite convincing as an example of what a good hotlist can do!

You can find more good hotlists on the Web than you can shake a stick at. Dan Kegel's collection of ISDN references is one of the true "seven wonders" of the Web: `www.alumni.caltech.edu/~dank/isdn/`.

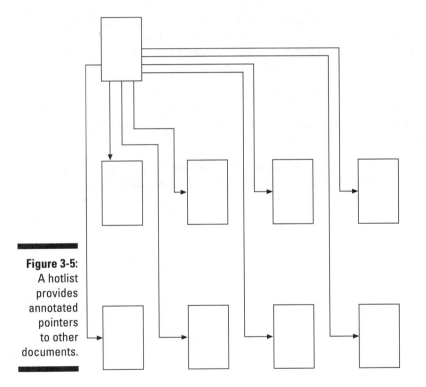

Figure 3-5:
A hotlist provides annotated pointers to other documents.

Extending the Web, a piece at a time

Another kind of Web page solicits input from users, who help to create an open-ended document. Users contribute comments, additional text, and hypermedia, or they add to an ongoing narrative. The structure of such a document is hard to predict and, therefore, hard to depict. Suffice it to say that this kind of Web document can grow like a coral colony, more by accretion than by prior organization or design.

For an example of this kind of living, ongoing document, consult the following URL: `bug.village.virginia.edu/`.

WAXweb is a hypermedia implementation of a feature-length, independent film, *WAX or the discovery of television among the bees* (David Blair, 85:00, 1991). WAXweb is a large hypermedia database available over the Internet. It features an authoring interface that lets users collaborate in adding onto the story. WAXweb includes thousands of individual elements, ranging from text to music, motion videos, and video transcriptions of motion picture clips. For users with VRML-capable browsers, WAXweb also offers a pretty nifty three-dimensional VRML implementation, as well.

The only limitations on how you structure documents are those imposed by your need to communicate effectively with your audience. After you realize that, you can use the various page flow and organizational techniques that we've outlined here for their best effects.

Now that you know the first building blocks of Web page design — layout and organization — it's time to initiate you into the world of markup languages. In Chapter 4, you discover what HTML looks like and how to create a simple document. Here comes the good stuff!!

Chapter 4

Building Your First Web Page

*A*t this point, you've read enough about HTML that you're probably itching to go out and build a page of your own. Your understanding of the details and the many capabilities of HTML will improve as you tackle the next sections in the book, but you've learned enough to try a few simple exercises. That's what we cover in this short, but tightly focused, chapter.

HTML consists of nothing more than plain ASCII text files, filled with special character sequences, called markup, and whatever content you might wish to communicate with your audience. (For more on the basics of HTML, check out Chapter 5.) In this chapter, we focus on the mechanics of putting the necessary pieces together to build a minimal, but working, HTML page. We also describe the typical process of creating the text, viewing it in a Web browser, making corrections or changes, and so on (which we call the "Edit-Review" cycle).

Building good Web pages means understanding how they're created the first time and maintained thereafter. Roll up your sleeves! This is a strictly hands-on set of exercises to get you up to your elbows in HTML.

Start with the Right Tools

Although you can find a myriad of tools built specifically to help you create and manage HTML pages, we think that a plain text editor does the job pretty well. That's why we recommend that you include a favorite text editor in your HTML toolbox, even if you use other tools. Because even if you decide to use an HTML editor like HoTMetaL, HotDog, FrontPage, or some other HTML-savvy piece of software to create pages, nothing beats a plain vanilla text editor for rapid post-creation tweaking or maintenance tasks. Even though we have lots of options available to us for building HTML pages, we still use a plain text editor as our tool of choice for most circumstances.

For more discussion of HTML tools of all kinds, please consult the CD-ROM that accompanies this book. (You find a general tool discussion there, along with discussions of our personal favorites, plus separate chapters for PC, Macintosh, and UNIX users.)

For PC users, a text editor like NotePad does the job quite nicely; for Mac users, SimpleText works pretty well; and for UNIX-heads, an ordinary text editor like *vi* is more than adequate for the task. We base the examples we show in this chapter on the version of Notepad that ships with Windows 95 and Windows NT.

If you absolutely must use a word processor of some kind, be aware that most such programs do not produce plain text files by default. That's why you have to remember to save any HTML files you create within your program as "text only" or "plain text." And no fair using the built-in "Convert to HTML" option, either!

The Edit-Review Cycle

The process of building an HTML file consists of typing in some HTML markup and some plain old text at the keyboard, saving the file, and then opening that file within a Web browser so you can see what you've wrought. Because seeing things you missed, misspelled, or just plain don't like is not unusual, you may end up continuing from that point in a cycle, like this:

1. **Make some changes in the text editor.**

2. **Save the changes in the text editor.**

3. **Open (or refresh) the file in a Web browser to check your work.**

This three-step activity typically continues until you obtain the results you want (or until the dinner bell, or some other interruption, pulls you from your work).

Time has no meaning when you build or tweak Web pages. Be prepared to lose hours, days, and sometimes even months of your life!

Check out this example. We start with the basic text that any well-formed Web page needs to make it both viewable and legal. Type the following characters into your favorite text editor, and save the resulting file as `test.htm` or `test.html`:

```
<HTML>
<HEAD>
<TITLE>My very first Web Page!</TITLE>
</HEAD>
<BODY>
"Hello World!"
</BODY>
</HTML>
```

After you type this material and save the file as test.htm, open your Web browser and look in the File menu for an entry that says something like Open (Internet Explorer lets you point at a file on your hard drive from this entry) or Open File (Netscape Navigator accepts a local file name here). Figure 4-1 shows what test.htm looks like from Internet Explorer.

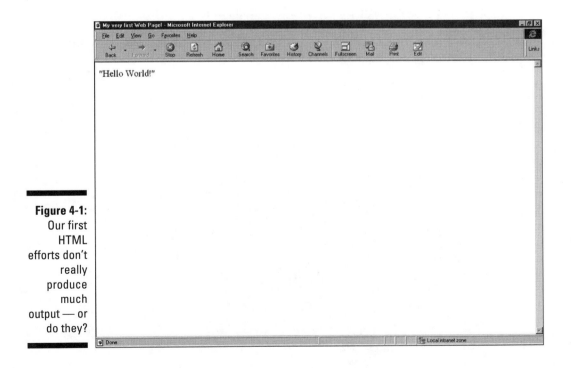

Figure 4-1: Our first HTML efforts don't really produce much output — or do they?

While the text that shows up in the browser's display window doesn't amount to much, you can see several noteworthy elements about this figure. First, notice that the text between the <TITLE> and </TITLE> tags appears in the title bar at the top of the Internet Explorer window. Also notice that the location of the HTML file you're viewing appears as C:\test.htm in the text box labeled "Address" just beneath the toolbar above the text display area. Notice also that one of the buttons on that toolbar is labeled "Refresh." From here on out, the Edit-Review cycle works like this:

1. **Switch to the text editor, enter some text.**

2. **Save the file in the text editor.**

3. **Switch to your Web browser, and hit the Refresh button.**

4. **Check your most recent efforts; if further changes are necessary, go back to Step 1!**

The most often overlooked elements of this process are (a) saving the file after making changes in the text editor and (b) remembering to refresh the browser display so that it shows the most recent version of your file. If you can remember to do these things every time, the Edit-Review cycle becomes a part of your basic page creation and maintenance activities!

Now, give the example a bit more substance. Return to your text editor, and make your test.htm file look like this one:

```
<HTML>
<HEAD>
<TITLE>Home Page: The Institute of Silly Research</TITLE>
</HEAD>
<BODY>
<H1>Welcome to the ISR!</H1>
The ISR is the world's best-known repository of truly tri-
fling and insignificant research results. Visit our pages
regularly to keep up with the exciting efforts of our team
of talented scholars, and their magnificent efforts to
extend the boundaries of science and technology to ever
more meaningless ends.
<H2>The ISR Staff</H2>
Dr. Maury Singleton-Smith, PhD, Director<BR>
Dr. Gwyneth Gastropolis, PhD, Chief of Research<BR>
Dr. Simon Schuster, MD, PhD, Head, Impracticality Dept.<BR>
<H2>ISR's Current Projects</H2>
Beyond Charm and Strangeness: The Nerdon<BR>
Lukewarm Fusion<BR>
Harnessing the Power of Stilton Cheese<BR>
The Dancing Louie Masters<BR>
```

```
<HR>
For more information about the ISR, please contact
<A HREF=mailto:nerdboy@isr.org>Dr. Singleton-Smith</A>.
All financial contributions are cheerfully accepted.
</BODY>
</HTML>
```

As you enter this text, you may find yourself dealing with HTML mistakes (remember to enclose all tags with < and >, and to precede the text for closing tags with a /). You may also find yourself dealing with typos, omissions, and other kinds of content errors as well. Just remember: Each time you make a change, shift back into your text editor to make the necessary changes. Then, save the new version of the file. When you return to your Web browser, refresh the page, and you see the results of your latest efforts. Keep at it, and you soon have a page every bit as insignificant and meaningless as the one shown in Figure 4-2.

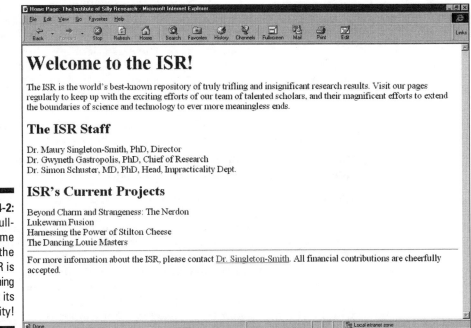

Figure 4-2:
The full-blown home page for the ISR is overwhelming in its triviality!

The real point behind the exercise, of course, is to familiarize yourself with what's involved in creating and editing an HTML document as you build a page to include on a Web site. As the process becomes more familiar, you can forget about most of these operational issues and concentrate on the content and formatting of your documents. By the time you create a few pages, all of this will become second nature to you.

Working with Templates

To make the job of building a Web page easier, we include a number of template files on the CD that accompanies this book (you'll find a collection of files in the /Template directory on the CD). You can use these files as a point of departure in your own Web page creation efforts, simply by copying them to your hard drive, and then editing them to get yourself started into the Edit-Review cycle that's so necessary to Web page creation.

Whenever you want to use a template as a point of departure for your work, save it under a different name as soon as you open it in your text editor. That way, you won't have to recopy the files from the CD each time you want to reuse the same template.

What Comes Next?

After you build an HTML document that looks just right and works the way you want, you have to move it from your local hard drive to a Web server somewhere to share it with anyone else. The exact details on how to do this varies tremendously, depending on where your Web pages live and what kinds of systems and services your Internet service provider offers. But in general, the process works something like this:

1. **Transfer the HTML file(s) and any graphics or programs they reference to a Web-accessible directory on your ISP's machine.**

2. **Access the files through the Web to note any relocation-related problems, and make any necessary changes.**

3. **Announce your new pages to the world!**

This general description doesn't do justice to the necessary details involved. Suffice it to say, we've seen FTP and e-mail based methods used widely to transfer collections of files, graphics, and programs from users to Web sites, and we've witnessed varying degrees of ISP support and involvement in bringing those materials onto the Web where other people can see them. The best way to understand and master those details is to talk to the technical support folks at your ISP. At least you know how to build an HTML document that you can look at and tweak on your own machine to your heart's content!

Part II
A Tour of the HTML Basics

The 5th Wave — By Rich Tennant

"We're researching molecular/digital technology that moves massive amounts of information across binary pathways that interact with free-agent programs capable of making decisions and performing logical tasks. We see applications in really high-end doorbells."

In this part . . .

In this part of the book, we cover markup in general, and HTML in particular. This includes logical groupings for HTML tags and a complete dictionary of HTML tags.

Chapter 5
What's a Markup Language?

*I*n this chapter, you get to see most of what HTML looks like. Hopefully, you also begin to appreciate what's involved in a markup language and better understand how to use HTML to create Web pages. Because this chapter is an overview, you won't be able to run right out and start building complex pages after you read it, but you should have a pretty good idea what pieces and parts make HTML do its thing.

A Markup Language Is Not a Form of Graffiti

HTML represents a way to take ordinary text and turn it into hypertext, just by adding special elements — called *markup tags* — that tell Web browsers how to display a Web page's contents.

A markup language gives programs (or humans) clues about the structure, content, and behavior of a document. Markup comes in two types: descriptive and procedural. A descriptive markup language, like HTML, describes the structure and behavior of a document. This lets authors concentrate more on content and structure, and less on formatting and presentation. Here's an example:

```
<H1>Cooking for One</H1> -- display level-one header
<OL> -- begin ordered (numbered) list
<LI>Take Lean Cuisine out of fridge.
<LI>Place in microwave.
<LI>Set timer for 5 min.
</OL> -- end ordered list
```

The tags H1, OL, and LI describe an object and its components. It's up to a browser to render these properly on your screen. In fact, from browser to browser, each of these objects could be rendered differently. But the important thing is that each browser has a meaningful way to display a first-level header (H1) and a numbered list (OL and LI). From a portability standpoint, this is a good thing.

The other kind of markup language, procedural, describes formatting rather than structure. An example is *troff,* a dinosaur UNIX markup language, which looks like this:

```
.center .12 .Helvetica .bold Table of Contents
```

troff tags tell the output device to render an object as "centered, 12 point Helvetica bold," like this:

Table of Contents

As you can imagine, this type of markup is not very portable and is difficult to maintain.

HTML tags not only govern how a browser displays the contents of an HTML document, they also control how a browser uses graphics, video, sound, and so on, to create a multimedia experience.

In the same vein, still other HTML tags tell browsers how to handle and display hypertext links, either within the same HTML file or to other documents or Web-accessible services. The key to building attractive, readable Web pages is knowing how to use HTML markup to highlight and organize your content.

Syntax is not a levy on cigarettes!

When it comes to any kind of formal, computer-readable language, invariably a set of rules governs its terms and their order of placement. This set of rules is called the *syntax* of the language. HTML syntax describes how a Web browser recognizes and interprets the instructions contained in the markup tags.

What makes HTML particularly interesting is that it's all pure text — in fact, HTML can work completely within the confines of the ASCII 7-bit character set (ISO 646), which contains only 128 distinct viewable characters. Nevertheless, HTML can handle display of so-called higher-order ASCII characters, which normally require 8 bits to represent directly and are sometimes called the 8-bit ASCII or Latin-1 character set (ISO 8859/1). Quite a bit of work is under way to permit HTML to handle the Unicode character set, which supports up to 65,535 different characters (of which over 34,000 are defined). The Unicode set includes non-Roman alphabets like Chinese (Han) ideograms, Hebrew characters, and lots of other interesting stuff.

This diversity lets HTML display things like accents, umlauts, and other diacritical marks often associated with non-English languages (or loan words, like *résumé*), by including instructions on what characters to represent as a part of the markup. In other words, HTML can provide instructions to a browser even if you can't always see things in the same format when you're writing the HTML. For example, <OL> and <LI> don't look like a numbered list inside a text file, but they do when the browser interprets them.

Elements of HTML syntax

The special control characters that separate HTML markup from ordinary text are the left and right angle brackets: < (left bracket) and > (right bracket). These characters indicate that the browser should pay special attention to what they enclose. And here's your big chance to learn another buzzword: *parser*. Inside the browser software, a parser reads and constructs display information. In other words, the parser examines characters in an HTML file, decides which elements are markup and which ones aren't, and instructs the browser to take appropriate action based on the markup it finds.

In HTML, left and right angle brackets can enclose all kinds of special instructions called *tags*. We devote the next several chapters of this book to introducing, explaining, and demonstrating the majority of HTML tags.

In the meantime, here's a formal introduction to the way HTML tags look and behave. A tag takes a generic form that looks something like this:

```
<TAG NAME {ATTRIBUTE{="VALUE"} ... }>Text{</TAG NAME>}
```

(By the way, text within tags is case insensitive, but for readability, we use caps to make HTML tags stand apart from other text.)

Take a look at the pieces of this generic form:

 ✔ <TAG NAME>: All HTML tags have names. For example, H1 is a level-one header; OL is an ordered list. Tags are surrounded by angle brackets to mark their contents for special attention from the parser.

✔ `{ATTRIBUTE{="VALUE"}...}`: Some HTML tags require or permit named attributes to be associated with them. Here the notation using curly braces — for example, `{ATTRIBUTE}` — indicates that attributes may be present for some tags, but not for others. In the same vein, some attributes require that values be associated with them, such as when supplying the name of an HTML document for a link; other attributes may not require associated values at all, which is why `{="VALUE"}` is also in curly braces.

For example, in an `<IMG>` tag used to point to a graphics file, a required attribute is `SRC` (source), to provide a pointer to the file where the graphic resides, as in `<IMG SRC="../gifs/redball.gif.">` This syntax proves yet again how important it is to stay close to your source! Finally, an ellipsis (. . .) indicates that some HTML tags may include multiple attributes, each of which may or may not take a value.

✔ **Text:** This is content that's modified by a tag. For example, if the tag were a document title, the HTML string

```
<TITLE>HTML For Dummies Home Page</TITLE>
```

would display the words "HTML For Dummies Home Page" in the title bar at the top of a graphical browser's window. Enclosing text within `<TITLE>` and `</TITLE>` tags marks it as the document's title.

✔ `{</TAG NAME>}`: A closing tag name is denoted by a left angle bracket (`<`), followed by a forward slash (`/`), then the tag name, and finally a closing right angle bracket (`>`). Curly braces indicate that this element does not always occur. Because over 70 percent of HTML tags require a closing tag as well as an opening tag, the omission of a closing tag is an exception, rather than a rule. Don't worry: Most, if not all, browsers simply ignore closing tags if they're not necessary.

The ampersand (&) is another special HTML control character. You can use it to denote a special character for HTML content that may not belong to a 7-bit ASCII character set (like an accent grave or an umlaut), or that may otherwise be interpreted as markup (like a left or right angle bracket). Such tagged items are called character entities and can be expressed in a number of ways. For example, the string `&egrave` produces a lowercase E with a grave accent mark (è), while the string `&lt` produces a left angle bracket (<).

Chapter 7 supplies the complete set of HTML character entities. If you work in a language other than English, you may consider building macros to replace familiar higher-order ASCII characters in your HTML files. Such macros allow you to automate a search-and-replace maneuver as a post-processing step. Then you can avoid keying seven or eight characters of HTML to produce one output character. (This is what computer science nerds like to call *an unfavorable input-output ratio!*) Even better, check out some of the HTML authoring tools described on the CD-ROM at the back of this book. Most of them automate this kind of thing for you.

TECHNICAL STUFF

Warning: Entering the Acronym Zone

Nearly any writing, speech, or documentation that has to do with computers is rife with technical jargon and gibberish, no matter the subject. To make matters even more confusing, the cognoscenti would much rather abbreviate frequently used technical terms — like HyperText Markup Language as HTML or Standard Generalized Markup Language as SGML — instead of having to say all the words for the concept each time.

The use of strings of first letters for technical terms — like ROM for Read-Only Memory, RAM for Random Access Memory, CPU for Central Processing Unit, and so on — happens across the board in the computer world, so you may as well get used to it! Because this kind of shorthand is called an acronym (which literally means *from the point or head of the name* in Greek), we have to warn you that you've entered a world where acronyms are commonplace. To make your lives a little easier, dear readers, we tried to include all of the acronyms that we use in this book in the Glossary on the CD-ROM. That way, if you forget what a particular string of letters means, you can at least look it up!

Standard Generalized Markup Language (SGML)

Technically speaking, HTML is not a programming language, nor can an HTML document be called a program, which is normally defined as a set of instructions and operations to be applied to external data (usually called the input).

HTML combines instructions with data to tell a display program, called a *browser,* how to render the data that a document contains. Even though it's not a programming language *per se,* HTML provides structure and layout controls to manage a document's appearance as well as the linkage mechanisms necessary to provide hypertext capabilities.

Actually, HTML is defined by a particular type of document — called a *Document Type Definition,* or *DTD* — within the context of SGML. Thus, any HTML document is also an SGML document that represents a specific subset of SGML capability.

Generalized Markup Covers Many Sins

SGML originated with work begun at IBM in the 1960s to overcome the problems inherent in moving documents across multiple hardware platforms and operating systems. IBM's efforts were called GML, for *General Markup Language*. GML was originally targeted for local use at IBM, rather than as a generic way of representing documents. This development was the first publish-once, multiplatform strategy for document preparation — a concept that's extremely popular today.

GML's originators — Charles Goldfarb, Ed Mosher, and Ray Lorie (the original "GML") — realized by the 1970s that a general version of markup would make documents portable across systems. Their work led ultimately to the definition and birth of SGML in the 1980s, which is today covered by the International Standards Organization (ISO) 8879 standard.

SGML is a powerful and complex tool for representing documents of all kinds. SGML offers the ability to create document specifications that can then be used to define and build individual documents that conform to those specifications.

Some commercial and government institutions, like the Department of Defense (DoD), have adopted SGML. The DoD mandates that contractors and subcontractors now submit all documentation to the government in SGML. The DoD even mandates the DTDs to which the contractors' documents must conform.

Several quotes from the SGML standard, ISO 8879, should help to illustrate its aims while underscoring its relationship to HTML. First, about the markup process:

> Text processing and word processing systems typically require additional information to be interspersed among the natural text of the document being processed. This added information, called "markup" serves two purposes:
>
> a) Separating the logical elements of the document; and
>
> b) Specifying the processing functions to be performed on those elements.
>
> Charles F. Goldfarb, *The SGML Handbook*, (Clarendon Press, Oxford, 1990) p. 5.

In stature and in scope, SGML far outstrips HTML; it is used to define complex document types like those used for military standard (Milspec) documents or aircraft maintenance manuals, whose specifications alone can run into thousands of pages.

The notion of *generalized markup* is what makes SGML's document definition system so all-encompassing and powerful. Goldfarb has this to say on that subject:

> . . . "generalized markup" . . . does not restrict documents to a single application, formatting style, or processing system. Generalized markup is based on two novel postulates:
>
> a) Markup should describe a document's structure and other attributes rather than specify processing to be performed on it, as descriptive markup need be done only once and will suffice for all future processing.
>
> b) Markup should be rigorous so that the techniques available for processing rigorously defined objects like programs and databases can be used for processing documents as well. (Goldfarb 7–8)

Even though SGML, like HTML, is oriented toward producing documents, its goal is to make those documents behave more like programs — that is, to behave predictably in a computer-oriented world.

Building better pieces and parts

The whole idea behind SGML is to create a formal method to describe the sections, headings, styles, and other components that make up a document so that references to individual items or entries in a document remain subject to such definitions. This definition lets a document be rendered consistently, no matter what platform displays it. In simplistic terms, SGML is a general-purpose tool to describe documents of just about any kind.

In its most generic form, an SGML document comes in three parts:

- ✔ A description of the legal character set and the characters used to distinguish plain text from markup tags.
- ✔ A declaration of the document type, including a listing of the legal markup tags it may contain.
- ✔ The document itself, which includes actual references to markup tags, mixed with the content for the document.

Where HTML fits under the SGML umbrella

All three document parts (see preceding bulleted list) do not have to be included in the same physical file. In fact, HTML works from the same set of definitions for the first two items so that only the contents and tags that make up an HTML document need to be included with the document itself, as described in the third item above.

For HTML, the ISO Latin-1 character set defines character entities for higher-order ASCII characters, along with the angle brackets and forward slash used to indicate markup tags. The declaration of document type comes from a standard DTD for HTML.

Therefore, HTML can be conveyed by pure ASCII text files that conform to the definitions and requirements covered in the first two bulleted items to create instances of documents, the third bulleted item. In other words, all that HTML consists of is content text, character entities, and markup tags.

Welcome to HTML!

Despite its more limited nature, HTML shares several important characteristics with its SGML *parent:*

- A character-based method for describing and expressing content
- A desire to deliver that content equally to multiple platforms
- A method for linking document components (and documents) together to compose compound documents

While HTML may be less general than SGML, it still leaves plenty of room for unique and powerful expressions, as any perusal of Web pages illustrates. Though it may be less than completely general, HTML's tags and entities can still do justice to a broad range of content!

Delivering content to a variety of platforms

HTML's tremendous power and appeal come from its capacity to service character-mode and graphical browsers with identical content. The look and feel of any document's content remains the same, subject only to the display limitations of your browser.

When you add the capability to group multiple, related sources of information together — text, graphics, sound, and video — and the capacity to link documents together, you get *hypertext.* HTML's combination of a simple concise form, powerful controls, and hypertext linkages helps to explain the overwhelming popularity of the Web as an information retrieval and investigation tool.

The many faces of HTML

In a manner of speaking, all that HTML contains, besides content, is a collection of character entities and markup tags. Some purists insist on remaining within the confines of an SGML DTD for HTML, but the number and kinds of tags and entities used in various Web environments (especially in some of the more advanced browsers) continues to expand with each passing day and each new version of browser software.

While some browsers recognize tags and entities unknown to other browsers, HTML includes the convention that all unrecognized markup is ignored. You may lose some of the finer formatting controls with some browsers (like the `<BLINK>` tag), but users still see the content.

Today, HTML has several standardization levels, numbered zero through four, plus a collection of code names:

0 The original text-only markup language developed for prototype browsers at CERN (Centre Européene pour la Reserche Nucléaire — the French acronym for the European Laboratory for Particle Physics in Geneva, where the Web began) prior to HTML's release to the general public. You shouldn't see any tools that remain at this level, except for historical curiosities.

1 The initial public implementation of HTML markup, which included the ability to reference graphical elements in addition to text controls. Many browsers — for example, Lynx and Cello — still operate at level 1 HTML.

2 The prior "official" implementation of HTML markup, which included all markup elements for level 1 plus tags for interactive forms. Most graphical browsers — like Mosaic, Navigator, and Internet Explorer — support level 2 HTML (and beyond).

3.2 The current "official" implementation of HTML. Throughout this book, HTML 3.2 is the foundation for what most browsers can handle today. HTML 3.2 was once known by the code name Wilbur.

4.0 This emerging HTML level is the primary focus of this book. Also known as Cougar, HTML 4.0 includes many significant, already well-defined enhancements and capabilities, particularly for style sheets and frames. We cover all of its aspects in various parts of this book.

To find out what's current for HTML, you can always go trolling on the Web itself. You should be able to find the current specification, in the form of an HTML DTD, along with online documentation on HTML markup, as well as current information on SGML.

HTML Elements!

Well-structured HTML documents come in these three parts:

- **A head** that identifies a document as HTML and establishes its title.

- **A body** that contains the content for a Web page. This part holds all displayed text on a page (except for the title), as well as most links to graphics, multimedia, locations inside the same file, and to other Web documents.

- **A footer** that labels a page by identifying its author, date of creation, and version number (if applicable).

In reality, most Web browsers are very forgiving, so you may "get away with" skipping some of these elements. As a matter of good style and practice, however, we strongly recommend that any pages you design begin with the information necessary for all three elements.

Go to the head of the document

You should bracket an entire HTML document by the identification tags <HTML>, to open the document, and </HTML>, to close it. These tags identify the DTD for the document to an SGML-sensitive program, to allow the program to interpret a document's contents properly. You can omit this tag for most browsers, but with the increasing convergence of HTML and SGML, doing so may limit the shelf-life of your Web pages.

An optional line may sometimes precede a document head. It is called a *document type prolog* and describes, in SGML, that the HTML document complies to the indicated level of the HTML DTD. Here is an example:

```
<!DOCTYPE HTML PUBLIC "-//IETF//DTD HTML 3.2//EN">
```

Deciphering this line indicates that the HTML document conforms to the HTML 3.2 DTD distributed by the Internet Engineering Task Force (IETF). You can also tell that the DTD is PUBLIC and is not system dependent. Finally, you can tell that the HTML tag set is defined by the English language (the EN in the DOCTYPE statement above). Local SGML parsers can also use this DOCTYPE statement to validate the HTML document; that is, the parsers check the document's syntax for conformance and correctness. This prolog will become increasingly important in the future.

A document title is embraced by two HTML tags: <TITLE> opens the title string, and </TITLE> closes it. The important thing about an HTML title is that it should identify itself in an informative and catchy way.

HTML also includes a pair of tags, <HEAD> and </HEAD>, that identify the head of a document. As with the <HTML> and </HTML> tags, many browsers happily let you omit these tags, but for readability and structure, we recommend including it. Within this section, you find an actual title and other document head tags (we cover them in detail in Chapter 6).

The bulk's in the body

The real content for any HTML document occurs in the body section, which is enclosed between <BODY> and </BODY> tags. The body is where you describe your document's layout and structure by using a variety of tags for text headings, embedded graphics, text paragraphs, lists, and other elements. Not surprisingly, the majority of HTML tags occur within a document's body, simply because that's where all the beef is!

Chapter 6 covers all HTML tags in brief form, and Parts II and III of this book provide lots of examples. Remember, this is just the overview.

The good stuff's in the graphics and links

You also find nearly all hypertext within a document's body section. This content can take the form of references to graphics or other files, as indicated by appropriate use of text tags like <IMG> for inline graphics. Or you can have links to other points within the same document or to outside documents by using the *anchor* tags (<A>, </A>) with appropriate attributes. In fact, because anchors point to generalized URLs (not just other HTML documents), you can also use them to invoke services like FTP to transfer files from within your Web pages.

Chapters 6 and 10-14 offer lots of details about using graphics within HTML documents, including good sources for material, appropriate usage, and other sorts of graphical information. After you come to understand all the topics of this book, you'll be slinging HTML graphics around with the best webmasters!

A footer may be optional, but it's still a good idea

Technically speaking, HTML doesn't include a separate tag to denote a page footer — that is, there's no <FOOT> and </FOOT> pair to label the information that would typically appear in a footer. Nevertheless, we strongly recommend that you include a footer on every Web page that you create, just for the record.

"What's in a footer," you ask? Well, it should contain information to describe the page and its author(s), as well as a copyright notice for your protection. A good footer helps to identify a document's vintage and contents and lets interested readers contact the author if they spot errors or want to provide feedback.

For your own sake, you would be smart to include copyright, date, and version information in each of your HTML files. Doing this enables you to recognize what version you're dealing with whenever you look at a page, and provides a great reminder of how stale your pages may be. As any Web-head knows, the older the page, the more likely that it's out-of-date!

Chapter 8 provides numerous details about footers and includes a fine example of what a good footer looks like. Be sure not to miss it.

Ladies and Gentlemen, Start Your Engines!

Okay, in this chapter we introduce HTML's basic elements. In the chapters that follow, we introduce you to the details, including more tags than you'll see at a Red Tag sale at your department store. As you come to know and love HTML, you can apply what you learn to build great Web pages of your own.

Chapter 6

Pigeonholing Page Contents: HTML Categories

---

*A*t last you've arrived at the first in-depth, no-holds-barred look at HTML markup that appears in this book. In this chapter, we talk some serious turkey about HTML syntax to make sure you can keep up with all the gory details. We also establish some categories for what HTML can do and group the markup tags in meaningful categories (to make them easier to learn and use). The remainder of the chapter is a reference tool, where we describe all the HTML tags in alphabetical order for easy access. Buckle up, and let's go!

HTML Syntax Redux

In the preceding chapter, we talk about the following general syntax for HTML tags:

✔ Tags are enclosed in left and right angle brackets; for example, <HEAD> marks the beginning of the head of an HTML document.

✔ By convention only (HTML itself has no requirement for upper- or lowercase) we present all tags in uppercase for readability. That's why you see <HEAD> but not <Head> or <head> in the rest of this book, even though all three are perfectly legal — and equivalent — HTML tags. We recommend that you follow this practice yourself because doing so will help you distinguish the tags from the real text.

✔ Tags usually come in pairs, so `<HEAD>` marks the beginning of a document heading block, and `</HEAD>` marks the end. Your browser considers all the text that occurs between opening and closing tags the focus of that tag and handles the text appropriately. Because the majority of HTML tags work this way, we flag all of the possible exceptions as we introduce them.

✔ Tags can sometimes take on one or more attributes to define data sources or destinations, to specify URLs, or to further specify the characteristics of the text to which a tag will be applied. For example, the `<IMG>` tag for placing graphics can use the following attributes to help specify the source and placement of an image on a page:

- `SRC` = source for image, same as URL.

- `ALT` = alternate text to display inline if browser isn't graphics-capable, or graphics are turned off.

- `ALIGN` = (`TOP`|`MIDDLE`|`BOTTOM`) **and** (`\WIDTH=number` and `HEIGHT=number\`) controls placement of a graphic. We explain this in more detail later when we tell you what you don't already know!

- `ISMAP` If this attribute is present, it indicates that the graphic is a clickable image map with one or more links to other locations built onto the image. If it's absent, it means the image is not a map.

Some attributes take on values — in this case, `SRC`, `ALT`, and `ALIGN` all require at least one value — while others, like `ISMAP`, do not. Attributes that don't require values are usually true ("turned on") if present and false ("turned off") when omitted. Also, tags may have default values for required attributes that are omitted, so make sure that you check the HTML specification to determine how such defaults are handled.

At this point, you may already know quite a bit about HTML syntax and layout. But you'll need to know quite a bit of additional stuff, some of which we had to use in our discussion in the preceding bullet item. Discussions of this additional stuff contain some goofy characters that aren't part of HTML itself, but are necessary to explain it formally.

In the sections that follow, we begin with formal syntax conventions and then move on to more interesting properties of HTML itself.

Syntax conventions are no party!

While we're providing formal definitions of the various HTML commands, we use typographical notation in an equally formal way. What this means (in plain language) is that you better pay attention to how we write some things down because we intend for the notation to describe how you should combine, construct, and use terms.

Describing a formal syntax means using certain characters in a special way to talk about how to treat elements that appear in conjunction with these characters. This is nearly identical to these HTML notions:

- ✔ Angle brackets surround a tag (`<HEAD>`).

- ✔ A forward slash following the left angle bracket denotes a closing tag (`</HEAD>`).

- ✔ An ampersand leads off a character entity and a semicolon closes it (`&egrave;`).

These special characters clue us (and our browser software) into the need for special handling. Chapter 7 provides in-depth information about character entities and their special formatting, while we focus on the HTML tags in this chapter.

The characters we're going to use for our HTML syntax come from conventions developed for a formal syntax — called a Backus-Naur Form (or BNF grammar, for short) — that was developed to completely and formally describe programming languages. Because we're forced to deviate somewhat from BNF, we lay out all of the special characters we use to describe HTML syntax. Table 6-1 contains these characters (which, by the way, are called metacharacters) and their definitions, plus an example for each one.

Table 6-1		The HTML Syntax Metacharacter Set	
Char(s)	*Name(s)*	*Definition*	*Example*
		vertical bar	Separates legal choices	`ITEM1|ITEM2|ITEM3`
( )	parentheses	Defines a set of items to treat as a unit	`(ITEM1|ITEM2)` or `(ITEM3|ITEM4)`
\ \	backslashes	Indicates that one or more items can be selected	`\ITEM1|ITEM2|ITEM3\`
<u>and</u>	logical and	Indicates that both items must be selected	`(ITEM1|ITEM2)` and `(ITEM3|ITEM4)`
<u>or</u>	logical or	Indicates that one or the other item must be selected	`ITEM1` or `ITEM2`
&r	and/or	Indicates that one or both items must be selected	`ITEM1 &r ITEM2`

(continued)

Table 6-1 *(continued)*

Char(s)	Name(s)	Definition	Example
[]	square brackets	Indicates nonstandard items, not supported by all browsers	[WIDTH=number]
integer	integer	Indicates whole numbers only	1, 2944, -40
...	ellipsis	Repeat elements as needed	ITEM1|ITEM2| ...
{}	curly braces	Contain optional elements, not required	{ITEM1|ITEM2}

Decoding a complex metacharacter example: ALIGN = ?

Nothing beats an example to make some sense out of this potential gibberish. Recall our definition of the ALIGN attribute for the <IMG> tag:

```
ALIGN = (TOP|MIDDLE|BOTTOM) and (WIDTH=number &r
          HEIGHT=number\)
```

To make sure you understand what this formalism means, we relate the example as follows:

ALIGN = TOP|MIDDLE|BOTTOM means that ALIGN can take one of the three values: TOP, MIDDLE, or BOTTOM. Basically, you use it to say whether you want an image at the top, middle, or bottom of a display area onscreen.

Also, ALIGN can take a member of the set (TOP|MIDDLE|BOTTOM), and it can sometimes take one or both members of the set (\WIDTH=number|HEIGHT=number\).

Sometimes, ALIGN can take either or both of a WIDTH and HEIGHT setting. The backslashes (\ \) around the WIDTH and HEIGHT and the logical and/or (&r) entries indicate either or both. Each of those two entries must be assigned some integer value corresponding to a position relative to the current display area, as indicated by the number part.

As you can see, what we described in a single complex line of type takes three paragraphs of details to explain completely. The brevity and compactness of formal syntax makes it appealing to computer nerds; as you review the various tags, we hope that you can work your way through this syntax to fully grasp what HTML can do. If not, never fear — we provide plenty of examples for each tag throughout so that you can absorb by osmosis what you can't grasp through formalism! Ouch!

Interesting HTML properties

In addition to the formal syntax for HTML that we use throughout the book, the markup language itself has some interesting general properties that are worth covering before you encounter the tags directly.

No embedded blanks, please!

All HTML tags require that the characters in a name be contiguous. You can't insert extra blanks within a tag or its surrounding markup without causing that tag to be ignored (which is what browsers do with tags they can't recognize).

This requirement means that $\langle/\text{HEAD}\rangle$ is a valid closing tag for a document heading, but that none of the following is legal:

```
< /HEAD>
</ HEAD>
</H EAD>
</HE AD>
</HEA D>
</HEAD >
```

We hope that you get the idea: Don't use blanks inside tags, except where you use a blank deliberately to separate a tag name from an attribute name (for example `<IMG SRC="sample.gif">` is legal, but `<IMGSRC="sample.gif">` is not).

When assigning values to attributes, however, spaces are okay. Therefore, all four of the following variants for this `SRC` assignment are legal:

```
<IMG SRC="sample.gif">
<!-- Previous line: no spaces before or after = sign -->
<IMG SRC = "sample.gif">
<!-- Previous line: spaces before and after = sign -->
<IMG SRC= "sample.gif">
<!-- Previous line: no space before, one after = sign -->
<IMG SRC ="sample.gif">
<!-- Previous line: one space before, none after = sign -->
```

Where one space is legal, multiple spaces are legal. Don't get carried away with what's legal or not, though — try to make your HTML documents as readable as possible and everything else should flow naturally.

We sneaked some more HTML markup into the preceding example. After each <IMG> tag line, we inserted readable HTML comments to describe what occurred on the preceding line. This lets you infer that the HTML markup to open a comment is the string <!-- and the string --> closes the comment. As you go through the markup section later on, we cover some style guidelines for using comments effectively and correctly.

What's the default?

If a tag can support an attribute, what does it mean when the attribute isn't present? For ISMAP on the <IMG> tag, for example, you already know that when the ISMAP attribute is present, it means *the image is a clickable map*. If ISMAP is absent, this means *the image is not a clickable map*.

This is a way of introducing the concept of a *default,* which is not a way of assigning blame, but rather a way of deciding what to assume when an attribute is not supplied for a particular tag. For ISMAP, the default is absent; that is, an image is only assumed to be a clickable map when the ISMAP attribute is explicitly supplied.

But how do images get displayed if the ALIGN attribute isn't defined? As a quick bit of experimentation shows you, the default for most graphical browsers is to insert the graphic at the left-hand margin. These kinds of defaults are important, too, and we'll try to tell you what to expect from them as well.

The nesting instinct

Sometimes it's necessary to insert one set of markup tags within another. You might want a few words within a sentence already marked for special emphasis to be the trigger for a hyperlink. For example, the entire heading "Other Important Numbers: Emergency Phone Numbers" will draw the readers attention if it is rendered in boldface, but you only want the words *Emergency Phone Numbers* to be "clickable" and lead to another HTML document listing relevant emergency numbers.

Enclosing one set of markup within another is called *nesting*. When the nesting instinct strikes you, the best rule of thumb is to close first what you opened most recently. For example, the text tags <A HREF="ephone.html"> ... </A> provide a way of bracketing text linking to another HTML document. If this occurred within strongly emphasized text, <STRONG> ... </STRONG>, the proper way to handle the hyperlink is like this:

```
<STRONG>Other Important Numbers: <A HREF:"ephone.html">
          Emergency Phone Numbers</A></STRONG>
```

That way, you close the nested <A> tag with its mate before you close out the <STRONG> heading. Some browsers may let you violate this rule, but others may behave unpredictably if you don't open and close tags in the right order. Figure 6-1 shows what this combination of tags looks like. (Notice that the words *Emergency Phone Numbers* appear in heavier type than the rest of the heading.)

Figure 6-1:
Using nested tags to create a hyperlink within strongly emphasized text.

Other Important Numbers: Emergency Phone Numbers	
Ed Tittel	454-3878
Santa Clause	1-800-ELF-HELP
The Good Fairy	1-800-MS-TOOTH

Nesting just doesn't make sense for some tags. For instance, within <TITLE> ... </TITLE>, you deal with information that shows up only on a window title, rather than on a particular Web page. Text and layout controls clearly do not apply here (and are cheerfully ignored by some browsers, while making others curl up and die).

Always look back to the left as you start closing tags you already opened. Close the closest one first, the next one next, and so on. Check the tag details (later on in this chapter) to find out which tags you can nest within your outermost open tag. If the tag you want to use doesn't appear on the okay list, then don't try to nest that tag inside the current open ones. Close out what you have open and then open the tag you need.

Keeping your tags in the right nests keeps your readers' browsers from getting confused! It also makes sure that you hatch only good-looking Web pages.

As you learn which tags can appear inside other tags, you begin to develop an appreciation for the controls and capabilities offered by HTML. In our alphabetical list (later in this chapter) we cover the nesting compatibilities under the heading "Context" to indicate which tags are okay to nest (and by exclusion, which are not).

HTML Categories

Before we take you through the HTML tags in alphabetical order, we'd like to introduce them to you grouped by category. These categories help to explain how and when you can use the tags, and what functions the tags provide.

We hope that the categories presented in Table 6-2 also help you to organize and understand HTML's numerous tags. (For a complete listing of the HTML character entities, please consult Chapter 7.) Because so many tags come in pairs, we use an ellipsis (...) between opening and closing tags to indicate where text and other elements can appear.

Table 6-2	HTML Categories and Their Respective Tags	
Tags	*Tag Names*	*Brief Explanation*
Global Structure	Basic document layout and linkage structures	
`<!DOCTYPE>`	Document type	Specifies the version of HTML used in the document
`<ADDRESS> ... </ADDRESS>`	Address	Author contact information
`<BODY> ... </BODY>`	Body	Blocks out a document's body
`<DIV> ... </DIV>`	Logical	Marks divisions in a divisions document and allows you to apply styles to those divisions
`<H1> ... </H1>`	Level 1 head	First-level heading
`<H2> ... </H2>`	Level 2 head	Second-level heading
`<H3> ... </H3>`	Level 3 head	Third-level heading
`<H4> ... </H4>`	Level 4 head	Fourth-level heading
`<H5> ... </H5>`	Level 5 head	Fifth-level heading
`<H6> ... </H6>`	Level 6 head	Sixth-level heading
`<HEAD> ... </HEAD>`	Head	Blocks out a document's head
`<HTML> ... </HTML>`	HTML document	Blocks out an entire HTML document
`<META>`	Meta-information	Describes aspects of the page's information structure
`<SPAN> ... </SPAN>`	Span	Applies a style as specified in the `<STYLE>` tag to the contained text

Tags	Tag Names	Brief Explanation
`<TITLE> ... </TITLE>`	Document title	Supplies the title that labels the entire document
`<!-- ... -->`	Comment	Inserts author comments and is ignored by the browser
Language Definition Defines language-related handlers		
`<BDO> ... </BDO>`	Bidirectional algorithm	Defines language and direction
Text Tags Control document appearance and add elements to a document		
`<ABBR> ... </ABBR>`	Abbreviation	Indicates an abbreviation
`<BLOCKQUOTE> ... </BLOCKQUOTE>`	Blockquote	Sets off long quotations or citations
` `	Line break	Forces a line break in the on-screen text flow
`<CITE> ... </CITE>`	Short citation	Marks distinctive text for citations
`<CODE> ... </CODE>`	Code	Identifies code samples
`<DEL> ... </DEL>`	Deleted section	Identifies sections of a Web page that have been deleted in revision
`<DFN> ... </DFN>`	Defined term	Emphasizes a term about to be defined in the following text
`<EM> ... </EM>`	Emphasis	Adds emphasis to enclosed text
`<INS> ... </INS>`	Inserted section	Identifies sections of a Web page that have been inserted in revision
`<KBD> ... </KBD>`	Keyboard text	Marks text to be entered by the user at the keyboard
`<P> ... </P>`	Paragraph	Breaks up text into content blocks
`<PRE> ... </PRE>`	Preformatted text	Preserves spacing and layout of original `text in monospaced font`
`<Q> ... </Q>`	Short quotation	Marks a short quotation within a sentence
`<SAMP> ... </SAMP>`	Sample text	Indicates sample output from a program or script

(continued)

Table 6-2 *(continued)*

Tags	Tag Names	Brief Explanation
`<STRONG>` ... `</STRONG>`	Strong emphasis	Provides maximum emphasis to enclosed text
`<SUB>` ... `</SUB>`	Subscript	Renders text smaller and slightly lowered
`<SUP>` ... `</SUP>`	Superscript	Renders text smaller and slightly raised
`<VAR>` ... `</VAR>`	Variable text	Marks variable or substitution for some other value
Lists Provide methods to lay out item or element sequences in document content		
`<DD>`	Definition	Marks the definition description for a term in a glossary list
`<DIR>` ... `</DIR>`	Directory list	Marks unbulleted list of short elements
`<DL>` ... `</DL>`	Definition list	Marks a special format for terms and their definitions
`<DT>`	Definition term	Marks the term being defined in a glossary list
`<LI>`	List item	Marks a member item within a list of any type
`<MENU>` ... `</MENU>`	Menu list	Marks a pickable list of elements
`<OL>` ... `</OL>`	Ordered list	Marks a numbered list of elements
`<UL>` ... `</UL>`	Unordered list	Marks bulleted list of elements
Tables Provide controls for table structure		
`<CAPTION>` ... `</CAPTION>`	Table caption	Defines the text and location information for a table caption
`<COL>`	Columns	Sets the properties of a single column within a column group
`<COLGROUP>`	Column group properties	Sets the properties for a group of columns
`<TABLE>` ... `</TABLE>`	Table	Creates a table
`<TBODY>` ... `</TBODY>`	Table body	Defines the table body when headers and footers are also defined

Tags	Tag Names	Brief Explanation
`<TD> ... </TD>`	Table cell	Contains table cell data and formatting controls
`<TFOOT> ... </TFOOT>`	Table footer	Defines the table footer when headers and body are also defined
`<TH> ... </TH>`	Table head	Contains the table head data and formatting controls
`<THEAD> ... </THEAD>`	Table head	Defines the table header when body and footers are also defined
`<TR> ... </TR>`	Table row	Contains table row data and formatting controls

Links   Create links to other Web resources

Tags	Tag Names	Brief Explanation
`<A> ... </A>`	Anchor	Visible control that links one Web resource to another
`<BASE> ... </BASE>`	Relative addressing base	Explicitly establishes a document's location for relative addressing
`<LINK> ... </LINK>`	Link	Sets relationships between the current document and other documents

Inclusions   Object inclusions

Tags	Tag Names	Brief Explanation
`<APPLET> ... </APPLET>`	Applet	Inserts calls for inclusion of a Java applet into an HTML document
`<AREA>`	Image map hot spot	Defines a client-side image map hot spot
`<IMG>`	Inline image	Inserts a graphic into the document
`<MAP> ... </MAP>`	Image map	Groups `<AREA>` tags into a single client-side image map definition
`<OBJECT> ... </OBJECT>`	Object embedding	Inserts nonstandard objects into documents
`<PARAM>`	Object parameter	Provides command-line arguments to a Java applet

Style Sheet Tags   Include style sheet rules within an HTML document

Tags	Tag Names	Brief Explanation
`<STYLE> ... </STYLE>`	Inline style information	Includes style rules directly within the Web page

(continued)

Table 6-2 *(continued)*

Tags	Tag Names	Brief Explanation
Presentation Controls Text presentation tags		
`<B> ... </B>`	Boldface	Produces bold text
`<BASEFONT>`	Base font	Specifies the base font color, typeface, and size
`<BIG> ... </BIG>`	Big text	Makes text larger
`<CENTER> ... </CENTER>`	Center	Centers enclosed text
`<FONT> ... </FONT>`	Font appearance	Sets the size, color, and typeface of text
`<HR>`	Horizontal rule	Draws a horizontal line across the page
`<I> ... </I>`	Italic	Produces italic text
`<S> ... </S>`	Strikethrough	Produces text that has been struck through
`<SMALL> ... </SMALL>`	Small text	Makes text smaller
`<STRIKE> ... </STRIKE>`	Strikethrough	Produces text that has been struck through
`<TT> ... </TT>`	Teletype text	Produces a typewriter font
`<U> ... </U>`	Underlined text	Underlines enclosed text
Frames Divides HTML pages into multiple, scrollable regions		
`<FRAME>`	Frame definition	Defines a single frame in a frameset
`<FRAMESET> ... </FRAMESET>`	Frame group definition	Containers for frame elements
`<IFRAME> ... </IFRAME>`	Inline frame	Defines an inline frame
`<NOFRAMES> ... </NOFRAMES>`	Frame alternative	Indicates content is viewable by browsers that do not support frames
Forms Forms-related markup tags		
`<BUTTON> ... </BUTTON>`	Form button	Creates an input button in an HTML form
`<FIELDSET>`	Set of fields	Groups related form controls
`<FORM> ... </FORM>`	User input form	Marks beginning and end of form block

Tags	Tag Names	Brief Explanation
`<INPUT>`	Input object	Defines type and appearance of input objects
`<ISINDEX>`	Single line input	Solicits a single line of input from users
`<LABEL> ... </LABEL>`	Control label	Identifies form controls
`<LEGEND> ... </LEGEND>`	Fieldset caption	Provides a caption to a set of related form controls
`<OPTION>`	Selectable item	Assigns a value or default to an input item
`<SELECT> ... </SELECT>`	Select input list	Creates a menu or scrolling list of input items
`<TEXTAREA> ... </TEXTAREA>`	Text input area	Multiline text entry area
Scripts Includes client-side scripts within HTML documents		
`<NOSCRIPT> ... </NOSCRIPT>`	No script	Specifies content for browsers unable to process scripts
`<SCRIPT> ... </SCRIPT>`	Inline script	Specifies inclusion of a script

Now, review the HTML categories we just introduced before we provide detailed syntax for each tag:

- **Global structure:** This includes document structure tags that you use to apply required structural elements to HTML documents.

- **Language definition:** You use language definition tags to define the language used to interpret a page's content.

- **Text tags:** Text tags provide a logical structure for content. This structure may or may not alter that content's display properties.

- **Lists:** You use list tags to define a variety of different lists.

- **Tables:** Table tags define the structure and layout of tables. Tables can be used to arrange data or to aid page layout and design.

- **Links:** Link tags create connections, such as hyperlinks, image links, and links to style sheets, between Web resources.

- **Inclusions:** You use these tags to include non-HTML objects, like Java applets and multimedia files, within Web documents.

- **Style sheet tags:** These HTML elements define how content is rendered in the browser.

✔ **Presentation controls:** Presentation tags alter the display of content by affecting properties such as font styles and horizontal rules.

✔ **Frames:** Frame tags define and control frames within the display area of a browser.

✔ **Forms:** Form tags control the input of data from a user and transmission of that data to a background CGI or similar application.

✔ **Scripts:** You use these tags to embed programming language scripts into Web documents.

From managing document structure to controlling the look and feel of text on a page, HTML includes tags to make these things happen. In the next section, we examine the nitty-gritty details of all the various HTML tags.

HTML Tags

The remainder of this chapter is devoted to an alphabetical listing of all the tags in the HTML Cougar DTD.

Because so many browser builders are adding extensions to HTML for their own use, and because future standards will introduce significant changes and enhancements to HTML, you should consider this list neither exhaustive nor complete. Although this listing was complete at press time, the Web changes more quickly than we can write and books can be published. For the latest and most up-to-date information on HTML, consult the World Wide Web Consortium Web site at `www.w3.org/`.

The rundown on attributes

In HTML, attributes typically take one of two forms within a tag:

✔ `ATTRIBUTE="value"`: Where `value` is typically enclosed in quotes (" ") and may be one of the following kinds of elements:

- URL: A uniform resource locator

- Name: A user-supplied name, probably for an input field

- Number: A user-supplied numeric value

- Text: User-supplied text

- Server: Server-dependent name (for example, page name defaults)

- (X|Y|Z): One member of a set of fixed values

- #rrggbb: Hexadecimal color notation

✔ ATTRIBUTE: Where the name itself provides information about how the tag should behave (for example, ISMAP in <IMG> indicates that the graphic is a clickable map).

As we discuss attributes for individual tags, you see them in a section under the tag name. For each one we provide a definition. We also indicate choices for predefined sets of values or provide an example for open-ended value assignments.

Common attributes

You'll find six attributes listed for more than 85 percent of the tags. We list them here, along with a brief description, to save a few trees and avoid being redundant. All of these attributes have implied values, which means that you don't have to actually list them in your tags unless you want to change their values. For example, the implied value for the DIR attribute is ltr, which stands for "left to right," the direction the tag and its contents will be read. If for some reason you wanted to change the value to rtl ("right to left"), then you would need to include the attribute and its value.

✔ ID="name": A document-wide identifier that you can use to give an HTML element a unique identifier within a document.

✔ CLASS="text": A comma-separated list of class names, which indicates that the element belongs to a specific class or classes of style definitions.

✔ STYLE="text": Provides rendering information specific to this element, such as the color, size, and font specifics.

✔ TITLE="text": Defines an advisory title that will display additional help. Balloon text around hyperlinks and graphics are generated using this attribute.

✔ DIR="(LTR|RTL)": Indicates the direction the text will be read in, left to right or right to left.

✔ LANG="name": Specifies the language that the element and its contents are written in.

Intrinsic events

The designers of HTML 4.0 included numerous intricacy event triggers to support programming and scripting mechanisms. Basically, one of several intrinsic events, like an onmouseover, when tied to an HTML tag causes a script to run without needing a hyperlink. The user simply performs the event, such as moving a mouse over a tag with the onmouseover attribute, and the script is automatically called. While we don't discuss the advanced topic of scripting in this book, Chapter 11 of our *MORE HTML For Dummies,* 2nd Edition (IDG Books Worldwide, Inc.), describes scripting in detail. Because you'll see intrinsic events listed for many of the tags, we wanted to warn you ahead of time that they are scripting related. A quick look at intrinsic events shows that

✔ You can use the onreset, onsubmit intrinsic events with the following markup tag: <FORM>.

✔ You can use the onload, onunload intrinsic events with the following markup tags: <FRAMESET> and <BODY>.

✔ You can use the onchange, onselect intrinsic events with the following markup tags: <INPUT>, <SELECT>, and <TEXTAREA>.

✔ You can use the onblur, onfocus intrinsic events with the following markup tags: <BUTTON>, <INPUT>, <LABEL>, <SELECT>, and <TEXTAREA>.

✔ You can use the onclick, ondblclick, onkeydown, onkeypress, onkeyup, onmousedown, onmousemove, onmouseout, onmouseover, onmouseup intrinsic events with the following markup tags: <A>, <ABBR>, <ADDRESS>, <B>, <BIG>, <BLOCKQUOTE>, <BODY>, <BUTTON>, <CAPTION>, <CENTER>, <CITE>, <CODE>, <COL>, <COLGROUP>, <DD>, <DEL>, <DFN>, <DIR>, <DIV>, <DL>, <DT>, <EM>, <FIELDSET>, <FORM>, <H*>, <HR>, <I>, <IMG>, <INPUT>, <INS>, <KBD>, <LABEL>, <LEGEND>, <LI>, <LINK>, <MENU>, <OBJECT>, <OL>, <OPTION>, <P>, <PRE>, <Q>, <S>, <SAMP>, <SELECT>, <SMALL>, <SPAN>, <STRIKE>, <STRONG>, <SUB>, <SUP>, <TABLE>, <TBODY>, <TD>, <TEXTAREA>, <TFOOT>, <TH>, <THEAD>, <TR>, <TT>, <U>, <UL>, and <VAR>.

For now that's all you need to know about intrinsic events. We will say that this is a way cool technology that adds interactivity to Web pages in a relatively simple way and is well worth exploring after you get your feet firmly planted in HTML land.

Tag information layout

Before we provide our alphabetical list of tags, you need to understand what information we present and how we present it. Using the by-now-familiar image tag (<IMG>), here's what a typical listing looks like:

<IMG> Inline image

Definition: Supplies image source, placement, and behavior information. Used to place graphics in a page.

Attributes:

ALT="text"

Supplies an alternative string of text if the browser has no graphics capability, or if graphics are turned off.

ALIGN=LEFT|RIGHT|TOP|MIDDLE|BOTTOM

[Depreciated] Sets the image or surrounding text alignment. The alignment type can be one of these values:

Note: Tags or attributes that are labeled as *depreciated* are obsolete and will soon be removed from the HTML DTD entirely. If a tag or attribute is labeled as depreciated, you can still use it, but don't get overly attached. The majority of these obsolete tags have been depreciated in favor of style sheet properties. For more information on style sheets, check out Chapter 13.

LEFT: The picture is drawn as a flush-left image and text flows around it.

RIGHT: The picture is drawn as a flush-right image and text flows around it.

TOP: The top of the surrounding text is aligned with the top of the image.

MIDDLE: The baseline of the surrounding text is aligned with the middle of the image.

BOTTOM: The baseline of the surrounding text is aligned with the bottom of the image.

BORDER=number

Specifies the size of a border to be drawn around the image. For a hyperlink image, the border is drawn in the appropriate hyperlink color. If the image is not a hyperlink, the border is invisible. Setting this to "0" hides hyperlink borders.

HEIGHT=pixels

Along with WIDTH=, specifies the size to which the image is scaled. If the picture's actual dimensions differ from those specified, the picture is stretched to match the specifications.

HSPACE=number

With VSPACE=, specifies extra blank space or margins around the image.

ISMAP

Indicates that the image (or its text replacement) should be a clickable map. This often invokes special map-handling software through the CGI interface on the Web server handling the request.

SRC="URL"

SRC is a required attribute. URL is a standard Uniform Resource Locator specifying the location of the image file.

USEMAP=map-name

Identifies the picture as a client-side image map and specifies a <MAP> to be used for acting on the user's clicks.

VSPACE=number

With HSPACE=, specifies extra blank space or margins around the image.

WIDTH=pixels

With HEIGHT=, specifies the size at which the image is scaled. If the picture's actual dimensions differ from those specified, the picture is stretched to match the specifications.

Context:

<IMG> is legal within the following tags:

```
<A>, <ABBR>, <ADDRESS>, <APPLET>, <B>, <BDO>, <BIG>,
<BLOCKQUOTE>, <BODY>, <BUTTON>, <CAPTION>, <CENTER>, <CITE>,
<CODE>, <DD>, <DEL>, <DFN>, <DIV>, <DT>, <EM>, <FIELDSET>, <FONT>,
<FORM>, <H*>, <I>, <IFRAME>, <INS>, <KBD>, <LABEL>, <LEGEND>,
<LI>, <NOFRAMES>, <NOSCRIPT>, <OBJECT>, <P>, <Q>, <S>, <SAMP>,
<SMALL>, <SPAN>, <STRIKE>, <STRONG>, <SUB>, <SUP>, <TD>, <TH>,
<TT>, <U>, <VAR>
```

The <IMG> tag is a singleton tag. No additional markup can be used within <IMG>:

Note: When referring to heading tags <H1> through <H6>, we abbreviate the whole series as <H*> as we did in the preceding paragraph.

Suggested style/usage: Keep images small and use them judiciously; graphics should add impact and interest to pages without adding too much bulk (or wait time).

Examples: See file /h4d4e/examples/ch06/img.htm.

Note: Rather than include code snippets and screen shots, we thought you might like to see HTML at work yourself. We included example code for each and every tag, and attribute where possible, on the CD. Using your browser, just open the file list under the "Examples" section to see how tag information is rendered. To view the HTML, choose View Source in your browser or open the .htm file with a text editor.

Tag layout commentary

You'll notice the use of our HTML syntax notation in the "Attributes" section most often. Because <IMG> is a stand-alone tag (that is, it doesn't need a closing </IMG> tag) we don't show a pair of tags here, but tags will be shown in pairs whenever appropriate.

Also, you'll notice a few tags and attributes marked as "Deprecated." In plain English, this means they are obsolete and will be removed from the next HTML specification. Most of these tags and attributes have been deprecated in favor of style sheet properties and values, and the folks at the W3C would prefer you use style sheets rather than these tags to mark up your document.

The last item for discussion is the "Context" section. In this section, you see where it's legal to put <IMG> tags inside other markup, between <PRE> ... </PRE> tags, for example. Just because you can use this tag in such a way doesn't mean you have to; as always, use markup judiciously to add impact or value to information. Complex compositions seldom delight anyone other than their makers, so try to keep things simple whenever you can.

The HTML tag team

This section shows an alphabetical listing of the most common and widely used HTML tags — taken from HTML 4.0 DTD. The 4.0 DTD is 100 percent supported by Netscape Navigator 4.0 or greater.

<!-- ... --> Comments

Definition: Indicates a comment. The browser ignores the text between the elements.

Attributes: None

Context:

<!-- ... --> is legal within all markup tags.

You can use all markup within <!-- ... -->.

Suggested style/usage: Use to document your markup, make notes for future reference, or provide extra information for others who view your source. You can use comments to temporarily remove sections of a document by simply adding a comment tag pair around the removed text.

Examples: See file /h4d4e/examples/ch06/comment.htm.

<!DOCTYPE> Document type

Definition: This is not technically an HTML tag, but rather an SGML tag. It specifies the version of HTML used in the document through SGML declaration. `<!DOCTYPE>` should be the first element within any HTML document and is a required element for all HTML DTD-compliant documents.

Attributes:

`HTML PUBLIC "version name"`

> This required attribute must contain a proper and complete HTML version name. A list of proper version names can be found at `www.webtechs.com/html-tk/src/lib/catalog`.

Context:

`<!DOCTYPE>` is not legal within any markup tag. It must appear before the `<HTML>` tag.

No additional markup can be used within `<!DOCTYPE>`; it is a singleton tag.

Suggested style/usage: All documents should contain a `<!DOCTYPE>` declaration to aid browsers, validation tools, and other software in determining the version of HTML used in the document.

Examples: See file /h4d4e/examples/ch06/doctype.htm.

<A> ... </A> Anchor

Definition: Provides a clickable link to another Web resource or to a specific point on a Web page.

Attributes:

`ACCESSKEY="text"`

> Specifies the character to be used as part of a keyboard shortcut to activate the link.

`CHARSET="text"`

> Defines the character set of the linked Web resource. The default is ISO-8859-1.

`COORDS="X1, Y1, X2, Y2, and so on."`

> Specifies the coordinates defining the shape of the hot spot. See the `SHAPE` attribute for details.

HREF="URL"

> URL stands for Uniform Resource Locator, which specifies the location of any type of Internet resource, including HTML files, non-HTML files, Telnet, e-mail, and Gopher resources.

NAME="text"

> This marks a hypertext link destination within a document. The text supplied for this attribute acts just like an anchor, "holding a place" to which a link can attach.

REL="text"

> Indicates the source end of a link and specifies the link's type. For example REL="STYLESHEET" lets the browser know the linked document is a style sheet.

REV="text"

> Indicates the destination end of a link and specifies the link's type.

SHAPE=(RECT|CIRCLE|POLY|DEFAULT)

> Specifies the shape of a hot spot in a client-side image map.

RECT

> A rectangle is defined by its top-left corner and its bottom-right corner. **Example:** <AREA SHAPE=rect COORDS="0,0,9,9">.

CIRCLE

> A circle is defined by its center, and then its radius. Example: <AREA SHAPE=circle COORDS="10,10,5">.

POLY

> A polygon is built from a list of coordinates, all connected in the order you present, with the last coordinate pair connected to the first. **Example:** <AREA SHAPE=POLY COORDS="10,50,15,20,20,50">.

DEFAULT

> The default location has no coordinates and should be used only once in the map. It indicates the outcome if the user selects a coordinate that is undefined in any of the other elements.

`TABINDEX="number"`

Indicates the link's place in the tabbing order.

`TARGET="window"`

Specifies loading the link into the targeted window. You can use TARGET with a FRAMESET in which you name a frame in the FRAME element. The targeted window can be one of the following values:

`window`: Specifies loading the link into the targeted window. The window must begin with an alphanumeric character to be valid, with the following four exceptions:

`_blank`: Loads the link into a new (unnamed) blank window.

`_parent`: Loads the link into the immediate parent of the document in which the link is found.

`_self`: Loads the link into the same window as the link.

`_top`: Loads the link into the full body of the window.

Context:

`<A> ... </A>` is legal within the following tags:

`<ABBR>`, `<ADDRESS>`, `<APPLET>`, `<B>`, `<BDO>`, `<BIG>`, `<BLOCKQUOTE>`, `<BODY>`, `<CAPTION>`, `<CENTER>`, `<CITE>`, `<CODE>`, `<DD>`, `<DEL>`, `<DFN>`, `<DIV>`, `<DT>`, `<EM>`, `<FIELDSET>`, `<FONT>`, `<FORM>`, `<H*>`, `<I>`, `<IFRAME>`, `<INS>`, `<KBD>`, `<LABEL>`, `<LEGEND>`, `<LI>`, `<NOFRAMES>`, `<NOSCRIPT>`, `<OBJECT>`, `<P>`, `<PRE>`, `<Q>`, `<S>`, `<SAMP>`, `<SMALL>`, `<SPAN>`, `<STRIKE>`, `<STRONG>`, `<SUB>`, `<SUP>`, `<TD>`, `<TH>`, `<TT>`, `<U>`, `<VAR>`

You can use the following tags within `<A> ... </A>`:

`<A>`, `<ABBR>`, `<APPLET>`, `<B>`, `<BASEFONT>`, `<BDO>`, `<BIG>`, `<BR>`, `<BUTTON>`, `<CITE>`, `<CODE>`, `<DFN>`, `<EM>`, `<FONT>`, `<I>`, `<IFRAME>`, `<IMG>`, `<INPUT>`, `<KBD>`, `<LABEL>`, `<MAP>`, `<OBJECT>`, `<Q>`, `<S>`, `<SAMP>`, `<SCRIPT>`, `<SELECT>`, `<SMALL>`, `<SPAN>`, `<STRIKE>`, `<STRONG>`, `<SUB>`, `<SUP>`, `<TEXTAREA>`, `<TT>`, `<U>`, `<VAR>`

Suggested style/usage: Anchors should be the innermost elements used in nested markup, except when you also use embedded character controls, font styles, or line breaks. However, you cannot nest anchors with other anchors. Relative URLs provide more compact references, but require more maintenance. A closing tag (`</A>`) is required.

Examples: See file /h4d4e/examples/ch06/a.htm.

<ABBR> ... </ABBR> Abbreviation

Definition: Marks the enclosed text as an abbreviation, such as WWW or TCP/IP.

Attributes:

```
TITLE="text"
```

> Provides the expanded version of the abbreviation and appears in a pop-up box when the mouse is over the acronym.

Content:

`<ABBR> ... </ABBR>` is legal within the following tags:

> `<A>, <ABBR>, <ADDRESS>, <APPLET>, <B>, <BDO>, <BIG>, <BLOCKQUOTE>, <BODY>, <BUTTON>, <CAPTION>, <CENTER>, <CITE>, <CODE>, <DD>, <DEL>, <DFN>, <DIV>, <DT>, <EM>, <FIELDSET>, <FONT>, <FORM>, <H*>, <I>, <IFRAME>, <INS>, <KBD>, <LABEL>, <LEGEND>, <LI>, <NOFRAMES>, <NOSCRIPT>, <OBJECT>, <P>, <PRE>, <Q>, <S>, <SAMP>, <SMALL>, <SPAN>, <STRIKE>, <STRONG>, <SUB>, <SUP>, <TD>, <TH>, <TT>, <U>, <VAR>`

You can use the following tags within `<ABBR> ... </ABBR>`:

> `<A>, <ABBR>, <APPLET>, <B>, <BASEFONT>, <BDO>, <BIG>, <BR>, <BUTTON>, <CITE>, <CODE>, <DFN>, <EM>, <FONT>, <I>, <IFRAME>, <IMG>, <INPUT>, <KBD>, <LABEL>, <MAP>, <OBJECT>, <Q>, <S>, <SAMP>, <SCRIPT>, <SELECT>, <SMALL>, <SPAN>, <STRIKE>, <STRONG>, <SUB>, <SUP>, <TEXTAREA>, <TT>, <U>, <VAR>`

Suggested style/usage: Use to highlight acronyms so readers can quickly identify them. If you are using an uncommon acronym for the first time, be sure to spell it out so users recognize its meaning later in the document.

Examples: See file /h4d4e/examples/ch06/acronym.htm.

<ADDRESS> ... </ADDRESS> Attribution information

Definition: Enclose credit and reference information about an HTML document and usually include such things as the author's name and address, signature files, contact information, and the like. The items included in this tag set are often rendered in an italics font.

Attributes: None

Context:

`<ADDRESS>` ... `</ADDRESS>` is legal within the following markup tags:

> `<BLOCKQUOTE>`, `<BODY>`, `<BUTTON>`, `<CENTER>`, `<DD>`, `<DIV>`,
> `<FIELDSET>`, `<FORM>`, `<IFRAME>`, `<LI>`, `<NOFRAMES>`, `<NOSCRIPT>`,
> `<OBJECT>`, `<TD>`, `<TH>`

The following markup tags can be used within `<ADDRESS>` ... `</ADDRESS>`:

> `<A>`, `<ABBR>`, `<APPLET>`, `<B>`, `<BASEFONT>`, `<BDO>`, `<BIG>`, `<BR>`,
> `<BUTTON>`, `<CITE>`, `<CODE>`, `<DFN>`, `<EM>`, `<FONT>`, `<I>`, `<IFRAME>`,
> `<IMG>`, `<INPUT>`, `<KBD>`, `<LABEL>`, `<MAP>`, `<OBJECT>`, `<P>`, `<Q>`, `<S>`,
> `<SAMP>`, `<SCRIPT>`, `<SELECT>`, `<SMALL>`, `<SPAN>`, `<STRIKE>`, `<STRONG>`,
> `<SUB>`, `<SUP>`, `<TEXTAREA>`, `<TT>`, `<U>`, `<VAR>`

Suggested style/usage: You can include this tag at the end of any document to supply author contact information for questions or feedback. You can use the `<ADDRESS>` tag as you would a footer because there is no `<FOOTER>` markup tag.

Examples: See file /h4d4e/examples/ch06/address.htm.

<APPLET> ... </APPLET> Applet

Definition: Used to include a Java applet within an HTML document.

Attributes:

`ALIGN="(LEFT|RIGHT|TOP|MIDDLE|BOTTOM)"`

> Sets the horizontal or vertical alignment for the applet.

`ALT="text"`

> May contain text that will display if the applet cannot run.

`ARCHIVE="text"`

> A comma-delimited string of archive names containing classes or other resources to be "preloaded."

`CODE="URL"`

> Indicates the name of the resource that contains the applet's compiled applet sub-class. This value must be a relative URL with respect to the `CODEBASE`.

CODEBASE="URL"

This is similar to the BASE element for HTML documents and can be used to specify an absolute URL for an applet. The location indicated in CODEBASE indicates where to search for other classes for this applet. The current URL will be used if this location is not specified.

HEIGHT=number

Specifies the height of the applet's window.

HSPACE=number

Controls horizontal blank space in pixels around the applet.

NAME="text"

Specifies the name of the applet.

OBJECT="text"

Identifies the name of the resource containing a serialized version of the applet.

VSPACE=number

Controls vertical blank space in pixels around the applet.

WIDTH=(number|"%")

Specifies the width of the applet's window.

Context:

<APPLET> ... </APPLET> is legal within the following tags:

<A>, <ABBR>, <ADDRESS>, <APPLET>, <B>, <BDO>, <BIG>, <BLOCKQUOTE>, <BODY>, <BUTTON>, <CAPTION>, <CENTER>, <CITE>, <CODE>, <DD>, <DEL>, <DFN>, <DIV>, <DT>, <EM>, <FIELDSET>, <FONT>, <FORM>, <H*>, <I>, <IFRAME>, <INS>, <KBD>, <LABEL>, <LEGEND>, <LI>, <NOFRAMES>, <NOSCRIPT>, <OBJECT>, <P>, <PRE>, <Q>, <S>, <SAMP>, <SMALL>, <SPAN>, <STRIKE>, <STRONG>, <SUB>, <SUP>, <TD>, <TH>, <TT>, <U>, <VAR>

You can use the following tags within `<APPLET> ... </APPLET>`:

```
<A>, <ABBR>, <APPLET>, <B>, <BASEFONT>, <BDO>, <BIG>, <BR>,
<BUTTON>, <CITE>, <CODE>, <DFN>, <EM>, <FONT>, <I>, <IFRAME>,
<IMG>, <INPUT>, <KBD>, <LABEL>, <MAP>, <OBJECT>, <PARAM>, <Q>,
<S>, <SAMP>, <SCRIPT>, <SELECT>, <SMALL>, <SPAN>, <STRIKE>,
<STRONG>, <SUB>, <SUP>, <TEXTAREA>, <TT>, <U>, <VAR>
```

Suggested style/usage: Always provide alternative text for those users without Java-enabled browsers and for those who have disabled Java.

Examples: See file /h4d4e/examples/ch06/applet.htm.

<AREA> Client-side image map hot spot

Definition: Specifies a hot spot's shape in a client-side image map.

Attributes:

`ACCESSKEY="character"`

Specifies a single-key stroke to activate the defined hot spot; is case-insensitive.

`ALT="text"`

Used by text browsers to present the image map's URLs in a more readable fashion.

`COORDS="X1, Y1, X2, Y2, and so on."`

Specifies the coordinates defining the shape of the hot spot. See the `SHAPE` attribute for details.

`HREF="URL"`

Links the hot spot on the image map to a specific resource.

`NOHREF`

Indicates that when the defined area of the map is clicked on, it should not link to any URL, including the current document or default URL.

`SHAPE=(RECT|CIRCLE|POLY|DEFAULT)`

Please refer to the `<A>` tag for details on this attribute.

`RECT: left-x, top-y, right-x, bottom-y`

A rectangle is defined by its top-left corner and its bottom-right corner. **Example:** <AREA SHAPE=rect COORDS="0,0,9,9">.

CIRCLE: center-x, center-y, radius

A circle is defined by its center and then radius. **Example:** <AREA SHAPE=circle COORDS="10,10,5">.

POLY: x1, y1, x2, y2, ... , x**N**, y**N**

A polygon is built from a list of coordinates, all connected in the order you present, with the last coordinate pair connected to the first. **Example:** <AREA SHAPE=POLY COORDS="10,50,15,20,20,50">.

DEFAULT

The default location has no coordinates and should be used only once in the map. It is used to indicate what should happen if the user selects one of the coordinates that are undefined in any other element.

TABINDEX=**number**

Specifies the tabbing or navigation order of the element. The number can be a positive or negative integer.

TARGET="window"

Specifies that the link should be loaded into the targeted window. You can use this attribute with a frame set in which you've named a frame in the <FRAME> element. The window can be one of these values:

window: Specifies loading the link into the targeted window, which must begin with an alphanumeric character to be valid, except in the case of the following four windows:

_blank: Loads the link into a new, unnamed empty window.

_parent: Loads the link into the immediately previous or originating document in which the link is found.

_self: Loads the link into the same window as that in which the link was clicked.

_top: Loads the link into the full body of the window.

Context:

<AREA> is legal within the following tag:

<MAP>

<AREA> is a singleton tag.

Suggested style/usage: When creating image maps, design your graphics so as to make defining geographic areas easier. Numerous image map creation tools simplify coordinate definitions by using a point-and-click interface that automates the process. See the Appendix for examples of these utilities.

Examples: See file /h4d4e/examples/ch06/area.htm.

<B> ... </B> Bold text

Definition: Indicates that the enclosed text is in boldface type.

Attributes: None

Context:

`<B> ... </B>` is legal within the following tags:

> `<A>, <ABBR>, <ADDRESS>, <APPLET>, <B>, <BDO>, <BIG>,`
> `<BLOCKQUOTE>, <BODY>, <BUTTON>, <CAPTION>, <CENTER>, <CITE>,`
> `<CODE>, <DD>, <DEL>, <DFN>, <DIV>, <DT>, <EM>, <FIELDSET>, <FONT>,`
> `<FORM>, <H*>, <I>, <IFRAME>, <INS>, <KBD>, <LABEL>, <LEGEND>,`
> `<LI>, <NOFRAMES>, <NOSCRIPT>, <OBJECT>, <P>, <PRE>, <Q>, <S>,`
> `<SAMP>, <SMALL>, <SPAN>, <STRIKE>, <STRONG>, <SUB>, <SUP>, <TD>,`
> `<TH>, <TT>, <U>, <VAR>`

You can use the following tags within `<B> ... </B>`:

> `<A>, <ABBR>, <APPLET>, <B>, <BASEFONT>, <BDO>, <BIG>, <BR>,`
> `<BUTTON>, <CITE>, <CODE>, <DFN>, <EM>, <FONT>, <I>, <IFRAME>,`
> `<IMG>, <INPUT>, <KBD>, <LABEL>, <MAP>, <OBJECT>, <Q>, <S>, <SAMP>,`
> `<SCRIPT>, <SELECT>, <SMALL>, <SPAN>, <STRIKE>, <STRONG>, <SUB>,`
> `<SUP>, <TEXTAREA>, <TT>, <U>, <VAR>`

Suggested style/usage: To provide specific focus on words or phrases in text.

Examples: See file /h4d4e/examples/ch06/b.htm.

<BASE> Basis for relative addressing

Definition: Occurs within `<HEAD> ... </HEAD>` and establishes the URL basis for subsequent URL references in `<LINK>` or anchor statements in the document body. With the `<BASE>` providing a good starting point for other references, you can write URLs more quickly and compactly.

Attributes:

`HREF="URL"`

States the absolute or relative URL for the current document.

`TARGET="window"`

Specifies loading the link into the targeted window. You can use `TARGET` with a `FRAMESET` in which you've named a frame in the `FRAME` element. The targeted window can be one of the following values:

`window`: Specifies loading the link into the targeted window. The window must begin with an alphanumeric character to be valid, with the following four exceptions:

`_blank`: Loads the link into a new (unnamed) blank window.

`_parent`: Loads the link into the immediate parent of the document in which the link is found.

`_self`: Loads the link into the same window as the link.

`_top`: Loads the link into the full body of the window.

Context:

`<BASE>` is legal within the following tag:

`<HEAD>`

`<BASE>` is a singleton tag and permits no enclosed tags.

Suggested style/usage: When building complex, multipage Web sites, it's a good idea to use the `<BASE>` tag on each page, building an easy-to-use and easy-to-navigate directory structure. `<BASE>` helps maintain the integrity of a site by specifically defining the common portion of every resource's URL. Sites that do not use the `<BASE>` tag must be more rigidly defined and controlled to ensure proper hyperlinking and resource association. Sites with `<BASE>` are a bit more stable; sites without `<BASE>` are more location-independent.

Examples: See file /h4d4e/examples/ch06/base.htm.

<BASEFONT> Base font

Definition: [Depreciated] Sets the base font parameters to be used as a default for any text that is not otherwise formatted by a style sheet or by using the `<FONT>` element.

Attributes:

`COLOR="(#RRGGBB|colorname)"`

[Depreciated] Defines the color of the base font.

FACE=name

> [Depreciated] Specifies the base font face.

SIZE="number"

> [Depreciated] Defines the size of the base font. The value of *number* can be between 1 and 7 inclusive; the default is 3, and 7 is the largest. Relative font size settings (for example, <FONT SIZE=+3>) are set according to this value throughout the document.

Context:

<BASEFONT> is legal within the following tags:

> <A>, <ABBR>, <ADDRESS>, <APPLET>, <B>, <BDO>, <BIG>, <BLOCKQUOTE>, <BODY>, <BUTTON>, <CAPTION>, <CENTER>, <CITE>, <CODE>, <DD>, <DEL>, <DFN>, <DIV>, <DT>, <EM>, <FIELDSET>, <FONT>, <FORM>, <H*>, <I>, <IFRAME>, <INS>, <KBD>, <LABEL>, <LEGEND>, <LI>, <NOFRAMES>, <NOSCRIPT>, <OBJECT>, <P>, <PRE>, <Q>, <S>, <SAMP>, <SMALL>, <SPAN>, <STRIKE>, <STRONG>, <SUB>, <SUP>, <TD>, <TH>, <TT>, <U>, <VAR>

You cannot use additional tags within <BASEFONT> because it is a singleton tag.

Suggested style/usage: This tag is depreciated in HTML 4.0 in favor of the style sheet rules that you can write for the <BODY> tag to define the same font characteristics for an entire Web document. <BASEFONT> is still supported by the current browsers, but make an effort to replace it with appropriate style rules.

Examples: See file /h4d4e/examples/ch06/basefont.htm.

<BDO> ... </BDO> Bidirectional algorithm

Definition: Establishes, alters, or reverses the default algorithm used for language and display direction.

Attributes:

LANG=language-code

> Defines the language to be used. See LANG attribute earlier in this chapter.

```
DIR=LTR|RTL
```

Sets the direction of interoperation and display of content. This is a mandatory attribute. See DIR attribute earlier in this chapter.

Context:

<BDO> is legal within the following markup tags:

```
<A>, <ABBR>, <ADDRESS>, <APPLET>, <B>, <BDO>, <BIG>,
<BLOCKQUOTE>, <BODY>, <BUTTON>, <CAPTION>, <CENTER>, <CITE>,
<CODE>, <DD>, <DEL>, <DFN>, <DIV>, <DT>, <EM>, <FIELDSET>, <FONT>,
<FORM>, <H*>, <I>, <IFRAME>, <INS>, <KBD>, <LABEL>, <LEGEND>,
<LI>, <NOFRAMES>, <NOSCRIPT>, <OBJECT>, <P>, <PRE>, <Q>, <S>,
<SAMP>, <SMALL>, <SPAN>, <STRIKE>, <STRONG>, <SUB>, <SUP>, <TD>,
<TH>, <TT>, <U>, <VAR>
```

You can use the following markup tags within <BDO> ... </BDO>:

```
<A>, <ABBR>, <APPLET>, <B>, <BASEFONT>, <BDO>, <BIG>, <BR>,
<BUTTON>, <CITE>, <CODE>, <DFN>, <EM>, <FONT>, <I>, <IFRAME>,
<IMG>, <INPUT>, <KBD>, <LABEL>, <MAP>, <OBJECT>, <Q>, <S>, <SAMP>,
<SCRIPT>, <SELECT>, <SMALL>, <SPAN>, <STRIKE>, <STRONG>, <SUB>,
<SUP>, <TEXTAREA>, <TT>, <U>, <VAR>
```

Suggested style/usage: You should use this tag when displaying varying sections of nondefault language and direction content.

Examples: See file /h4d4e/examples/ch06/bdo.htm.

<BIG> ... </BIG> Big text

Definition: Makes text font one size larger than the <BASEFONT> size.

Attributes: None

Context:

<BIG> ... </BIG> is legal within the following tags:

```
<A>, <ABBR>, <ADDRESS>, <APPLET>, <B>, <BDO>, <BIG>,
<BLOCKQUOTE>, <BODY>, <BUTTON>, <CAPTION>, <CENTER>, <CITE>,
<CODE>, <DD>, <DEL>, <DFN>, <DIV>, <DT>, <EM>, <FIELDSET>,
<FONT>, <FORM>, <H*>, <I>, <IFRAME>, <INS>, <KBD>, <LABEL>,
<LEGEND>, <LI>, <NOFRAMES>, <NOSCRIPT>, <OBJECT>, <P>, <Q>,
<S>, <SAMP>, <SMALL>, <SPAN>, <STRIKE>, <STRONG>, <SUB>, <SUP>,
<TD>, <TH>, <TT>, <U>, <VAR>
```

You can use the following tags within `<BIG>` ... `</BIG>`:

> `<A>`, `<ABBR>`, `<APPLET>`, `<B>`, `<BASEFONT>`, `<BDO>`, `<BIG>`, `<BR>`,
> `<BUTTON>`, `<CITE>`, `<CODE>`, `<DFN>`, `<EM>`, `<FONT>`, `<I>`, `<IFRAME>`,
> `<IMG>`, `<INPUT>`, `<KBD>`, `<LABEL>`, `<MAP>`, `<OBJECT>`, `<Q>`, `<S>`, `<SAMP>`,
> `<SCRIPT>`, `<SELECT>`, `<SMALL>`, `<SPAN>`, `<STRIKE>`, `<STRONG>`, `<SUB>`,
> `<SUP>`, `<TEXTAREA>`, `<TT>`, `<U>`, `<VAR>`

Suggested style/usage: Nesting `<BIG>` tags can produce text in a larger font than using only one `<BIG>` tag, but the specs do not require this. However, you can use style sheet rules to achieve the same effect as using multiple nested `<BIG>` tags.

Examples: See file /h4d4e/examples/ch06/big.htm.

`<BLOCKQUOTE>` ... `</BLOCKQUOTE>` *Quote style*

Definition: `<BLOCKQUOTE>` ... `</BLOCKQUOTE>` sets off large chunks of material quoted from external sources, publications, or other materials.

Attributes:

`CITE="text"`

> Provides information about the source of the quote.

Context:

`<BLOCKQUOTE>` ... `</BLOCKQUOTE>` is legal within the following tags:

> `<BLOCKQUOTE>`, `<BODY>`, `<BUTTON>`, `<CENTER>`, `<DD>`, `<DIV>`,
> `<FIELDSET>`, `<FORM>`, `<IFRAME>`, `<LI>`, `<NOFRAMES>`, `<NOSCRIPT>`,
> `<OBJECT>`, `<TD>`, `<TH>`

You can use the following tags within `<BLOCKQUOTE>` ... `</BLOCKQUOTE>`:

> `<A>`, `<ABBR>`, `<ADDRESS>`, `<APPLET>`, `<B>`, `<BASEFONT>`, `<BDO>`, `<BIG>`,
> `<BLOCKQUOTE>`, `<BR>`, `<BUTTON>`, `<CENTER>`, `<CITE>`, `<CODE>`, `<DFN>`,
> `<DIR>`, `<DIV>`, `<DL>`, `<EM>`, `<FIELDSET>`, `<FONT>`, `<FORM>`, `<H*>`, `<HR>`,
> `<I>`, `<IFRAME>`, `<IMG>`, `<INPUT>`, `<ISINDEX>`, `<KBD>`, `<LABEL>`, `<MAP>`,
> `<MENU>`, `<NOFRAMES>`, `<NOSCRIPT>`, `<OBJECT>`, `<OL>`, `<P>`, `<PRE>`, `<Q>`,
> `<S>`, `<SAMP>`, `<SCRIPT>`, `<SELECT>`, `<SMALL>`, `<SPAN>`, `<STRIKE>`,
> `<STRONG>`, `<SUB>`, `<SUP>`, `<TABLE>`, `<TEXTAREA>`, `<TT>`, `<U>`, `<UL>`, `<VAR>`

Suggested style/usage: When you quote from an external source (more than one line long), use `<BLOCKQUOTE>` to offset the text from both left and right margins. Always attribute your sources. Remember to use `<CITE>` to highlight the actual publication, if applicable.

Examples: See file /h4d4e/examples/ch06/block.htm.

<BODY> ... </BODY> Document body

Definition: Identifies the body of an HTML document and completely encloses its contents.

Attributes:

ALINK=(#RRGGBB|colorname)

> **[Depreciated]** Sets the color for the active (currently selected) link.

BACKGROUND="URL"

> **[Depreciated]** Points to an image location that is used as the (tiled) background of the document.

BGCOLOR=(#RRGGBB|colorname)

> **[Depreciated]** Sets the background color.

LINK=(#RRGGBB|colorname)

> **[Depreciated]** Sets the color for links.

TEXT=(#RRGGBB|colorname)

> **[Depreciated]** Sets the color for text.

VLINK=(#RRGGBB|colorname)

> **[Depreciated]** Sets the color for visited links.

Context:

<BODY> ... </BODY> is legal within the following markup tags:

> <HTML>, <NOFRAMES>

You can use the following markup tags within <BODY> ... </BODY>:

> <A>, <ABBR>, <ADDRESS>, <APPLET>, <B>, <BASEFONT>, <BDO>, <BIG>,
> <BLOCKQUOTE>, <BR>, <BUTTON>, <CENTER>, <CITE>, <CODE>, <DFN>,
> <DIR>, <DIV>, <DL>, <EM>, <FIELDSET>, <FONT>, <FORM>, <H*>, <HR>,
> <I>, <IFRAME>, <IMG>, <INPUT>, <ISINDEX>, <KBD>, <LABEL>, <MAP>,
> <MENU>, <NOFRAMES>, <NOSCRIPT>, <OBJECT>, <OL>, <P>, <PRE>, <Q>,
> <S>, <SAMP>, <SCRIPT>, <SELECT>, <SMALL>, <SPAN>, <STRIKE>,
> <STRONG>, <SUB>, <SUP>, <TABLE>, <TEXTAREA>, <TT>, <U>, <UL>, <VAR>

Suggested style/usage: <BODY> ... </BODY> has only one use; it sets off (defines) the body of an HTML document. This explicit structure tag is required for strictly interpreted HTML.

Examples: See file /h4d4e/examples/ch06/body.htm.

*
 Force line break*

Definition: Forces a line break in HTML text.

Attributes:

CLEAR=(LEFT|ALL|RIGHT|NONE)

> LEFT inserts space that aligns the following text with the left margin directly below a left-aligned floating image.
>
> ALL places the following text past all floating images.
>
> RIGHT inserts space that aligns the following text with the right margin directly below a right-aligned floating image.
>
> NONE is the default, which does nothing.

Context:

 is legal within the following tags:

> <A>, <ABBR>, <ADDRESS>, <APPLET>, <B>, <BDO>, <BIG>,
> <BLOCKQUOTE>, <BODY>, <BUTTON>, <CAPTION>, <CENTER>, <CITE>,
> <CODE>, <DD>, <DEL>, <DFN>, <DIV>, <DT>, <EM>, <FIELDSET>, <FONT>,
> <FORM>, <H*>, <I>, <IFRAME>, <INS>, <KBD>, <LABEL>, <LEGEND>,
> <LI>, <NOFRAMES>, <NOSCRIPT>, <OBJECT>, <P>, <PRE>, <Q>, <S>,
> <SAMP>, <SMALL>, <SPAN>, <STRIKE>, <STRONG>, <SUB>, <SUP>, <TD>,
> <TH>, <TT>, <U>, <VAR>

 is a singleton tag. No tags can be used within it.

Suggested style/usage:
 forces line breaks in text. This tag is useful for creating short lines of text, or for text that must be broken in specific places, such as verse.

Examples: See file /h4d4e/examples/ch06/br.htm.

<BUTTON> ... </BUTTON> Form button

Definition: Creates a submission input element similar to the standard "submit" and "reset" buttons, but is graphically more interesting.

Attributes:

DISABLED

> Renders the button unclickable by the user.

NAME="name"

> Specifies a name for the button.

TABINDEX="number"

> Identifies the element's place in the tabbing order.

TYPE=BUTTON|SUBMIT|RESET

> Specifies the type of button. The type can be one of these values:
>
> TYPE=button: **Creates a button that calls a script. You can have more than one button in a form, but each should have a different** NAME.
>
> TYPE=submit: **Produces a button that sends the contents of the form to the server. You can have more than one submit button in the form, but each should have a different** NAME. **The name and value of the pressed button will be sent to the server as well.**
>
> TYPE=reset: **Produces a button that restores the form to its original state and erases any data the user has entered.**

VALUE="value"

> Specifies the value of the control.

Context:

<BUTTON> ... </BUTTON> is legal within the following tags:

> <A>, <ABBR>, <ADDRESS>, <APPLET>, <B>, <BDO>, <BIG>,
> <BLOCKQUOTE>, <BODY>, <CAPTION>, <CENTER>, <CITE>, <CODE>, <DD>,
> <DEL>, <DFN>, <DIV>, <DT>, <EM>, <FIELDSET>, <FONT>, <FORM>, <H*>,
> <I>, <IFRAME>, <INS>, <KBD>, <LABEL>, <LEGEND>, <LI>, <NOFRAMES>,
> <NOSCRIPT>, <OBJECT>, <P>, <PRE>, <Q>, <S>, <SAMP>, <SMALL>,
> <SPAN>, <STRIKE>, <STRONG>, <SUB>, <SUP>, <TD>, <TH>, <TT>, <U>,
> <VAR>

You can use the following tags within `<BUTTON>` ... `</BUTTON>`:

```
<A>, <ABBR>, <ADDRESS>, <APPLET>, <B>, <BASEFONT>, <BDO>, <BIG>,
<BLOCKQUOTE>, <BR>, <BUTTON>, <CENTER>, <CITE>, <CODE>, <DFN>,
<DIR>, <DIV>, <DL>, <EM>, <FIELDSET>, <FONT>, <FORM>, <H*>, <HR>,
<I>, <IFRAME>, <IMG>, <INPUT>, <ISINDEX>, <KBD>, <LABEL>, <MAP>,
<MENU>, <NOFRAMES>, <NOSCRIPT>, <OBJECT>, <OL>, <P>, <PRE>, <Q>,
<S>, <SAMP>, <SCRIPT>, <SELECT>, <SMALL>, <SPAN>, <STRIKE>,
<STRONG>, <SUB>, <SUP>, <TABLE>, <TEXTAREA>, <TT>, <U>, <UL>,
<VAR>
```

Suggested style/usage: The `<BUTTON>` tag is the preferred choice when creating input objects that contain graphics. If you use the `<INPUT>` tag to create a graphical input object, the graphic is flat against the screen, as with other images. `<BUTTON>` raises the image so it looks like, and depresses like, an actual button.

Examples: See file /h4d4e/examples/ch06/button.htm.

<CAPTION> ... </CAPTION> Table caption

Definition: Used in captioning a `<TABLE>` and can appear above or below the table. You can indicate the location of the caption with the `ALIGN` attribute. A table caption is usually centered and in boldface type or is otherwise emphasized by the browser.

Attributes:

`ALIGN=(LEFT|RIGHT|TOP|BOTTOM)`

> Sets the caption alignment within the table. The align type can be `LEFT`, `RIGHT`, `TOP`, or `BOTTOM`. The default centers the caption at the bottom of the table.

Context:

`<CAPTION>` ... `</CAPTION>` is legal within the following tag:

`<TABLE>`

You can use the following tags within `<CAPTION>` ... `</CAPTION>`:

```
<A>, <ABBR>, <APPLET>, <B>, <BASEFONT>, <BDO>, <BIG>, <BR>,
<BUTTON>, <CITE>, <CODE>, <DFN>, <EM>, <FONT>, <I>, <IFRAME>,
<IMG>, <INPUT>, <KBD>, <LABEL>, <MAP>, <OBJECT>, <Q>, <S>, <SAMP>,
<SCRIPT>, <SELECT>, <SMALL>, <SPAN>, <STRIKE>, <STRONG>, <SUB>,
<SUP>, <TEXTAREA>, <TT>, <U>, <VAR>
```

Suggested style/usage: The <CAPTION> tag should appear directly below the <TABLE> tag and before the first <TR>. You can use all text-level tags inside a <CAPTION>. Keep it brief; avoid using images or large blocks of text.

Examples: See file /h4d4e/examples/ch06/caption.htm.

<CENTER> ... </CENTER> *Centered text*

Definition: [Depreciated] Indicates that the text should be centered horizontally in the display window.

Attributes: None

Context:

<CENTER> ... </CENTER> is legal within the following tags:

> <BLOCKQUOTE>, <BODY>, <BUTTON>, <CENTER>, <DD>, <DIV>,
> <FIELDSET>, <FORM>, <IFRAME>, <LI>, <NOFRAMES>, <NOSCRIPT>,
> <OBJECT>, <TD>, <TH>

You can use the following tags within <CENTER> ... </CENTER>:

> <A>, <ABBR>, <ADDRESS>, <APPLET>, <B>, <BASEFONT>, <BDO>, <BIG>,
> <BLOCKQUOTE>, <BR>, <BUTTON>, <CENTER>, <CITE>, <CODE>, <DFN>,
> <DIR>, <DIV>, <DL>, <EM>, <FIELDSET>, <FONT>, <FORM>, <H*>, <HR>,
> <I>, <IFRAME>, <IMG>, <INPUT>, <ISINDEX>, <KBD>, <LABEL>, <MAP>,
> <MENU>, <NOFRAMES>, <NOSCRIPT>, <OBJECT>, <OL>, <P>, <PRE>, <Q>,
> <S>, <SAMP>, <SCRIPT>, <SELECT>, <SMALL>, <SPAN>, <STRIKE>,
> <STRONG>, <SUB>, <SUP>, <TABLE>, <TEXTAREA>, <TT>, <U>, <UL>,
> <VAR>

Suggested style/usage: <CENTER> has been depreciated in favor of similar style sheet properties as well as the ALIGN=CENTER attribute that can be applied to many block-level elements.

Examples: See file /h4d4e/examples/ch06/center.htm.

<CITE> ... </CITE> *Citation markup*

Definition: Use <CITE> ... </CITE> to highlight external resource citations for documents, publications, and so on.

Attributes: None

Context:

<CITE> ... </CITE> is legal within the following tags:

```
<A>, <ABBR>, <ADDRESS>, <APPLET>, <B>, <BDO>, <BIG>,
<BLOCKQUOTE>, <BODY>, <BUTTON>, <CAPTION>, <CENTER>, <CITE>,
<CODE>, <DD>, <DEL>, <DFN>, <DIV>, <DT>, <EM>, <FIELDSET>, <FONT>,
<FORM>, <H*>, <I>, <IFRAME>, <INS>, <KBD>, <LABEL>, <LEGEND>,
<LI>, <NOFRAMES>, <NOSCRIPT>, <OBJECT>, <P>, <PRE>, <Q>, <S>,
<SAMP>, <SMALL>, <SPAN>, <STRIKE>, <STRONG>, <SUB>, <SUP>, <TD>,
<TH>, <TT>, <U>, <VAR>
```

You can use the following tags within `<CITE>` ... `</CITE>`:

```
<A>, <ABBR>, <APPLET>, <B>, <BASEFONT>, <BDO>, <BIG>, <BR>,
<BUTTON>, <CITE> <CODE>, <DFN>, <EM>, <FONT>, <I>, <IFRAME>,
<IMG>, <INPUT>, <KBD>, <LABEL>, <MAP>, <OBJECT>, <Q>, <S>, <SAMP>,
<SCRIPT>, <SELECT>, <SMALL>, <SPAN>, <STRIKE>, <STRONG>, <SUB>,
<SUP>, <TEXTAREA>, <TT>, <U>, <VAR>
```

Suggested style/usage: Use to highlight short citations or other references.

Examples: See file /h4d4e/examples/ch06/cite.htm.

<CODE> ... </CODE> Program code text

Definition: `<CODE>` ... `</CODE>` is used to enclose programs or samples of code to offset them from normal text and is usually displayed in a monospaced font.

Attributes: None.

Context:

`<CODE>` ... `</CODE>` is legal within the following tags:

```
<A>, <ABBR>, <ADDRESS>, <APPLET>, <B>, <BDO>, <BIG>,
<BLOCKQUOTE>, <BODY>, <BUTTON>, <CAPTION>, <CENTER>, <CITE>,
<CODE>, <DD>, <DEL>, <DFN>, <DIV>, <DT>, <EM>, <FIELDSET>, <FONT>,
<FORM>, <H*>, <I>, <IFRAME>, <INS>, <KBD>, <LABEL>, <LEGEND>,
<LI>, <NOFRAMES>, <NOSCRIPT>, <OBJECT>, <P>, <PRE>, <Q>, <S>,
<SAMP>, <SMALL>, <SPAN>, <STRIKE>, <STRONG>, <SUB>, <SUP>, <TD>,
<TH>, <TT>, <U>, <VAR>
```

You can use the following tags within `<CODE>` ... `</CODE>`:

```
<A>, <ABBR>, <APPLET>, <B>, <BASEFONT>, <BDO>, <BIG>, <BR>,
<BUTTON>, <CITE>, <CODE>, <DFN>, <EM>, <FONT>, <I>, <IFRAME>,
<IMG>, <INPUT>, <KBD>, <LABEL>, <MAP>, <OBJECT>, <Q>, <S>, <SAMP>,
<SCRIPT>, <SELECT>, <SMALL>, <SPAN>, <STRIKE>, <STRONG>, <SUB>,
<SUP>, <TEXTAREA>, <TT>, <U>, <VAR>
```

Suggested style/usage: Use <CODE> ... </CODE> to set off samples of program code or other computer-based information within the text body of a document.

Examples: See file /h4d4e/examples/ch06/code.htm.

<COL> Column properties

Definition: Sets the properties of a column. Use this element with a <COLGROUP> element to set the properties of a single column among a number of columns.

Attributes:

ALIGN=(LEFT|RIGHT|CENTER|JUSTIFY|CHAR)

Specifies the horizontal text alignment in the column's cells. The align type can be one of these values:

LEFT: The text is left-aligned. This is the default alignment.

RIGHT: The text is right-aligned.

CENTER: The text is centered.

JUSTIFY: The text is justified.

CHAR: The text is aligned to the character specified by the CHAR attribute.

CHAR="text"

Specifies the character that the text will be aligned to when using ALIGN=CHAR and when the CHAROFF attribute is present.

CHAROFF=number

Defines how far, in pixels, the remainder of text in a line should be offset from the first occurrence of the alignment character specified by CHAR=.

SPAN="number"

Sets the number of consecutive columns for which the properties are defined.

VALIGN=TOP|MIDDLE|BOTTOM|BASELINE

Specifies the vertical text alignment in the column's cells. The valign type can be one of these values:

TOP: The text is aligned with the top of the cell.

MIDDLE: The text is aligned with the middle of the cell.

BOTTOM: The text is aligned with the bottom of the cell.

BASELINE: The text is aligned with the baseline common to all the cells in the row.

WIDTH=number

Sets the width for each column.

Context:

<COL> is legal within the following tags:

<COLGROUP>, <TABLE>

<COL> is a singleton tag, and no tags can be used within it.

Suggested style/usage: Column markup is a convenient way to define a set of common properties for several columns. The <COL> tag is a subset of <COLGROUP>.

Examples: See file /h4d4e/examples/ch06/col.htm.

<COLGROUP> Column group

Definition: Sets the properties of one or more columns. If different columns in a group of columns will require different properties, use <COLGROUP> in conjunction with one or more <COL> elements to set the properties for the columns individually. This element affects how rules are drawn within a table when groups are specified with the RULES= attribute in the <TABLE> element.

Attributes:

ALIGN=(LEFT|RIGHT|CENTER|JUSTIFY|CHAR)

Specifies the horizontal text alignment in the column cells. The align type can be one of these values:

LEFT: The text is left-aligned. This is the default alignment.

RIGHT: The text is right-aligned.

CENTER: The text is centered.

JUSTIFY: The text is double-justified.

CHAR: The text is aligned to the character specified by the CHAR attribute.

CHAR="text"

Specifies the character the text will be aligned to when using ALIGN=CHAR and when the CHAROFF attribute is present.

CHAROFF=number

Defines how far, in pixels, the remainder of text in a line should be offset from the first occurrence of the alignment character specified by CHAR=.

SPAN="number"

Sets the number of consecutive columns that make up the group and for which the properties are defined.

VALIGN= TOP|MIDDLE|BOTTOM|BASELINE

Specifies the vertical text alignment in the column cells. The VALIGN type can be one of these values:

TOP: The text is aligned with the top of the cell.

MIDDLE: The text is aligned with the middle of the cell.

BOTTOM: The text is aligned with the bottom of the cell.

BASELINE: The text is aligned with the baseline common to all the cells in the row.

WIDTH=number

Sets the width for each column.

Context:

<COLGROUP> is legal within the following tag:

    <TABLE>

<COLGROUP> is a singleton tag, and no tags can be used within it.

Suggested style/usage: Column groups allow you to specify formatting for several columns in a like group, just as table row formatting applies formatting to a collection of table cells.

Examples: See file /h4d4e/examples/ch06/colgroup.htm.

<DD> Definition description

Definition: The descriptive or definition part of a definition list element. This element is displayed indented below the term item.

Attributes: None

Context:

<DD> is legal within the following tag:

<DL>

You can use the following tags within <DD>:

<A>, <ABBR>, <ADDRESS>, <APPLET>, <B>, <BASEFONT>, <BDO>, <BIG>, <BLOCKQUOTE>, <BR>, <BUTTON>, <CENTER>, <CITE>, <CODE>, <DFN>, <DIR>, <DIV>, <DL>, <EM>, <FIELDSET>, <FONT>, <FORM>, <H*>, <HR>, <I>, <IFRAME>, <IMG>, <INPUT>, <ISINDEX>, <KBD>, <LABEL>, <MAP>, <MENU>, <NOFRAMES>, <NOSCRIPT>, <OBJECT>, <OL>, <P>, <PRE>, <Q>, <S>, <SAMP>, <SCRIPT>, <SELECT>, <SMALL>, <SPAN>, <STRIKE>, <STRONG>, <SUB>, <SUP>, <TABLE>, <TEXTAREA>, <TT>, <U>, <UL>, <VAR>

The <DD> tag is a singleton tag.

Suggested style/usage: For glossaries or other lists in which a single term or line needs to be associated with a block of indented text.

Examples: See file /h4d4e/examples/ch06/dd.htm.

<DEL> ... </DEL> Deleted text

Definition: Marks text that has been deleted from a previous version of the Web document.

Attributes:

CITE="URL"

Points to another document that describes why the text was deleted.

DATETIME=YYYY-MM-DDThh:mm:ssTZD

Marks the time when you changed the document. This attribute's value must use a specific format, shown above, that conforms to the ISO8601 time/date specification. The abbreviations shown above refer to the following date and time information:

YYYY = The year

MM = The two-digit month — for example, "03" for March

DD = The day

T = Indicates the beginning of the time section

hh = The hour, in military time (0–23 hours), without a.m. or p.m. specifications

mm = The minute

ss = The second

TZD = The time zone

Z = The Coordinated Universal Time (CUT)

+hh:mm = The local time that is hours (hh) and minutes (mm) ahead of the CUT

-hh:mm = The local time that is hours (hh) and minutes (mm) behind the CUT

Context:

<DEL> ... </DEL> is legal within the following tag:

<BODY>

You can use the following tags within <DEL> ... </DEL>:

<A>, <ABBR>, <APPLET>, <B>, <BASEFONT>, <BDO>, <BIG>, <BR>, <BUTTON>, <CITE>, <CODE>, <DFN>, <EM>, <FONT>, <I>, <IFRAME>, <IMG>, <INPUT>, <KBD>, <LABEL>, <MAP>, <OBJECT>, <Q>, <S>, <SAMP>, <SCRIPT>, <SELECT>, <SMALL>, <SPAN>, <STRIKE>, <STRONG>, <SUB>, <SUP>, <TEXTAREA>, <TT>, <U>, <VAR>

Suggested style/usage: <DEL> ... </DEL> and its companion tag <INS> ... </INS> were created to show revisions to Web pages. Use <DEL> ... </DEL> when several people are working on a Web document to highlight text that has been removed, including when and why.

Examples: See file /h4d4e/examples/ch06/del.htm.

<DFN> ... </DFN> Definition of a term

Definition: You use <DFN> ... </DFN> to mark terms that appear for the first time in the Web document. These definitions are often in italics so the user can identify the first occurrence of the term.

Attributes: None

Context:

<DFN> ... </DFN> is legal within the following tags:

        <A>, <ABBR>, <ADDRESS>, <APPLET>, <B>, <BDO>, <BIG>,
        <BLOCKQUOTE>, <BODY>, <BUTTON>, <CAPTION>, <CENTER>, <CITE>,
        <CODE>, <DD>, <DEL>, <DFN>, <DIV>, <DT>, <EM>, <FIELDSET>, <FONT>,
        <FORM>, <H*>, <I>, <IFRAME>, <INS>, <KBD>, <LABEL>, <LEGEND>,
        <LI>, <NOFRAMES>, <NOSCRIPT>, <OBJECT>, <P>, <PRE>, <Q>, <S>,
        <SAMP>, <SMALL>, <SPAN>, <STRIKE>, <STRONG>, <SUB>, <SUP>, <TD>,
        <TH>, <TT>, <U>, <VAR>

You can use the following tags within <DFN> ... </DFN>:

        <A>, <ABBR>, <APPLET>, <B>, <BASEFONT>, <BDO>, <BIG>, <BR>,
        <BUTTON>, <CITE>, <CODE>, <DFN>, <EM>, <FONT>, <I>, <IFRAME>,
        <IMG>, <INPUT>, <KBD>, <LABEL>, <MAP>, <OBJECT>, <Q>, <S>, <SAMP>,
        <SCRIPT>, <SELECT>, <SMALL>, <SPAN>, <STRIKE>, <STRONG>, <SUB>,
        <SUP>, <TEXTAREA>, <TT>, <U>, <VAR>

Suggested style/usage: Use this tag sparingly. Not all browsers may interpret this tag correctly.

Examples: See file /h4d4e/examples/ch06/dfn.htm.

<DIR> ... </DIR> Directory list

Definition: [Depreciated] A style typically used for lists made up of short elements, such as filenames.

Attributes: None

Context:

<DIR> ... </DIR> is legal within the following tags:

        <BLOCKQUOTE>, <BODY>, <BUTTON>, <CENTER>, <DD>, <DIV>,
        <FIELDSET>, <FORM>, <IFRAME>, <LI>, <NOFRAMES>, <NOSCRIPT>,
        <OBJECT>, <TD>, <TH>

You can use the following tag within <DIR> ... </DIR>:

        <LI>

Suggested style/usage: Use to build lists of short elements (usually shorter than 20 characters long). Use this tag sparingly due to depreciation.

Examples: See file /h4d4e/examples/ch06/dir.htm.

<DIV> ... </DIV> Logical division

Definition: Indicates divisions in a document. You can use this block-level element to group other block elements.

Attributes:

```
ALIGN=(LEFT|CENTER|RIGHT|JUSTIFY)
```

Specifies the default horizontal alignment for the contents of the <DIV> element.

```
STYLE="text"
```

You can also use <SPAN> to add margins, paragraph width, and other related width options to text. See Chapter 10 for <STYLE> attribute details.

Context:

<DIV> ... </DIV> is legal within the following markup tags:

```
<BLOCKQUOTE>, <BODY>, <BUTTON>, <CENTER>, <DD>, <DIV>,
<FIELDSET>, <FORM>, <IFRAME>, <LI>, <NOFRAMES>, <NOSCRIPT>,
<OBJECT>, <TD>, <TH>
```

You can use the following markup tags within <DIV> ... </DIV>:

```
<A>, <ABBR>, <ADDRESS>, <APPLET>, <B>, <BASEFONT>, <BDO>, <BIG>,
<BLOCKQUOTE>, <BR>, <BUTTON>, <CENTER>, <CITE>, <CODE>, <DFN>,
<DIR>, <DIV>, <DL>, <EM>, <FIELDSET>, <FONT>, <FORM>, <H*>, <HR>,
<I>, <IFRAME>, <IMG>, <INPUT>, <ISINDEX>, <KBD>, <LABEL>, <MAP>,
<MENU>, <NOFRAMES>, <NOSCRIPT>, <OBJECT>, <OL>, <P>, <PRE>, <Q>,
<S>, <SAMP>, <SCRIPT>, <SELECT>, <SMALL>, <SPAN>, <STRIKE>,
<STRONG>, <SUB>, <SUP>, <TABLE>, <TEXTAREA>, <TT>, <U>, <UL>,
<VAR>
```

Suggested style/usage: The align attribute on a block element inside <DIV> overrides the align value of the <DIV> element. Use <CENTER> instead of <DIV ALIGN=CENTER>, even though HTML DTD defines the two as being identical. You cannot use <DIV> in conjunction with <P> because a <DIV>

element will terminate a paragraph. However, the <CENTER> tag has been depreciated in favor of the text-align: center style rule, and we suggest getting into the habit of using the style rule method instead of the <CENTER> tag.

Examples: See file /h4d4e/examples/ch06/div.htm.

<DL> ... </DL> Definition list

Definition: <DD> encloses a collection of definition items in a definition list. You would usually use the <DD> tag for glossaries or other situations where short, left-aligned terms precede longer blocks of indented text. Browsers usually render definition lists with the term (<DT>) in the left margin and the definition (<DD>) on one or more lines indented slightly from the term.

Attributes:

COMPACT

> **[Depreciated]** Renders the list as compactly as possible by reducing line leading and spacing.

Context:

<DL> ... </DL> is legal within the following tags:

> <BLOCKQUOTE>, <BODY>, <BUTTON>, <CENTER>, <DD>, <DIV>, <FIELDSET>, <FORM>, <IFRAME>, <LI>, <NOFRAMES>, <NOSCRIPT>, <OBJECT>, <TD>, <TH>

You can use the following tags within <DL> ... </DL>:

> <DD>, <DT>

Suggested style/usage: For lists where left-justified elements (for example, terms and definitions) precede longer, indented blocks of text, such as glossaries or a dictionary. Do not use <DL> to create an indented section of text. This is syntactically invalid HTML and is not guaranteed to work.

Examples: See file /h4d4e/examples/ch06/dl.htm.

<DT> Definition term

Definition: The term part of a definition entry.

Attributes: None

Context:

`<DT>` is legal within the following tag:

> `<DL>`

The `<DT>` tag is a singleton tag.

Suggested style/usage: For situations where left-justified, short entries pair up with longer blocks of indented text, such as glossaries or definition lists.

Examples: See file /h4d4e/examples/ch06/dt.htm.

<EM> ... </EM> Emphasis

Definition: `<EM>` provides typographic emphasis, usually rendered as italics.

Attributes: None

Context:

`<EM> ... </EM>` is legal within the following tags:

> `<A>, <ABBR>, <ADDRESS>, <APPLET>, <B>, <BDO>, <BIG>,`
> `<BLOCKQUOTE>, <BODY>, <BUTTON>, <CAPTION>, <CENTER>, <CITE>,`
> `<CODE>, <DD>, <DEL>, <DFN>, <DIV>, <DT>, <EM>, <FIELDSET>, <FONT>,`
> `<FORM>, <H*>, <I>, <IFRAME>, <INS>, <KBD>, <LABEL>, <LEGEND>,`
> `<LI>, <NOFRAMES>, <NOSCRIPT>, <OBJECT>, <P>, <PRE>, <Q>, <S>,`
> `<SAMP>, <SMALL>, <SPAN>, <STRIKE>, <STRONG>, <SUB>, <SUP>, <TD>,`
> `<TH>, <TT>, <U>, <VAR>`

You can use the following tags within `<EM> ... </EM>`:

> `<A>, <ABBR>, <APPLET>, <B>, <BASEFONT>, <BDO>, <BIG>, <BR>,`
> `<BUTTON>, <CITE>, <CODE>, <DFN>, <EM>, <FONT>, <I>, <IFRAME>,`
> `<IMG>, <INPUT>, <KBD>, <LABEL>, <MAP>, <OBJECT>, <Q>, <S>, <SAMP>,`
> `<SCRIPT>, <SELECT>, <SMALL>, <SPAN>, <STRIKE>, <STRONG>, <SUB>,`
> `<SUP>, <TEXTAREA>, <TT>, <U>, <VAR>`

Suggested style/usage: Use this tag wherever you need to add mild emphasis to text. Make certain to use sparingly, both in terms of the number of emphasized words and how often text emphasis occurs.

Examples: See file /h4d4e/examples/ch06/em.htm.

<FIELDSET> ... </FIELDSET> Set of fields

Definition: Groups similar form elements and controls.

Attributes: None

Context:

<FIELDSET> ... </FIELDSET> is legal within the following tags:

> <BLOCKQUOTE>, <BODY>, <CENTER>, <DD>, <DIV>, <FIELDSET>, <FORM>,
> <IFRAME>, <LI>, <NOFRAMES>, <NOSCRIPT>, <OBJECT>, <TD>, <TH>

You can use the following tags within <FIELDSET> ... </FIELDSET>:

> <A>, <ABBR>, <ADDRESS>, <APPLET>, <B>, <BASEFONT>, <BDO>, <BIG>,
> <BLOCKQUOTE>, <BR>, <BUTTON>, <CENTER>, <CITE>, <CODE>, <DFN>,
> <DIR>, <DIV>, <DL>, <EM>, <FIELDSET>, <FONT>, <FORM>, <H*>, <HR>,
> <I>, <IFRAME>, <IMG>, <INPUT>, <ISINDEX>, <KBD>, <LABEL>,
> <LEGEND>, <MAP>, <MENU>, <NOFRAMES>, <NOSCRIPT>, <OBJECT>, <OL>,
> <P>, <PRE>, <Q>, <S>, <SAMP>, <SCRIPT>, <SELECT>, <SMALL>, <SPAN>,
> <STRIKE>, <STRONG>, <SUB>, <SUP>, <TABLE>, <TEXTAREA>, <TT>, <U>,
> <UL>, <VAR>

Suggested style/usage: Including <FIELDSET> tags within forms helps users recognize related groups of controls and input items. Use the <LEGEND> tag to clearly identify each field set.

Examples: See file /h4d4e/examples/ch06/fieldset.htm.

<FONT> ... </FONT> Font appearance

Definition: Sets the size, font, and color of enclosed text.

Attributes:

COLOR="(#RRGGBB|colorname)"

> **[Depreciated]** Sets font color.

FACE="name[, name2[, name3]]"

> **[Depreciated]** Sets the font face. You can specify a list of font names. If the first font is available on the system, it will be used; otherwise, the second will be tried, and so on. If none are available, a default font will be used.

```
SIZE="number"
```

> **[Depreciated]** Specifies font size between 1 and 7 (7 is the largest). A plus or minus sign before the number indicates a size relative to the current font setting. Relative font sizes are not cumulative, so putting two `<FONT SIZE="+1">` elements in a row does not result in the size being increased by 2.

Context:

`<FONT> ... </FONT>` is legal within the following tags:

> `<A>, <ABBR>, <ADDRESS>, <APPLET>, <B>, <BDO>, <BIG>,`
> `<BLOCKQUOTE>, <BODY>, <BUTTON>, <CAPTION>, <CENTER>, <CITE>,`
> `<CODE>, <DD>, <DEL>, <DFN>, <DIV>, <DT>, <EM>, <FIELDSET>, <FONT>,`
> `<FORM>, <H*>, <I>, <IFRAME>, <INS>, <KBD>, <LABEL>, <LEGEND>,`
> `<LI>, <NOFRAMES>, <NOSCRIPT>, <OBJECT>, <P>, <Q>, <S>, <SAMP>,`
> `<SMALL>, <SPAN>, <STRIKE>, <STRONG>, <SUB>, <SUP>, <TD>, <TH>,`
> `<TT>, <U>, <VAR>`

You can use the following tags within `<FONT> ... </FONT>`:

> `<A>, <ABBR>, <APPLET>, <B>, <BASEFONT>, <BDO>, <BIG>, <BR>,`
> `<BUTTON>, <CITE>, <CODE>, <DFN>, <EM>, <FONT>, <I>, <IFRAME>,`
> `<IMG>, <INPUT>, <KBD>, <LABEL>, <MAP>, <OBJECT>, <Q>, <S>, <SAMP>,`
> `<SCRIPT>, <SELECT>, <SMALL>, <SPAN>, <STRIKE>, <STRONG>, <SUB>,`
> `<SUP>, <TEXTAREA>, <TT>, <U>, <VAR>`

Suggested style/usage: The `<FONT>` tag has been depreciated in favor of similar style sheet rules. Whenever specifying a font face, remember that if users don't have that particular font installed on their machines, the browser will use the system default instead.

Examples: See file /h4d4e/examples/ch06/font.htm.

<FORM> ... </FORM> User input form

Definition: Defines an area that contains objects soliciting user input, such as selection buttons or check boxes, or areas for text input.

Attributes:

```
ACCEPT="Internet media type"
```

> Provides a list of MIME types separated by commas, which the server processing the form recognizes.

ACCEPT-CHARSET="text"

Specifies the character set or sets that the server processing the form must recognize and accept.

ACTION="URL"

URL is a standard Uniform Resource Locator. ACTION specifies the name of a resource for the browser to execute as an action in response to clicking on an on-screen Submit or Reset button. The URL will typically point to a CGI script or other executable service on a Web server.

ENCTYPE="Internet media type"

Specifies the format of the submitted data in case the protocol does not itself impose a format. With the POST method, this attribute is a MIME type specifying the format of the posted data. The default value is "application/x-www-form-urlencoded".

METHOD=("GET"|"POST")

Tells the browser how to interact with the service designated by the ACTION's URL. GET is the default if no other method is specified.

If GET is used, the browser constructs a query URL consisting of the URL of the page that contains the form, followed by a question mark, followed by the values of the form's input areas and other objects. The browser sends the query URL to the target URL specified by ACTION. The WWW server in the specified target URL uses the information supplied to perform a search, process a query, or provide whatever services it has been programmed to deliver.

If you use POST, the browser sends a copy of the form's contents to the recipient URL as a data block to the standard input service (stdin or STDIN). This makes the form data easy to grab and process. POST is the preferred method for most HTML programmers, because it passes much more information in a cleaner fashion to the server than the GET method.

Whatever the recipient program writes to output will be returned as a new HTML document for further interaction. The recipient program can also save form data to a file on the local WWW server.

`TARGET="window"`

Specifies loading the link into the targeted window. You can use `TARGET` with a `FRAMESET` where you've named a frame in the `FRAME` element. The targeted window can be one of the following values:

`window`: Specifies loading the link into the targeted window. The window must begin with an alphanumeric character to be valid, with the following four exceptions:

`_blank`: Loads the link into a new (unnamed) blank window.

`_parent`: Loads the link into the immediate parent of the document in which the link is found.

`_self`: Loads the link into the same window as the link.

`_top`: Loads the link into the full body of the window.

Context:

`<FORM>` ... `</FORM>` is legal within the following tags:

> `<BLOCKQUOTE>`, `<BODY>`, `<CENTER>`, `<DD>`, `<DIV>`, `<FIELDSET>`, `<IFRAME>`, `<LI>`, `<NOFRAMES>`, `<NOSCRIPT>`, `<OBJECT>`, `<TD>`, `<TH>`

You can use the following tags within `<FORM>` ... `</FORM>`:

> `<A>`, `<ABBR>`, `<ADDRESS>`, `<APPLET>`, `<B>`, `<BASEFONT>`, `<BDO>`, `<BIG>`, `<BLOCKQUOTE>`, `<BR>`, `<BUTTON>`, `<CENTER>`, `<CITE>`, `<CODE>`, `<DFN>`, `<DIR>`, `<DIV>`, `<DL>`, `<EM>`, `<FIELDSET>`, `<FONT>`, `<FORM>`, `<H*>`, `<HR>`, `<I>`, `<IFRAME>`, `<IMG>`, `<INPUT>`, `<ISINDEX>`, `<KBD>`, `<LABEL>`, `<MAP>`, `<MENU>`, `<NOFRAMES>`, `<NOSCRIPT>`, `<OBJECT>`, `<OL>`, `<P>`, `<PRE>`, `<Q>`, `<S>`, `<SAMP>`, `<SCRIPT>`, `<SELECT>`, `<SMALL>`, `<SPAN>`, `<STRIKE>`, `<STRONG>`, `<SUB>`, `<SUP>`, `<TABLE>`, `<TEXTAREA>`, `<TT>`, `<U>`, `<UL>`, `<VAR>`

Suggested style/usage: Use `<FORM>` ... `</FORM>` whenever you want to solicit input from your readers or to provide additional back-end services through your Web pages.

Examples: See file /h4d4e/examples/ch06/form.htm.

<FRAME> Frame definition

Definition: Defines a single frame in a `<FRAMESET>`. This is not a container, so a matching end tag is not used.

Attributes:

`FRAMEBORDER=(1|0)`

Renders a 3-D border around the frame. The default (1) inserts a border; 0 displays no border.

`MARGINHEIGHT=(number|"%")`

Controls the margin height (in pixels) for the frame.

`MARGINWIDTH=(number|"%")`

Controls the margin width (in pixels) for the frame.

`NAME="text"`

Provides a target name for the frame. See `<A>`.

`NORESIZE`

Prevents the user from resizing the frame.

`SCROLLING=(yes|no|auto)`

Creates a scrolling frame.

`SRC="URL"`

Displays the source file for the frame.

Context:

`<FRAME>` is legal within the following tag:

`<FRAMESET>`

The `<FRAME>` tag is a singleton tag.

Suggested style/usage: Frame specifications vary widely from browser to browser, and it is difficult to anticipate how a particular browser will interpret frame information. If you use frames, be sure to offer an alternative route for your users via the `<NOFRAMES>` tag.

Examples: See file /h4d4e/examples/ch06/frame.htm.

<FRAMESET> ... </FRAMESET> Frame group definition

Definition: Hosts the <FRAME>, <FRAMESET>, and <NOFRAMES> elements. <FRAMESET> is used instead of the <BODY> tag.

Attributes:

COLS="col-widths|%|*"

Creates a frame document with columns. Specify the column dimensions by percentage (%), pixels, or relative size (*). If you use percentages or relative sizes, then enclose the associated values in double quotation marks.

ROWS="row-height|%|*"

Creates a frame document with rows. Specify the row dimensions by percentage (%), pixels, or relative size (*). The asterisk assigns the remaining unused portion of the display area. If you use percentages or relative sizes, enclose the associated values in double quotation marks.

Context:

<FRAMESET> is legal within the following tags:

 <FRAMESET>, <HTML>

You can use the following tags within <FRAMESET> ... </FRAMESET>:

 <FRAME>, <FRAMESET>, <NOFRAMES>

Suggested style/usage: You can nest frames within other frames. You can set both ROWS and COLS simultaneously to create a grid, or you can use nested <FRAMESET> pairs to construct complicated layouts.

Examples: See file /h4d4e/examples/ch06/frameset.htm.

<H> ... </H*> Heading level*

Definition: Headers come in different styles and sizes to help you organize your content and make it easier to read. The size and display characteristics of a heading is determined by the viewing browser. But by standard default convention, a level 1 heading is larger and more pronounced than a level 2 heading, and so on.

Attributes:

ALIGN=(LEFT|CENTER|RIGHT|JUSTIFY)

Sets the alignment of header text. LEFT is the default.

Context:

`<H*>` ... `</H*>` is legal within the following markup tags:

> `<BLOCKQUOTE>`, `<BODY>`, `<BUTTON>`, `<CENTER>`, `<DD>`, `<DIV>`,
> `<FIELDSET>`, `<FORM>`, `<IFRAME>`, `<LI>`, `<NOFRAMES>`, `<NOSCRIPT>`,
> `<OBJECT>`, `<TD>`, `<TH>`

You can use the following markup tags within `<H*>` ... `</H*>`:

> `<A>`, `<ABBR>`, `<APPLET>`, `<B>`, `<BASEFONT>`, `<BDO>`, `<BIG>`, `<BR>`,
> `<BUTTON>`, `<CITE>`, `<CODE>`, `<DFN>`, `<EM>`, `<FONT>`, `<I>`, `<IFRAME>`,
> `<IMG>`, `<INPUT>`, `<KBD>`, `<LABEL>`, `<MAP>`, `<OBJECT>`, `<Q>`, `<S>`, `<SAMP>`,
> `<SCRIPT>`, `<SELECT>`, `<SMALL>`, `<SPAN>`, `<STRIKE>`, `<STRONG>`, `<SUB>`,
> `<SUP>`, `<TEXTAREA>`, `<TT>`, `<U>`, `<VAR>`

Suggested style/usage: Using headings regularly and consistently helps add structure and divisions to your documents. Some experts recommend not using a subhead level unless you plan to use at least two of them beneath a parent level. In other words, don't use a single `<H3>` ... `</H3>` after an `<H2>` ... `</H2>` pair. This follows an outlining principle of not indenting unless you have at least two subtopics under a topic. Although we think the occasional exception is okay, this remains a good guideline.

Examples: See file /h4d4e/examples/ch06/h.htm.

<HEAD> ... </HEAD> Document head block

Definition: Defines information about an HTML document, including its title, meta-information, index information, next page pointer, and links to other HTML documents.

Attributes:

`Profile="URL"`

> Defines the location of a meta-dictionary or profile.

Context:

`<HEAD>` ... `</HEAD>` is legal within the following markup tag:

> `<HTML>`

You can use the following markup tags within `<HEAD>` ... `</HEAD>`:

> `<BASE>`, `<ISINDEX>`, `<LINK>`, `<META>`, `<SCRIPT>`, `<STYLE>`, `<TITLE>`

Suggested style/usage: <HEAD> ... </HEAD> is required at the head of an HTML document. Even though many browsers render documents without a <HEAD> ... </HEAD> block at the beginning, it's still good practice to include one, especially if you want to establish a base URL when you have numerous graphics or local document links in your page.

Note: Although the <HEAD> ... </HEAD> block produces no browser output other than a document title, it is an important component of proper HTML page design.

Examples: See file /h4d4e/examples/ch06/head.htm.

<HR> Horizontal rule

Definition: Draws a horizontal rule across the page, usually one or two pixels wide.

Attributes:

ALIGN=(LEFT|CENTER|RIGHT)

> Draws the rule left aligned, right aligned, or centered. The align type can be LEFT, RIGHT, or CENTER.

NOSHADE

> Draws the rule without 3-D shading.

SIZE=number

> **[Depreciated]** Sets the height of the rule in pixels.

WIDTH=(number|"%")

> **[Depreciated]** Sets the width of the rule in pixels or as a percentage of window width. To specify a percentage, the number must end with a percent (%) sign.

Context:

<HR> is legal within the following tags:

> <BLOCKQUOTE>, <BODY>, <BUTTON>, <CENTER>, <DD>, <DIV>,
> <FIELDSET>, <FORM>, <IFRAME>, <LI>, <NOFRAMES>, <NOSCRIPT>,
> <OBJECT>, <TD>, <TH>

You can't use any tags within <HR>, because it is a singleton tag.

Suggested style/usage: Wherever good design will benefit from placement of a horizontal rule — typically to emphasize natural divisions between text items or topics, or to separate a page header and footer from the body.

Examples: See file /h4d4e/examples/ch06/hr.htm.

<HTML> ... </HTML> HTML document

Definition: Should enclose an entire HTML document as the outermost layer of its structure.

Attributes:

```
VERSION="URL"
```

Specifies the URL of the DTD that's used for the interpretation of this document. This is usually the same information obtained in the `<!DOCTYPE>` declaration, thus making the usefulness of this attribute uncertain.

Context:

`<HTML> ... </HTML>` is not legal within any other markup tags.

You can use the following markup tags within `<HTML> ... </HTML>`:

```
<BODY>, <FRAMESET>, <HEAD>
```

Suggested style/usage: Use `<HTML> ... </HTML>` to enclose all HTML documents. The `<HTML>` tags should go around the entire document.

Examples: See file /h4d4e/examples/ch06/html.htm.

<I> ... </I> Italic text

Definition: [Depreciated] Italicizes all enclosed text.

Attributes: None

Context:

`<I> ... </I>` is legal within the following tags:

```
<A>, <ABBR>, <ADDRESS>, <APPLET>, <B>, <BDO>, <BIG>,
<BLOCKQUOTE>, <BODY>, <BUTTON>, <CAPTION>, <CENTER>, <CITE>,
<CODE>, <DD>, <DEL>, <DFN>, <DIV>, <DT>, <EM>, <FIELDSET>, <FONT>,
<FORM>, <H*>, <I>, <IFRAME>, <INS>, <KBD>, <LABEL>, <LEGEND>,
<LI>, <NOFRAMES>, <NOSCRIPT>, <OBJECT>, <P>, <PRE>, <Q>, <S>,
<SAMP>, <SMALL>, <SPAN>, <STRIKE>, <STRONG>, <SUB>, <SUP>, <TD>,
<TH>, <TT>, <U>, <VAR>
```

You can use the following tags within `<I>` ... `</I>`:

```
<A>, <ABBR>, <APPLET>, <B>, <BASEFONT>, <BDO>, <BIG>, <BR>,
<BUTTON>, <CITE>, <CODE>, <DFN>, <EM>, <FONT>, <I>, <IFRAME>,
<IMG>, <INPUT>, <KBD>, <LABEL>, <MAP>, <OBJECT>, <Q>, <S>, <SAMP>,
<SCRIPT>, <SELECT>, <SMALL>, <SPAN>, <STRIKE>, <STRONG>, <SUB>,
<SUP>, <TEXTAREA>, <TT>, <U>, <VAR>
```

Suggested style/usage: Use italics sparingly for emphasis or effect, remembering that its effectiveness fades quickly with overuse. If you are including a citation or bibliographic resource in your document, use `<CITE>` instead of `<I>`.

Examples: See file /h4d4e/examples/ch06/html.htm.

<IFRAME> ... </IFRAME> Inline frame

Definition: Defines an inline or floating frame.

Attributes:

`ALIGN=(LEFT|CENTER|RIGHT|TOP|MIDDLE|BOTTOM)`

> Sets the alignment of the frame or the surrounding text. The align-type can be one of these values:
>
> `LEFT`: The frame is drawn as a flush-left inline frame, and text flows around it.
>
> `CENTER`: The frame is drawn as a centered inline frame, and text flows around it.
>
> `RIGHT`: The frame is drawn as a flush-right inline frame, and text flows around it.
>
> `TOP`: Surrounding text is aligned with the top of the frame.
>
> `MIDDLE`: Surrounding text is aligned with the middle of the frame.
>
> `BOTTOM`: Surrounding text is aligned with the bottom of the frame.

`FRAMEBORDER=(1|0)`

> Renders a 3-D border around the frame. The default (1) inserts a border. To display no border, use 0.

`HEIGHT=(number|"%")`

> Controls the height (in pixels) of the inline frame.

`MARGINHEIGHT=(number|"%")`

> Controls the margin height (in pixels) for the frame.

`MARGINWIDTH=(number|"%")`

Controls the margin width (in pixels) for the frame.

`NAME="text"`

Provides a target name for the frame.

`SCROLLING=(yes|no)`

Creates a scrolling frame.

`SRC="URL"`

Displays the source file for the frame.

`WIDTH=(number|"%")`

Controls the width (in pixels) of the inline frame.

Context:

`<IFRAME> ... </IFRAME>` is legal within the following tags:

```
<A>, <ABBR>, <ADDRESS>, <APPLET>, <B>, <BDO>, <BIG>,
<BLOCKQUOTE>, <BODY>, <BUTTON>, <CAPTION>, <CENTER>, <CITE>,
<CODE>, <DD>, <DEL>, <DFN>, <DIV>, <DT>, <EM>, <FIELDSET>,
<FONT>, <FORM>, <H*>, <I>, <IFRAME>, <INS>, <KBD>, <LABEL>,
<LEGEND>, <LI>, <NOFRAMES>, <NOSCRIPT>, <OBJECT>, <P>, <PRE>,
<Q>, <S>, <SAMP>, <SMALL>, <SPAN>, <STRIKE>, <STRONG>, <SUB>,
<SUP>, <TD>, <TH>, <TT>, <U>, <VAR>
```

You can use the following tags within `<IFRAME> ... </IFRAME>`:

```
<A>, <ABBR>, <ADDRESS>, <APPLET>, <B>, <BASEFONT>, <BDO>, <BIG>,
<BLOCKQUOTE>, <BR>, <BUTTON>, <CENTER>, <CITE>, <CODE>, <DFN>,
<DIR>, <DIV>, <DL>, <EM>, <FIELDSET>, <FONT>, <FORM>, <H*>, <HR>,
<I>, <IFRAME>, <IMG>, <INPUT>, <ISINDEX>, <KBD>, <LABEL>, <MAP>,
<MENU>, <NOFRAMES>, <NOSCRIPT>, <OBJECT>, <OL>, <P>, <PRE>, <Q>,
<S>, <SAMP>, <SCRIPT>, <SELECT>, <SMALL>, <SPAN>, <STRIKE>,
<STRONG>, <SUB>, <SUP>, <TABLE>, <TEXTAREA>, <TT>, <U>, <UL>, <VAR>
```

Suggested style/usage: You can use inline or floating frames to create interesting effects within an HTML page. Any content placed between the `<IFRAME>` tags is displayed only if the browser can't render the frame. You cannot resize inline frames.

Examples: See file /h4d4e/examples/ch06/iframe.htm.

<IMG> Inline image

Definition: Supplies image source, placement, and behavior information. Used to place graphics in a page.

Attributes:

ALT="text"

> Supplies an alternative string of text if the browser has no graphics capability, or if graphics are turned off.

ALIGN=LEFT|RIGHT|TOP|MIDDLE|BOTTOM

> **[Depreciated]** Sets the image or surrounding text alignment. The alignment type can be one of these values:
>
> LEFT: The picture is drawn as a flush-left image and text flows around it.
>
> RIGHT: The picture is drawn as a flush-right image and text flows around it.
>
> TOP: The top of the surrounding text is aligned with the top of the image.
>
> MIDDLE: The baseline of the surrounding text is aligned with the middle of the image.
>
> BOTTOM: The baseline of the surrounding text is aligned with the bottom of the image.

BORDER=number

> Specifies the size of a border to be drawn around the image. For a hyperlink image, the border is drawn in the appropriate hyperlink color. If the image is not a hyperlink, the border is invisible. Setting this to "0" will hide hyperlink borders.

HEIGHT=pixels

> Along with WIDTH=, specifies the size to which the image is scaled. If the picture's actual dimensions differ from those specified, the picture is stretched to match the specifications.

HSPACE=number

> With VSPACE=, specifies extra blank space or margins around the image.

ISMAP

>   Indicates that the image (or its text replacement) should be a clickable
>   map. This often invokes special map-handling software through the CGI
>   interface on the Web server handling the request.

SRC="URL"

>   SRC is a required attribute. URL is a standard Uniform Resource Locator
>   specifying the location of the image file.

USEMAP=map-name

>   Identifies the picture as a client-side image map and specifies a <MAP>
>   to be used for acting on the user's clicks.

VSPACE=number

>   With HSPACE=, specifies extra blank space or margins around the
>   image.

WIDTH=pixels

>   With HEIGHT=, specifies the size at which the image is scaled. If the
>   picture's actual dimensions differ from those specified, the picture is
>   stretched to match the specifications.

Context:

<IMG> is legal within the following tags:

>   <A>, <ABBR>, <ADDRESS>, <APPLET>, <B>, <BDO>, <BIG>,
>   <BLOCKQUOTE>, <BODY>, <BUTTON>, <CAPTION>, <CENTER>, <CITE>,
>   <CODE>, <DD>, <DEL>, <DFN>, <DIV>, <DT>, <EM>, <FIELDSET>, <FONT>,
>   <FORM>, <H*>, <I>, <IFRAME>, <INS>, <KBD>, <LABEL>, <LEGEND>,
>   <LI>, <NOFRAMES>, <NOSCRIPT>, <OBJECT>, <P>, <Q>, <S>, <SAMP>,
>   <SMALL>, <SPAN>, <STRIKE>, <STRONG>, <SUB>, <SUP>, <TD>, <TH>,
>   <TT>, <U>, <VAR>

The <IMG> tag is a singleton tag.

Suggested style/usage: Keep images small and use them judiciously; you
should use graphics to add impact and interest to pages without adding too
much bulk (or wait time).

Examples: See file /h4d4e/examples/ch06/img.htm.

<INPUT> Input object

Definition: Defines an input object within an HTML form. These objects come in several different types and include several different ways of naming and specifying the data they contain.

Attributes:

ACCEPT="Internet media type"

> Provides a list of MIME types separated by commas, which the server processing the form recognizes.

ALIGN=(LEFT|CENTER|RIGHT|JUSTIFY)

> **[Depreciated]** Places the element left aligned, right aligned, centered, or justified on the page.

ALT="text"

> Provides an alternative text label for browsers that cannot render graphical form elements, such as buttons and images.

CHECKED

> Sets a check box or radio button to be "selected" when the form first loads.

DISABLED

> Renders the element unusable.

MAXLENGTH=number

> Indicates the maximum number of characters that the user can enter into a text control.

NAME="text"

> Specifies the name of the control.

READONLY

> The contents of the control or the control itself cannot be modified by the user. Any information contained within the control is automatically submitted with the form.

`SIZE="width|(width, height)"`

Specifies the size of the input window (in characters).

`SRC="URL"`

Specifies the address of the image to be used. Used in conjunction with `TYPE=IMAGE`.

`TABINDEX="number"`

Identifies the element's place in the tabbing order.

`TYPE=(TEXT|PASSWORD|CHECKBOX|RADIO|SUBMIT|RESET|FILE|HIDDEN|IMAGE|BUTTON)`

Specifies the type of control to use. The type can be one of these values:

`TYPE=text`: Generates an input field where the user can enter up to `MAXLENGTH` characters. The `SIZE` attribute lists the length of the input field (if the user enters more characters, the text scrolls).

`TYPE=password`: Same as `TYPE=text`, but the text will be hidden by "*" or similar characters as the user types.

`TYPE=checkbox`: Produces a check box. When it is checked and the form is submitted, it will be sent as `name=on`; otherwise it is ignored. If you use `CHECKED`, it will come up selected initially.

`TYPE=radio`: Produces a radio button. A radio button always exists in a group, and all members of this group should have the same `NAME` attribute and different `VALUE`s. The `VALUE` of the selected radio button will be sent to the server. You should specify `CHECKED` on exactly one radio button, which then comes up selected initially.

`TYPE=submit`: Produces a button that sends the contents of the form to the server. You can have more than one submit button in the form, but each should have a different `NAME`. The name and value of the pressed button will be sent to the server as well.

`TYPE=reset`: Produces a button that restores the form to its original state and erases any data the user has entered.

`TYPE=file`: Allows the user to upload a file. Be sure to provide an acceptable list of file types using the `ACCEPT` attribute.

`TYPE=hidden`: Allows you to embed information you do not want changed in the form. This is useful if the document is generated by a script and you need to store static information. The `NAME` and `VALUE` of this input field will be sent to the server without modifications.

TYPE=image: Functions similar to a SUBMIT button, but uses an image instead of a button. The ALIGN attribute controls the alignment of the image. The coordinates of the selected region will also be sent to the server in the form of "NAME.x=n&NAME.y=n." A text browser treats it identically to a normal submit button.

TYPE=button: Creates a button that has no specific use, but calls a script instead. This default control type is TEXT.

USEMAP="text"

Identifies a client-side image map to be used as a user input device.

VALUE="value"

For textual/numerical controls, specifies the default value of the control. For Boolean controls (AND, OR, and so on), specifies the value to be returned when the control is turned on. Also used to provide text labels for SUBMIT and RESET buttons.

Context:

<INPUT> is legal within the following tags:

```
<A>, <ABBR>, <ADDRESS>, <APPLET>, <B>, <BDO>, <BIG>,
<BLOCKQUOTE>, <BODY>, <CAPTION>, <CENTER>, <CITE>, <CODE>, <DD>,
<DEL>, <DFN>, <DIV>, <DT>, <EM>, <FIELDSET>, <FONT>, <FORM>, <H*>,
<I>, <IFRAME>, <INS>, <KBD>, <LABEL>, <LEGEND>, <LI>, <NOFRAMES>,
<NOSCRIPT>, <OBJECT>, <P>, <PRE>, <Q>, <S>, <SAMP>, <SMALL>,
<SPAN>, <STRIKE>, <STRONG>, <SUB>, <SUP>, <TD>, <TH>, <TT>, <U>,
<VAR>
```

<INPUT> is a singleton tag.

Suggested style/usage: <INPUT> is an essential ingredient for HTML forms of all kinds, because it provides the mechanism for soliciting input from readers and delivers it to the underlying forms-handling services provided by the related CGI script or other forms-handling programs.

Examples: See file /h4d4e/examples/ch06/input.htm.

<INS> ... </INS> Inserted text

Definition: Marks text that you've inserted since a previous version of the Web document.

Attributes:

CITE="URL"

> Points to another HTML document that further explains why the text was inserted.

DATETIME=YYYY-MM-DDThh:mm:ssTZD

> Marks the time when the document was changed. This attribute's value must use a specific format, shown above, that conforms to the ISO8601 time/date specification. The abbreviations shown above refer to the following date and time information:

> YYYY = The year

> MM = The two-digit month — for example, "03" for March

> DD = The day

> T = indicates the beginning of the time section

> hh = The hour, in military time (0–23 hours), without a.m. or p.m. specifications

> mm = The minute

> ss = The second

> TZD = The time zone

> Z = The Coordinated Universal Time (CUT)

> +hh:mm = The local time that is hours (hh) and minutes (mm) ahead of the CUT

> -hh:mm = The local time that is hours (hh) and minutes (mm) behind the CUT

Context:

<INS> ... </INS> is legal within the following tags:

> <BODY>

You can use the following tags within <INS> ... </INS>:

> <A>, <ABBR>, <APPLET>, <B>, <BASEFONT>, <BDO>, <BIG>, <BR>, <BUTTON>, <CITE>, <CODE>, <DFN>, <EM>, <FONT>, <I>, <IFRAME>, <IMG>, <INPUT>, <KBD>, <LABEL>, <MAP>, <OBJECT>, <Q>, <S>, <SAMP>, <SCRIPT>, <SELECT>, <SMALL>, <SPAN>, <STRIKE>, <STRONG>, <SUB>, <SUP>, <TEXTAREA>, <TT>, <U>, <VAR>

Suggested style/usage: ⟨INS⟩ ... ⟨/INS⟩ and its companion tag ⟨DEL⟩ ... ⟨/DEL⟩ were created to show revisions to Web pages. Use ⟨INS⟩ ... ⟨/INS⟩ when several people are working on a Web document to highlight text that has been inserted since the last version of the document, when it was added, and to refer others to an explanatory document that tells why it was added.

Examples: See file /h4d4e/examples/ch06/ins.htm.

⟨ISINDEX⟩ Single line input

Definition: [Depreciated] Prompts the user for a single line of input. This typically indicates that a searchable index for the document is available on the server. This index is usually in the form of a CGI script that allows searches and is normally supplied by a SEARCH button somewhere in the document.

Attributes:

PROMPT="text"

> **[Depreciated]** Specifies a prompt to be used instead of the default prompt.

Context:

⟨ISINDEX⟩ is legal within the following tags:

> ⟨BLOCKQUOTE⟩, ⟨BODY⟩, ⟨CENTER⟩, ⟨DD⟩, ⟨DIV⟩, ⟨FIELDSET⟩, ⟨FORM⟩, ⟨HEAD⟩, ⟨IFRAME⟩, ⟨LI⟩, ⟨NOFRAMES⟩, ⟨NOSCRIPT⟩, ⟨OBJECT⟩, ⟨TD⟩, ⟨TH⟩

No tags can be used within ⟨ISINDEX⟩.

Suggested style/usage: The ⟨ISINDEX⟩ tag has been depreciated in favor of a form and the ⟨INPUT⟩ tag, because the original implementation of ⟨ISINDEX⟩ is not developed enough to support multiple character sets. To create a searchable index in place of old ⟨ISINDEX⟩, create a form for users to enter search strings into and use the GET method to send the queries to the CGI script. This provides you with more options and allows you to provide more accurate search results to your users.

Examples: See file /h4d4e/examples/ch06/isindex.htm.

<KBD> ... </KBD> Keyboard text

Definition: Indicates text should be entered at a computer keyboard. `<KBD> ... </KBD>` changes the type style for all the text it contains, typically into a monospaced font like those used in character-mode computer terminal displays.

Attributes: None

Context:

`<KBD> ... </KBD>` is legal within the following tags:

> `<A>, <ABBR>, <ADDRESS>, <APPLET>, <B>, <BDO>, <BIG>,`
> `<BLOCKQUOTE>, <BODY>, <BUTTON>, <CAPTION>, <CENTER>, <CITE>,`
> `<CODE>, <DD>, <DEL>, <DFN>, <DIV>, <DT>, <EM>, <FIELDSET>, <FONT>,`
> `<FORM>, <H*>, <I>, <IFRAME>, <INS>, <KBD>, <LABEL>, <LEGEND>,`
> `<LI>, <NOFRAMES>, <NOSCRIPT>, <OBJECT>, <P>, <PRE>, <Q>, <S>,`
> `<SAMP>, <SMALL>, <SPAN>, <STRIKE>, <STRONG>, <SUB>, <SUP>, <TD>,`
> `<TH>, <TT>, <U>, <VAR>`

You can use the following tags within `<KBD> ... </KBD>`:

> `<A>, <ABBR>, <APPLET>, <B>, <BASEFONT>, <BDO>, <BIG>, <BR>,`
> `<BUTTON>, <CITE>, <CODE>, <DFN>, <EM>, <FONT>, <I>, <IFRAME>,`
> `<IMG>, <INPUT>, <KBD>, <LABEL>, <MAP>, <OBJECT>, <Q>, <S>, <SAMP>,`
> `<SCRIPT>, <SELECT>, <SMALL>, <SPAN>, <STRIKE>, <STRONG>, <SUB>,`
> `<SUP>, <TEXTAREA>, <TT>, <U>, <VAR>`

Suggested style/usage: Whenever you want to set off text that the user needs to type in from the body text, use `<KBD> ... </KBD>`. This is different from `<CODE>`, which indicates existing program text. This is also different from `<TT>`, which indicates computer output.

Examples: See file /h4d4e/examples/ch06/kbd.htm.

<LABEL> ... </LABEL> Control label

Definition: Assigns a label to a form control or element to provide more information about it in much the same way the `TITLE` attribute does for other HTML elements.

Attributes:

`ACCESSKEY="text"`

> Specifies the character to be used as part of a keyboard shortcut to move focus to the control.

DISABLED

Renders the element unusable.

FOR="text"

Associates the label explicitly with a form control using the form control's unique ID. If this attribute is not included, the label is automatically associated with the text it contains.

TABINDEX="number"

Identifies the element's place in the tabbing order.

Context:

<LABEL> ... </LABEL> is legal within the following tags:

<A>, <ABBR>, <ADDRESS>, <APPLET>, <B>, <BDO>, <BIG>, <BLOCKQUOTE>, <BODY>, <CAPTION>, <CENTER>, <CITE>, <CODE>, <DD>, <DEL>, <DFN>, <DIV>, <DT>, <EM>, <FIELDSET>, <FONT>, <FORM>, <H*>, <I>, <IFRAME>, <INS>, <KBD>, <LEGEND>, <LI>, <NOFRAMES>, <NOSCRIPT>, <OBJECT>, <P>, <PRE>, <Q>, <S>, <SAMP>, <SMALL>, <SPAN>, <STRIKE>, <STRONG>, <SUB>, <SUP>, <TD>, <TH>, <TT>, <U>, <VAR>

You can use the following tags within <LABEL> ... </LABEL>:

<A>, <ABBR>, <APPLET>, <B>, <BASEFONT>, <BDO>, <BIG>, <BR>, <BUTTON>, <CITE>, <CODE>, <DFN>, <EM>, <FONT>, <I>, <IFRAME>, <IMG>, <INPUT>, <KBD>, <LABEL>, <MAP>, <OBJECT>, <Q>, <S>, <SAMP>, <SCRIPT>, <SELECT>, <SMALL>, <SPAN>, <STRIKE>, <STRONG>, <SUB>, <SUP>, <TEXTAREA>, <TT>, <U>, <VAR>

Suggested style/usage: Use <LABEL> to provide users with more information about a form control. If users need to enter data in a specific way, such as MMDDYY instead of MM-DD-YY, you can use <LABEL> to pass this information along to users.

Examples: See file /h4d4e/examples/ch06/label.htm.

<LEGEND> ... </LEGEND> *Fieldset caption*

Definition: Provides a caption for a FIELDSET.

Attributes:

ALIGN=(LEFT|RIGHT|TOP|BOTTOM)

Sets the alignment of the legend within the <FIELDSET>. The align type can be LEFT, RIGHT, TOP, or BOTTOM. The default centers the legend at the bottom of the <FIELDSET>.

ACCESSKEY="text"

Specifies the character to be used as part of a keyboard shortcut to move focus to the control.

Context:

<LEGEND> ... </LEGEND> is legal within the following tag:

<FIELDSET>

You can use the following tags within <LEGEND> ... </LEGEND>:

<A>, <ABBR>, <APPLET>, <B>, <BASEFONT>, <BDO>, <BIG>, <BR>, <BUTTON>, <CITE>, <CODE>, <DFN>, <EM>, <FONT>, <I>, <IFRAME>, <IMG>, <INPUT>, <KBD>, <LABEL>, <MAP>, <OBJECT>, <Q>, <S>, <SAMP>, <SCRIPT>, <SELECT>, <SMALL>, <SPAN>, <STRIKE>, <STRONG>, <SUB>, <SUP>, <TEXTAREA>, <TT>, <U>, <VAR>

Suggested style/usage: You should include this tag to improve the accessibility of the information of a FIELDSET when it is not rendered in a graphical manner.

Examples: See file /h4d4e/examples/ch06/fieldset.htm.

<LI> List item

Definition: An element belonging to one of the HTML list styles.

Attributes:

TYPE=(DISC|SQUARE|CIRCLE) or (1|a|A|i|I)

When an ordered list <OL> is used, the <LI> element will be rendered with a number. You can control that number's appearance with the <TYPE> attribute. Similarly, inside an unordered list <UL>, you can control the type of bullet displayed with <TYPE>. You can't control <DIR> and <MENU> this way, because they are not required to be bulleted or numbered.

Shape types define a named shape for bullets:

DISC uses a filled circular shape for a bullet.

SQUARE uses a filled square shape for a bullet.

CIRCLE uses a circular outline shape for a bullet.

Outline style types define the numbering/labeling scheme used, as in an outline format:

1: Number using Arabic numerals (default starts with "1").

a: Enumerate using lowercase alphabetic characters (default starts with "a").

A: Enumerate using uppercase alphabetic characters (default starts with "A").

I: Enumerate using lowercase Roman numerals (default starts with "i").

I: Enumerate using uppercase Roman numerals (default starts with "I").

VALUE=number

Changes the count of ordered lists as they progress.

Context:

<LI> is legal within the following tags:

    <DIR>, <MENU>, <OL>, <UL>

<LI> is a singleton tag.

Suggested style/usage: Use to set off elements within lists.

Examples: See file /h4d4e/examples/ch06/li.htm.

<LINK> Link

Definition: Provides information that links the current document to other documents or resources.

Attributes:

HREF="URL"

The address of the current link destination, accessible through normal Web linkage mechanisms. Works in the same way as the anchor tag <A> ... </A>.

MEDIA=SCREEN|PRINT|PROJECTION|BRAILLE|SPEECH|ALL

Identifies the ideal environment for the Web page to be conveyed in. The default is ALL. Use SCREEN in most cases. Use PROJECTION for overhead presentations, and use SPEECH for a text-to-speech reader. Currently, this attribute provides information only and does not affect the way the style sheet is interpreted or the page rendered. You may include more than one media type, each separated by commas.

REL="text"

Indicates the source end of a link and specifies the link's type. For example REL="STYLESHEET" lets the browser know the linked document is a style sheet.

REV="text"

Indicates the destination end of a link and specifies the link's type.

TARGET="window"

Specifies loading the link into the targeted window. You can use TARGET with a FRAMESET in which you've named a frame in the FRAME element. The targeted window can be one of the following values:

window: Loads the link into the targeted window. The window must begin with an alphanumeric character to be valid, with the following four exceptions:

_blank: Loads the link into a new (unnamed) blank window.

_parent: Loads the link into the immediate parent of the document in which the link is found.

_self: Loads the link into the same window as the link.

_top: Loads the link into the full body of the window.

TYPE="text"

Specifies the Internet media type of linked resource. For example, the type for CSS1 sheets is "TEXT/CSS".

Context:

<LINK> is legal within the following tag:

<HEAD>

<LINK> is a singleton tag and permits no enclosed tags.

Suggested style/usage: Typical uses of links include authorship attributions, glossaries, tutorials, style sheet references, and information about outdated or more current versions of the document.

Examples: See file /h4d4e/examples/ch06/link.htm.

<MAP> ... </MAP> Client-side image map

Definition: Information concerning "hot spots" (clickable areas) in the image is defined here. You should mention every selectable area in an <AREA> tag inside the <MAP> tag. A client-side image map is the same as a server-side image map, except for where the hot spot definitions are stored — within the HTML document viewed in the client or in a map file on the server.

Attributes:

NAME="text"

Gives the <MAP> a name so it can be referred to later.

Context:

<MAP> ... </MAP> is legal within the following tags:

<A>, <ABBR>, <ADDRESS>, <APPLET>, <B>, <BDO>, <BIG>,
<BLOCKQUOTE>, <BODY>, <BUTTON>, <CAPTION>, <CENTER>, <CITE>,
<CODE>, <DD>, <DEL>, <DFN>, <DIV>, <DT>, <EM>, <FIELDSET>, <FONT>,
<FORM>, <H*>, <I>, <IFRAME>, <INS>, <KBD>, <LABEL>, <LEGEND>,
<LI>, <NOFRAMES>, <NOSCRIPT>, <OBJECT>, <P>, <PRE>, <Q>, <S>,
<SAMP>, <SMALL>, <SPAN>, <STRIKE>, <STRONG>, <SUB>, <SUP>, <TD>,
<TH>, <TT>, <U>, <VAR>

You can use the following tag within <MAP> ... </MAP>:

<AREA>

Suggested style/usage: Client-side image maps are becoming more popular, but not all browsers support them, so try to offer a textual alternative or use a server-side image map in addition. This is done by putting the <IMG> tag with the USEMAP attribute inside an <A> and by adding the ISMAP attribute.

Examples: See file /h4d4e/examples/ch06/map.htm.

<MENU> ... </MENU> Menu list

Definition: [Depreciated] Encloses a menu list in which each element is typically a word or short phrase that fits on a single line; this list is rendered more compactly than most other list types.

Attributes:

COMPACT

Renders the list as compactly as possible by reducing line leading and spacing.

Context:

<MENU> ... </MENU> is legal within the following tags:

<BLOCKQUOTE>, <BODY>, <BUTTON>, <CENTER>, <DD>, <DIV>,
<FIELDSET>, <FORM>, <IFRAME>, <LI>, <NOFRAMES>, <NOSCRIPT>,
<OBJECT>, <TD>, <TH>

You can use the following tag within <MENU> ... </MENU>:

<LI>

Suggested style/usage: Provides the most compact way for displaying information in short, simple lists. If you really need to squeeze things down, use the COMPACT attribute.

Examples: See file /h4d4e/examples/ch06/menu.htm.

<META> Meta-information

Definition: Used within the <HEAD> element to embed document meta-information (information about information in the document). Such information can be extracted by servers/clients and be used in identifying, indexing, and cataloging specialized document meta-information.

Attributes:

NAME="text"

Used to name a property such as author, publication date, and so on. If absent, the name can be assumed to be the same as the value of HTTP-EQUIV.

CONTENT="text"

Used to supply a value for a named property.

HTTP-EQUIV="text"

This attribute binds the element to an HTTP response header. If the HTTP response header is known, the contents can be processed. HTTP header names are not case-sensitive. If HTTP-EQUIV is absent, you should use the NAME attribute to identify this meta-information, and you shouldn't use it within an HTTP response header.

SCHEME="schemename"

Identifies a scheme to be used to interpret the property's values.

Context:

<META> is legal within the following markup tag:

> <HEAD>

You cannot use any markup tags within <META>; it is a singleton tag.

Suggested style/usage: Meta-information can make information more accessible to spiders and robots for automatic indexing. It also makes information more accessible to other programs you might use to help manage an HTML document collection. There are no universally defined HTTP-EQUIV values; instead, these are determined by the user and robot/ agent owners. Often when a robot/agent is declared to support a specific HTTP-EQUIV value, it quickly spreads around the Web. Some robots record all the meta-information so specialized or focused data searches can use the information, even it if is not standardized. Check Chapter 15 for more information on spiders and robots.

The Platform for Internet Content Selection (PICS) can also be used through the <META> tag to identify content, sign code, aid privacy, or identify intellectual property rights. Details are available at www.w3.org/PICS/.

Examples: See file /h4d4e/examples/ch06/meta.htm.

<NOFRAMES> ... </NOFRAMES> Frames alternative

Definition: Indicates content is viewable only by browsers that do not support frames. Browsers that support frames will not display content between the beginning and ending <NOFRAMES> tags. Browsers that do not support frames will also not recognize the <NOFRAMES> tag and, therefore, will interpret the enclosed tags normally. Thus, you can create a page that is compatible with both types of browsers by using <NOFRAMES>.

Attributes: None

Context:

<NOFRAMES> ... </NOFRAMES> is legal within the following tags:

> <BLOCKQUOTE>, <BODY>, <BUTTON>, <CENTER>, <DD>, <DIV>,
> <FIELDSET>, <FORM>, <FRAMESET>, <IFRAME>, <LI>, <NOFRAMES>,
> <NOSCRIPT>, <OBJECT>, <TD>, <TH>

You can use the following tags within <NOFRAMES> ... </NOFRAMES>:

```
<A>, <ABBR>, <ADDRESS>, <APPLET>, <B>, <BASEFONT>, <BDO>, <BIG>,
<BLOCKQUOTE>, <BODY>, <BR>, <BUTTON>, <CENTER>, <CITE>, <CODE>,
<DFN>, <DIR>, <DIV>, <DL>, <EM>, <FIELDSET>, <FONT>, <FORM>, <H*>,
<HR>, <I>, <IFRAME>, <IMG>, <INPUT>, <ISINDEX>, <KBD>, <LABEL>,
<MAP>, <MENU>, <NOFRAMES>, <NOSCRIPT>, <OBJECT>, <OL>, <P>,
<PRE>, <Q>, <S>, <SAMP>, <SCRIPT>, <SELECT>, <SMALL>, <SPAN>,
<STRIKE>, <STRONG>, <SUB>, <SUP>, <TABLE>, <TEXTAREA>, <TT>, <U>,
<UL>, <VAR>
```

Suggested style/usage: You can use the `<NOFRAMES>` tag to present alternative content for users who don't have frames-compatible browsers. You
should provide a complete non-frames version of your document here, or
point users to a non-frames path through your pages.

Examples: See file /h4d4e/examples/ch06/noframes.htm.

<NOSCRIPT> ... </NOSCRIPT> *No script*

Definition: Specifies alternative content to be used by browsers that do not
support scripts or the specific scripting language used.

Attributes:

```
TYPE=scripting language
```

Context:

`<NOSCRIPT>` ... `</NOSCRIPT>` is legal within the following markup tags:

```
<BLOCKQUOTE>, <BODY>, <BUTTON>, <CENTER>, <DD>, <DIV>,
<FIELDSET>, <FORM>, <IFRAME>, <LI>, <NOFRAMES>, <NOSCRIPT>,
<OBJECT>, <TD>, <TH>
```

You can use the following markup tags within `<NOSCRIPT>` ... `</NOSCRIPT>`:

```
<A>, <ABBR>, <ADDRESS>, <APPLET>, <B>, <BASEFONT>, <BDO>, <BIG>,
<BLOCKQUOTE>, <BR>, <BUTTON>, <CENTER>, <CITE>, <CODE>, <DFN>,
<DIR>, <DIV>, <DL>, <EM>, <FIELDSET>, <FONT>, <FORM>, <H*>, <HR>,
<I>, <IFRAME>, <IMG>, <INPUT>, <ISINDEX>, <KBD>, <LABEL>, <MAP>,
<MENU>, <NOFRAMES>, <NOSCRIPT>, <OBJECT>, <OL>, <P>, <PRE>, <Q>,
<S>, <SAMP>, <SCRIPT>, <SELECT>, <SMALL>, <SPAN>, <STRIKE>,
<STRONG>, <SUB>, <SUP>, <TABLE>, <TEXTAREA>, <TT>, <U>, <UL>,
<VAR>
```

Suggested style/usage: You should use `<NOSCRIPT>` to include content for
browsers unable to process the inline script.

Examples: See file /h4d4e/examples/ch06/noscript.htm.

<OBJECT> ... </OBJECT> Object embedding

Definition: Inserts an object, such as an image, document, or applet, into the HTML document. An object can contain any elements ordinarily used within the body of an HTML document, including section headings, paragraphs, lists, and forms.

Attributes:

`ALIGN=(baseline|center|left|middle|right|textbottom|textmiddle|texttop)`

> Sets the alignment for the object. Please refer to the W3C DTD for further details on the alignment attribute of this tag.

`BORDER=number`

> Specifies the width of the border.

`CLASSID="URL"`

> Identifies the resource to be used for object rendering.

`CODEBASE="URL"`

> Identifies the code base or the location of the programming code for the object. The URL syntax depends on the object.

`CODETYPE=codetype`

> Specifies the Internet Media Type (MIMETYPE) for code. For details, see `ftp://ftp.isi.edu/in-notes/iana/assignments/media-types/`.

`DATA="URL"`

> Identifies data for the object. The URL syntax depends on the object.

`DECLARE`

> Defines the object without activating it. Use when cross-referencing to an object later in the same document, or when using an object as a parameter in another object.

`HEIGHT=number`

> Specifies the suggested height for the object; some objects can violate this parameter.

HSPACE=n

Specifies the horizontal gutter. This is the extra, empty space between the object and any text or images to the left or right of the object.

NAME="URL"

Sets the name of the object when submitted as part of a form.

SHAPES

Specifies that the object has shaped hyperlinks.

STANDBY=message

Sets the message to show while loading the object.

TABINDEX=number

Specifies the element's navigation order. The number can be a positive or negative integer.

TYPE=type

Specifies the Internet Media Type (MIMETYPE) for data. For details, see `ftp://ftp.isi.edu/in-notes/iana/assignments/media-types/`.

USEMAP="URL"

Specifies the image map to use with the object.

VSPACE=number

Specifies the vertical gutter. This is the extra, empty space between the object and any text or images above or below the object.

WIDTH=number

Specifies the suggested width for the object.

Context:

`<OBJECT> ... </OBJECT>` is legal within the following tags:

```
<A>, <ABBR>, <ADDRESS>, <APPLET>, <B>, <BDO>, <BIG>,
<BLOCKQUOTE>, <BODY>, <BUTTON>, <CAPTION>, <CENTER>, <CITE>,
<CODE>, <DD>, <DEL>, <DFN>, <DIV>, <DT>, <EM>, <FIELDSET>, <FONT>,
<FORM>, <H*>, <I>, <IFRAME>, <INS>, <KBD>, <LABEL>, <LEGEND>,
```

```
<LI>, <NOFRAMES>, <NOSCRIPT>, <OBJECT>, <P>, <PRE>, <Q>, <S>,
<SAMP>, <SMALL>, <SPAN>, <STRIKE>, <STRONG>, <SUB>, <SUP>, <TD>,
<TH>, <TT>, <U>, <VAR>
```

You can use the following tags within `<OBJECT>` ... `</OBJECT>`:

```
<A>, <ABBR>, <ADDRESS>, <APPLET>, <B>, <BASEFONT>, <BDO>, <BIG>,
<BLOCKQUOTE>, <BR>, <BUTTON>, <CENTER>, <CITE>, <CODE>, <DFN>,
<DIR>, <DIV>, <DL>, <EM>, <FIELDSET>, <FONT>, <FORM>, <H*>, <HR>,
<I>, <IFRAME>, <IMG>, <INPUT>, <ISINDEX>, <KBD>, <LABEL>, <MAP>,
<MENU>, <NOFRAMES>, <NOSCRIPT>, <OBJECT>, <OL>, <P>, <PARAM>,
<PRE>, <Q>, <S>, <SAMP>, <SCRIPT>, <SELECT>, <SMALL>, <SPAN>,
<STRIKE>, <STRONG>, <SUB>, <SUP>, <TABLE>, <TEXTAREA>, <TT>, <U>,
<UL>, <VAR>
```

Suggested style/usage: Used to embed nonstandard objects into HTML that are handled by inline or external applications. In general, three types of information are used or required by rendering mechanisms: the mechanism's implementation, the data to be presented, and additional values required at runtime.

Examples: See file /h4d4e/examples/ch06/object.htm.

<OL> ... </OL> Ordered list

Definition: Numbers the elements in order of occurrence.

Attributes:

`TYPE=(1|a|A|i|I)`

Changes the style of the list.

`COMPACT`

[Depreciated] Renders the list as compactly as possible by reducing line leading and spacing.

`START="value"`

Indicates where the list numbering or lettering should begin.

Context:

`<OL>` ... `</OL>` is legal within the following tags:

```
<BLOCKQUOTE>, <BODY>, <BUTTON>, <CENTER>, <DD>, <DIV>,
<FIELDSET>, <FORM>, <IFRAME>, <LI>, <NOFRAMES>, <NOSCRIPT>,
<OBJECT>, <TD>, <TH>
```

You can use the following tag within `<OL>` ... `</OL>`:

`<LI>`

Suggested style/usage: Ordered lists work well for step-by-step instructions or other situations in which the order the information is presented is important.

Examples: See file /h4d4e/examples/ch06/ol.htm.

<OPTION> Selectable item

Definition: Defines the various options available within a `<SELECT>` ... `</SELECT>` tag pair for a forms definition, where users must select a value from a predefined list of options. Also provides a mechanism for selecting a default value if the user does not explicitly choose a value.

Attributes:

`DISABLED`

Renders the element unusable.

`SELECTED`

Defines a default value for a `<SELECT>` field within a form in cases where the user chooses no value explicitly.

`VALUE="text"`

Defines the value for a specific `<SELECT>` option, which equals the text string assigned to `VALUE`.

Context:

`<OPTION>` is legal within the following tag:

`<SELECT>`

`<OPTION>` is a singleton tag.

Suggested style/usage: For defining a set of values or options for a `<SELECT>` field, and for supplying a default for such sets where appropriate.

Examples: See file /h4d4e/examples/ch06/option.htm.

<P> ... </P> Paragraph

Definition: Defines paragraph boundaries for normal text. A line break and carriage return occurs where this tag is placed.

Attributes:

```
ALIGN=(LEFT|CENTER|RIGHT|JUSTIFY)
```

[Depreciated] Sets the alignment of the paragraph. The align type can be LEFT, CENTER, RIGHT, or JUSTIFY. The default alignment is LEFT.

Context:

<P> ... </P> is legal within the following tags:

<ADDRESS>, <BLOCKQUOTE>, <BODY>, <BUTTON>, <CENTER>, <DD>, <DIV>, <FIELDSET>, <FORM>, <IFRAME>, <LI>, <NOFRAMES>, <NOSCRIPT>, <OBJECT>, <TD>, <TH>

You can use the following tags within <P> ... </P>:

<A>, <ABBR>, <APPLET>, <B>, <BASEFONT>, <BDO>, <BIG>, <BR>, <BUTTON>, <CITE>, <CODE>, <DFN>, <EM>, <FONT>, <I>, <IFRAME>, <IMG>, <INPUT>, <KBD>, <LABEL>, <MAP>, <OBJECT>, <Q>, <S>, <SAMP>, <SCRIPT>, <SELECT>, <SMALL>, <SPAN>, <STRIKE>, <STRONG>, <SUB>, <SUP>, <TEXTAREA>, <TT>, <U>, <VAR>

Suggested style/usage: You use paragraphs to break the flow of ideas or information into related chunks. Each idea or concept should have its own paragraph for good writing style. The closing </P> tag is optional.

Examples: See file /h4d4e/examples/ch06/p.htm.

<PARAM> Object parameters

Definition: Used to provide "command-line" arguments to a Java applet embedded in a document with the <APPLET> tag.

Attributes:

```
NAME="text"
```

Specifies the property name, assumed to be known by the object. Case-sensitivity is determined by the object.

`VALUE=number|"text"`

> Specifies the property's value identified with the `NAME` attribute. The value does not change, except that the corresponding character values replace any character entities.

`VALUETYPE=(DATA|REF|OBJECT)`

> Specifies how to interpret the value. The type can be one of these values:
>
> `DATA`: Data; this is the default value type.
>
> `REF`: A URL.
>
> `OBJECT`: A URL of an object in the same document.

`TYPE=type`

> Specifies the Internet Media Type (MIMETYPE). For details, see `ftp://ftp.isi.edu/in-notes/iana/assignments/media-types/`.

Context:

`<PARAM>` ... `</PARAM>` is legal within the following tags:

> `<APPLET>`, `<OBJECT>`

No other tags may be used within `<PARAM>` ... `</PARAM>` markup.

Suggested style/usage: Argument names are case-sensitive in Java, so be sure you have the case right in the `<PARAM>` tag.

Examples: See file /h4d4e/examples/ch06/param.htm.

<PRE> ... </PRE> Preformatted text

Definition: Forces the browser to display the exact formatting, indentation, and white space that the original text contains. This is valuable in reproducing formatted tables or other text, such as code listings.

Attributes:

`WIDTH=number`

> This specifies the maximum number of characters for a line and allows the browser to select an appropriate font and indentation setting.

Context:

`<PRE> ... </PRE>` is legal within the following tags:

> `<BLOCKQUOTE>`, `<BODY>`, `<BUTTON>`, `<CENTER>`, `<DD>`, `<DIV>`,
> `<FIELDSET>`, `<FORM>`, `<IFRAME>`, `<LI>`, `<NOFRAMES>`, `<NOSCRIPT>`,
> `<OBJECT>`, `<TD>`, `<TH>`

You can use the following tags within `<PRE> ... </PRE>`:

> `<A>`, `<ABBR>`, `<APPLET>`, `<B>`, `<BASEFONT>`, `<BDO>`, `<BIG>`, `<BR>`,
> `<BUTTON>`, `<CITE>`, `<CODE>`, `<DFN>`, `<EM>`, `<FONT>`, `<I>`, `<IFRAME>`,
> `<IMG>`, `<INPUT>`, `<KBD>`, `<LABEL>`, `<MAP>`, `<OBJECT>`, `<Q>`, `<S>`, `<SAMP>`,
> `<SCRIPT>`, `<SELECT>`, `<SMALL>`, `<SPAN>`, `<STRIKE>`, `<STRONG>`, `<SUB>`,
> `<SUP>`, `<TEXTAREA>`, `<TT>`, `<U>`, `<VAR>`

Suggested style/usage: Within a `<PRE> ... </PRE>` block, you can break lines by pressing Enter, but try to keep line lengths at 80 characters or less, because `<PRE>` text is typically set in a monospaced font. This tag is great for presenting text-only information.

Examples: See file /h4d4e/examples/ch06/pre.htm.

<Q> ... </Q> Quotation markup

Definition: Use to highlight short quotations from outside resources.

Attributes:

`CITE="text"`

> Provides information about the source of the quote.

Context:

`<Q> ... </Q>` is legal within the following tags:

> `<A>`, `<ABBR>`, `<ADDRESS>`, `<APPLET>`, `<B>`, `<BDO>`, `<BIG>`,
> `<BLOCKQUOTE>`, `<BODY>`, `<BUTTON>`, `<CAPTION>`, `<CENTER>`, `<CITE>`,
> `<CODE>`, `<DD>`, `<DEL>`, `<DFN>`, `<DIV>`, `<DT>`, `<EM>`, `<FIELDSET>`, `<FONT>`,
> `<FORM>`, `<H*>`, `<I>`, `<IFRAME>`, `<INS>`, `<KBD>`, `<LABEL>`, `<LEGEND>`,
> `<LI>`, `<NOFRAMES>`, `<NOSCRIPT>`, `<OBJECT>`, `<P>`, `<PRE>`, `<Q>`, `<S>`,
> `<SAMP>`, `<SMALL>`, `<SPAN>`, `<STRIKE>`, `<STRONG>`, `<SUB>`, `<SUP>`, `<TD>`,
> `<TH>`, `<TT>`, `<U>`, `<VAR>`

You can use the following tags within `<Q> ... </Q>`:

```
<A>, <ABBR>, <APPLET>, <B>, <BASEFONT>, <BDO>, <BIG>, <BR>,
<BUTTON>, <CITE>, <CODE>, <DFN>, <EM>, <FONT>, <I>, <IFRAME>,
<IMG>, <INPUT>, <KBD>, <LABEL>, <MAP>, <OBJECT>, <Q>, <S>, <SAMP>,
<SCRIPT>, <SELECT>, <SMALL>, <SPAN>, <STRIKE>, <STRONG>, <SUB>,
<SUP>, <TEXTAREA>, <TT>, <U>, <VAR>
```

Suggested style/usage: When you use a short quote from an external source, include it within `<Q> ... </Q>` tags. Always attribute your sources. Remember to use `<CITE>` to highlight the actual publication, if applicable.

Examples: See file /h4d4e/examples/ch06/q.htm.

<S> ... </S> Strikethrough

Definition: [Depreciated] Renders enclosed text in strikethrough style. This tag is the same as `<STRIKE>`.

Attributes: None

Context:

`<S> ... </S>` is legal within the following tags:

```
<A>, <ABBR>, <ADDRESS>, <APPLET>, <B>, <BDO>, <BIG>,
<BLOCKQUOTE>, <BODY>, <BUTTON>, <CAPTION>, <CENTER>, <CITE>,
<CODE>, <DD>, <DEL>, <DFN>, <DIV>, <DT>, <EM>, <FIELDSET>, <FONT>,
<FORM>, <H*>, <I>, <IFRAME>, <INS>, <KBD>, <LABEL>, <LEGEND>,
<LI>, <NOFRAMES>, <NOSCRIPT>, <OBJECT>, <P>, <PRE>, <Q>, <S>,
<SAMP>, <SMALL>, <SPAN>, <STRIKE>, <STRONG>, <SUB>, <SUP>, <TD>,
<TH>, <TT>, <U>, <VAR>
```

You can use the following tags within `<S> ... </S>`:

```
<A>, <ABBR>, <APPLET>, <B>, <BASEFONT>, <BDO>, <BIG>, <BR>,
<BUTTON>, <CITE>, <CODE>, <DFN>, <EM>, <FONT>, <I>, <IFRAME>,
<IMG>, <INPUT>, <KBD>, <LABEL>, <MAP>, <OBJECT>, <Q>, <S>, <SAMP>,
<SCRIPT>, <SELECT>, <SMALL>, <SPAN>, <STRIKE>, <STRONG>, <SUB>,
<SUP>, <TEXTAREA>, <TT>, <U>, <VAR>
```

Suggested style/usage: This tag has been depreciated in favor of similar style sheet properties. Strikethrough text is difficult to read onscreen, so use this tag sparingly. It's most commonly used to show text removed from earlier versions of a document.

Examples: See file /h4d4e/examples/ch06/s.htm.

<SAMP> ... </SAMP> Sample output

Definition: You should use `<SAMP> ... </SAMP>` for sequences of literal characters or to represent output from a program or other data source.

Attributes: None

Context:

`<SAMP> ... </SAMP>` is legal within the following tags:

> `<A>, <ABBR>, <ADDRESS>, <APPLET>, <B>, <BDO>, <BIG>,`
> `<BLOCKQUOTE>, <BODY>, <BUTTON>, <CAPTION>, <CENTER>, <CITE>,`
> `<CODE>, <DD>, <DEL>, <DFN>, <DIV>, <DT>, <EM>, <FIELDSET>, <FONT>,`
> `<FORM>, <H*>, <I>, <IFRAME>, <INS>, <KBD>, <LABEL>, <LEGEND>,`
> `<LI>, <NOFRAMES>, <NOSCRIPT>, <OBJECT>, <P>, <PRE>, <Q>, <S>,`
> `<SAMP>, <SMALL>, <SPAN>, <STRIKE>, <STRONG>, <SUB>, <SUP>, <TD>,`
> `<TH>, <TT>, <U>, <VAR>`

You can use the following tags within `<SAMP> ... </SAMP>`:

> `<A>, <ABBR>, <APPLET>, <B>, <BASEFONT>, <BDO>, <BIG>, <BR>,`
> `<BUTTON>, <CITE>, <CODE>, <DFN>, <EM>, <FONT>, <I>, <IFRAME>,`
> `<IMG>, <INPUT>, <KBD>, <LABEL>, <MAP>, <OBJECT>, <Q>, <S>, <SAMP>,`
> `<SCRIPT>, <SELECT>, <SMALL>, <SPAN>, <STRIKE>, <STRONG>, <SUB>,`
> `<SUP>, <TEXTAREA>, <TT>, <U>, <VAR>`

Suggested style/usage: Use `<SAMP> ... </SAMP>` whenever you want to reproduce output from a program, script, or other data source.

Examples: See file /h4d4e/examples/ch06/samp.htm.

<SCRIPT> ... </SCRIPT> Inline script

Definition: Specifies inclusion of a script. Scripts execute and initiate objects in the order in which they appear in the HTML document. Named objects can be referenced only in the order in which they appear in the document.

Attributes:

`TYPE=scripting language`

> Specifies the script language type for the enclosed script text. This value must be an Internet Media Type (MIME); see `ftp://ftp.isi.edu/in-notes/iana/assignments/media-types/`. There is no default value.

```
LANGUAGE=scripting language
```

> **[Depreciated]** Indicates the scripting language in which the enclosed
> script was written, such as "VBScript" and "JavaScript."

```
SRC="URL"
```

> Specifies the location of an external script. If this value is defined, all
> text enclosed by the `<SCRIPT>` tags will be ignored.

Context:

`<SCRIPT> ... </SCRIPT>` is legal within the following markup tags:

> `<A>`, `<ABBR>`, `<ADDRESS>`, `<APPLET>`, `<B>`, `<BDO>`, `<BIG>`,
> `<BLOCKQUOTE>`, `<BODY>`, `<BUTTON>`, `<CAPTION>`, `<CENTER>`, `<CITE>`,
> `<CODE>`, `<DD>`, `<DEL>`, `<DFN>`, `<DIV>`, `<DT>`, `<EM>`, `<FIELDSET>`, `<FONT>`,
> `<FORM>`, `<H*>`, `<HEAD>`, `<I>`, `<IFRAME>`, `<INS>`, `<KBD>`, `<LABEL>`,
> `<LEGEND>`, `<LI>`, `<NOFRAMES>`, `<NOSCRIPT>`, `<OBJECT>`, `<P>`, `<PRE>`,
> `<Q>`, `<S>`, `<SAMP>`, `<SMALL>`, `<SPAN>`, `<STRIKE>`, `<STRONG>`, `<SUB>`,
> `<SUP>`, `<TD>`, `<TH>`, `<TT>`, `<U>`, `<VAR>`

No additonal HTML markup can be used with the script tags; only scripting
code is allowed.

Suggested style/usage: The scripting language must be defined through a
default declaration — see `<META>` — or a local declaration — `<SCRIPT>` with
type attribute. If you use both, the local declaration overrides the default
only for that instance of `<SCRIPT>`.

Because not all browsers support scripts or simply fail to support the
specific scripting language used, we highly recommend that you use the
`<NOSCRIPT>` tag for alternative nonscript content.

HTML also supports many intrinsic programming events; you can use these
in the same fashion as attributes for various other tags.

Examples: See file /h4d4e/examples/ch06/script.htm.

<SELECT> ... </SELECT> Select input object

Definition: Allows users to pick one or more options out of a list of possible
values supplied in an input form. Each alternative is represented by an
`<OPTION>` element.

Attributes:

DISABLED

> Renders the element unusable.

MULTIPLE

> This attribute appears when you allow users to select more than one element from the set of <OPTION> values supplied within a <SELECT> ... </SELECT> tag pair.

NAME="text"

> Specifies a name for the list.

SIZE=number

> Specifies the number of visible choices.

TABINDEX="number"

> Identifies the element's place in the tabbing order.

Context:

<SELECT> ... </SELECT> is legal within the following tags:

> <A>, <ABBR>, <ADDRESS>, <APPLET>, <B>, <BDO>, <BIG>, <BLOCKQUOTE>, <BODY>, <CAPTION>, <CENTER>, <CITE>, <CODE>, <DD>, <DEL>, <DFN>, <DIV>, <DT>, <EM>, <FIELDSET>, <FONT>, <FORM>, <H*>, <I>, <IFRAME>, <INS>, <KBD>, <LABEL>, <LEGEND>, <LI>, <NOFRAMES>, <NOSCRIPT>, <OBJECT>, <P>, <PRE>, <Q>, <S>, <SAMP>, <SMALL>, <SPAN>, <STRIKE>, <STRONG>, <SUB>, <SUP>, <TD>, <TH>, <TT>, <U>, <VAR>

You can use the following tag within <SELECT> ... </SELECT>:

> <OPTION>

Suggested style/usage: Use to provide lists of scalar values within HTML forms whenever users can pick only from a predetermined set of possible values.

Examples: See file /h4d4e/examples/ch06/option.htm.

<SMALL> ... </SMALL> Small text

Definition: Makes text one size smaller than the base font size.

Attributes: None

Context:

`<SMALL> ... </SMALL>` is legal within the following tags:

> `<A>, <ABBR>, <ADDRESS>, <APPLET>, <B>, <BDO>, <BIG>,`
> `<BLOCKQUOTE>, <BODY>, <BUTTON>, <CAPTION>, <CENTER>, <CITE>,`
> `<CODE>, <DD>, <DEL>, <DFN>, <DIV>, <DT>, <EM>, <FIELDSET>,`
> `<FONT>, <FORM>, <H*>, <I>, <IFRAME>, <INS>, <KBD>, <LABEL>,`
> `<LEGEND>, <LI>, <NOFRAMES>, <NOSCRIPT>, <OBJECT>, <P>, <Q>,`
> `<S>, <SAMP>, <SMALL>, <SPAN>, <STRIKE>, <STRONG>, <SUB>, <SUP>,`
> `<TD>, <TH>, <TT>, <U>, <VAR>`

You can use the following tags within `<SMALL> ... </SMALL>`:

> `<A>, <ABBR>, <APPLET>, <B>, <BASEFONT>, <BDO>, <BIG>, <BR>,`
> `<BUTTON>, <CITE>, <CODE>, <DFN>, <EM>, <FONT>, <I>, <IFRAME>,`
> `<IMG>, <INPUT>, <KBD>, <LABEL>, <MAP>, <OBJECT>, <Q>, <S>, <SAMP>,`
> `<SCRIPT>, <SELECT>, <SMALL>, <SPAN>, <STRIKE>, <STRONG>, <SUB>,`
> `<SUP>, <TEXTAREA>, <TT>, <U>, <VAR>`

Suggested style/usage: Nesting `<SMALL>` tags can produce text in a smaller font than using only one `<SMALL>` tag, but the specs do not require this. However, you can use style sheet rules to achieve the same effect as using multiple nested `<SMALL>` tags.

Examples: See file /h4d4e/examples/ch06/small.htm.

<SPAN> ... </SPAN> Localized style formatting

Definition: Applies style information to text within a document. You can use `<SPAN>` for localized text formatting using `<STYLE>` as an attribute.

Attributes:

`ALIGN=(LEFT|CENTER|RIGHT|JUSTIFY)`

> Specifies the default horizontal alignment for the contents of the `<DIV>` element.

`STYLE="text"`

> You can use `<SPAN>` to add margins, paragraph width, and other related width options to text. See Chapter 10 for `<STYLE>` attribute details.

Context:

<SPAN> ... </SPAN> is legal within the following markup tags:

> <A>, <ABBR>, <ADDRESS>, <APPLET>, <B>, <BDO>, <BIG>,
> <BLOCKQUOTE>, <BODY>, <BUTTON>, <CAPTION>, <CENTER>, <CITE>,
> <CODE>, <DD>, <DEL>, <DFN>, <DIV>, <DT>, <EM>, <FIELDSET>, <FONT>,
> <FORM>, <H*>, <I>, <IFRAME>, <INS>, <KBD>, <LABEL>, <LEGEND>,
> <LI>, <NOFRAMES>, <NOSCRIPT>, <OBJECT>, <P>, <PRE>, <Q>, <S>,
> <SAMP>, <SMALL>, <SPAN>, <STRIKE>, <STRONG>, <SUB>, <SUP>, <TD>,
> <TH>, <TT>, <U>, <VAR>

You can use the following markup tags within <SPAN> ... </SPAN>:

> <A>, <ABBR>, <APPLET>, <B>, <BASEFONT>, <BDO>, <BIG>, <BR>,
> <BUTTON>, <CITE>, <CODE>, <DFN>, <EM>, <FONT>, <I>, <IFRAME>,
> <IMG>, <INPUT>, <KBD>, <LABEL>, <MAP>, <OBJECT>, <Q>, <S>, <SAMP>,
> <SCRIPT>, <SELECT>, <SMALL>, <SPAN>, <STRIKE>, <STRONG>, <SUB>,
> <SUP>, <TEXTAREA>, <TT>, <U>, <VAR>

Suggested style/usage: <SPAN> is an inline division element. It applies no change to standard rendering to surrounded content without a <STYLE> attribute definition. You can use <SPAN> within paragraphs, unlike <DIV>, but you cannot use it to group block elements.

Examples: See file /h4d4e/examples/ch06/span.htm.

<STRIKE> ... </STRIKE> Strikethrough

Definition: [Depreciated] Renders enclosed text in strikethrough style. This is the style <S> is based on.

Attribute:

> None

Context:

<STRIKE> ... </STRIKE> is legal within the following tags:

> <A>, <ABBR>, <ADDRESS>, <APPLET>, <B>, <BDO>, <BIG>,
> <BLOCKQUOTE>, <BODY>, <BUTTON>, <CAPTION>, <CENTER>, <CITE>,
> <CODE>, <DD>, <DFN>, <DIV>, <DT>, <EM>, <FIELDSET>, <FONT>,
> <FORM>, <H*>, <I>, <IFRAME>, <INS>, <KBD>, <LABEL>, <LEGEND>,
> <LI>, <NOFRAMES>, <NOSCRIPT>, <OBJECT>, <P>, <PRE>, <Q>, <S>,
> <SAMP>, <SMALL>, <SPAN>, <STRIKE>, <STRONG>, <SUB>, <SUP>, <TD>,
> <TH>, <TT>, <U>, <VAR>

You can use the following tags within `<STRIKE>` ... `</STRIKE>`:

```
<A>, <ABBR>, <APPLET>, <B>, <BASEFONT>, <BDO>, <BIG>, <BR>,
<BUTTON>, <CITE>, <CODE>, <DFN>, <EM>, <FONT>, <I>, <IFRAME>,
<IMG>, <INPUT>, <KBD>, <LABEL>, <MAP>, <OBJECT>, <Q>, <S>, <SAMP>,
<SCRIPT>, <SELECT>, <SMALL>, <SPAN>, <STRIKE>, <STRONG>, <SUB>,
<SUP>, <TEXTAREA>, <TT>, <U>, <VAR>
```

Suggested style/usage: Strikethrough text is difficult to read onscreen, so use this tag sparingly. Use `<STRIKE>` to show text removed from earlier versions of a document; the old text will appear with a line through it.

Examples: See file /h4d4e/examples/ch06/strike.htm.

`<STRONG>` ... `</STRONG>` *Strong emphasis*

Definition: Provides strong emphasis for key words or phrases within normal body text, lists, and other block level elements.

Attributes: None

Context:

`<STRONG>` ... `</STRONG>` is legal within the following tags:

```
<A>, <ABBR>, <ADDRESS>, <APPLET>, <B>, <BDO>, <BIG>,
<BLOCKQUOTE>, <BODY>, <BUTTON>, <CAPTION>, <CENTER>, <CITE>,
<CODE>, <DD>, <DEL>, <DFN>, <DIV>, <DT>, <EM>, <FIELDSET>, <FONT>,
<FORM>, <H*>, <I>, <IFRAME>, <INS>, <KBD>, <LABEL>, <LEGEND>,
<LI>, <NOFRAMES>, <NOSCRIPT>, <OBJECT>, <P>, <PRE>, <Q>, <S>,
<SAMP>, <SMALL>, <SPAN>, <STRIKE>, <STRONG>, <SUB>, <SUP>, <TD>,
<TH>, <TT>, <U>, <VAR>
```

You can use the following tags within `<STRONG>` ... `</STRONG>`:

```
<A>, <ABBR>, <APPLET>, <B>, <BASEFONT>, <BDO>, <BIG>, <BR>,
<BUTTON>, <CITE>, <CODE>, <DFN>, <EM>, <FONT>, <I>, <IFRAME>,
<IMG>, <INPUT>, <KBD>, <LABEL>, <MAP>, <OBJECT>, <Q>, <S>, <SAMP>,
<SCRIPT>, <SELECT>, <SMALL>, <SPAN>, <STRIKE>, <STRONG>, <SUB>,
<SUP>, <TEXTAREA>, <TT>, <U>, <VAR>
```

Suggested style/usage: Use within running text to provide the strongest degree of inline emphasis available in HTML. Remember that overuse blunts the effect, so use emphatic text controls sparingly.

Examples: See file /h4d4e/examples/ch06/strong.htm.

<STYLE> ... </STYLE> Style information

Definition: Provides a means to include rendering and display information using style sheet notation. Cascading Style Sheets (CSS1) are currently the most widely supported standard and all references to style sheets refer to CSS1. Information in the <STYLE> tag works with the client's default configuration as well any externally referenced style sheets to provide an overall set of style rules for a given Web page.

Attributes:

TYPE="text"

> Specifies the type of style sheet in use. The type for CSS1 sheets is text/css.

MEDIA= SCREEN | PRINT | PROJECTION | BRAILLE | SPEECH | ALL

> Identifies the ideal environment for the Web page to be conveyed in. The default is ALL, and SCREEN will be used in most cases since Web pages are most often viewed on a computer screen. However, pages designed for presentations would use the PROJECTION value, while those meant to be read by a text-to-speech reader would use the SPEECH value. Currently this attribute provides information only and does not affect the way the style sheet is interpreted or the page rendered. You may include more than one media type, each separated by a comma.

Context:

<STYLE> ... </STYLE> is legal within the following markup tags:

> <HEAD>

You can't use any markup with <STYLE> ... </STYLE>.

Suggested style/usage: The tag should contain only valid style statements in the language indicated by the TYPE attribute. Style sheets are now formally part of the HTML 4.0 specification and are supported in full by Internet Explorer 4.0 and Netscape Navigator 4.0. Older versions of browsers that do not support style sheets ignore style markup. While style sheets provide Web designers with more control over Web pages than standard HTML, the technology is still in its infancy and will grow quickly.

Example: See file /h4d4e/examples/ch06/style.htm.

_{...} Subscript

Definition: Specifies that the enclosed text should be rendered in subscript, slightly lower than the surrounding text.

Attributes: None

Context:

`<SUB> ... </SUB>` is legal within the following tags:

```
<A>, <ABBR>, <ADDRESS>, <APPLET>, <B>, <BDO>, <BIG>,
<BLOCKQUOTE>, <BODY>, <BUTTON>, <CAPTION>, <CENTER>, <CITE>,
<CODE>, <DD>, <DEL>, <DFN>, <DIV>, <DT>, <EM>, <FIELDSET>,
<FONT>, <FORM>, <H*>, <I>, <IFRAME>, <INS>, <KBD>, <LABEL>,
<LEGEND>, <LI>, <NOFRAMES>, <NOSCRIPT>, <OBJECT>, <P>, <Q>,
<S>, <SAMP>, <SMALL>, <SPAN>, <STRIKE>, <STRONG>, <SUB>, <SUP>,
<TD>, <TH>, <TT>, <U>, <VAR>
```

You can use the following tags within `<SUB> ... </SUB>`:

```
<A>, <ABBR>, <APPLET>, <B>, <BASEFONT>, <BDO>, <BIG>, <BR>,
<BUTTON>, <CITE>, <CODE>, <DFN>, <EM>, <FONT>, <I>, <IFRAME>,
<IMG>, <INPUT>, <KBD>, <LABEL>, <MAP>, <OBJECT>, <Q>, <S>, <SAMP>,
<SCRIPT>, <SELECT>, <SMALL>, <SPAN>, <STRIKE>, <STRONG>, <SUB>,
<SUP>, <TEXTAREA>, <TT>, <U>, <VAR>
```

Suggested style/usage: Use subscript for scientific or mathematical notation.

Examples: See file /h4d4e/examples/ch06/sub.htm.

^{...} Superscript

Definition: Specifies that the enclosed text should be rendered in superscript, slightly higher than the surrounding text.

Attributes: None

Context:

`<SUP> ... </SUP>` is legal within the following tags:

```
<A>, <ABBR>, <ADDRESS>, <APPLET>, <B>, <BDO>, <BIG>,
<BLOCKQUOTE>, <BODY>, <BUTTON>, <CAPTION>, <CENTER>, <CITE>,
<CODE>, <DD>, <DEL>, <DFN>, <DIV>, <DT>, <EM>, <FIELDSET>,
<FONT>, <FORM>, <H*>, <I>, <IFRAME>, <INS>, <KBD>, <LABEL>,
```

```
<LEGEND>, <LI>, <NOFRAMES>, <NOSCRIPT>, <OBJECT>, <P>, <Q>,
<S>, <SAMP>, <SMALL>, <SPAN>, <STRIKE>, <STRONG>, <SUB>, <SUP>,
<TD>, <TH>, <TT>, <U>, <VAR>
```

You can use the following tags within `<SUP>` ... `</SUP>`:

```
<A>, <ABBR>, <APPLET>, <B>, <BASEFONT>, <BDO>, <BIG>, <BR>,
<BUTTON>, <CITE>, <CODE>, <DFN>, <EM>, <FONT>, <I>, <IFRAME>,
<IMG>, <INPUT>, <KBD>, <LABEL>, <MAP>, <OBJECT>, <Q>, <S>, <SAMP>,
<SCRIPT>, <SELECT>, <SMALL>, <SPAN>, <STRIKE>, <STRONG>, <SUB>,
<SUP>, <TEXTAREA>, <TT>, <U>, <VAR>
```

Suggested style/usage: Superscript is particularly useful when working with foreign languages and names, as well as with mathematical and scientific notations and footnotes.

Examples: See file /h4d4e/examples/ch06/sup.htm.

<TABLE> ... </TABLE> Table

Definition: Creates a table. The table is empty unless you create rows and cells using the `<TR>`, `<TD>`, and `<TH>` elements.

Attributes:

`ALIGN=(LEFT|RIGHT|CENTER)`

Specifies the table alignment in relation to the document. The align type can be one of these values:

`LEFT`: The table is aligned with the left side of the document. This is the default.

`RIGHT`: The table is aligned with the right side of the document. If the table width is less than the width of the window, text following the table wraps along the left side of the table.

`CENTER`: The table is centered.

`BGCOLOR=color`

[Depreciated] Sets the background color. The color is a hexadecimal, red-green-blue color value or is a predefined color name.

`BORDER=number`

Sets the size, in pixels, of the table border. The default is 1.

`CELLPADDING=number`

Sets the amount of space, in pixels, between the sides of a cell and its contents.

`CELLSPACING=number`

Sets the amount of space, in pixels, between the frame (exterior) of the table and the cells in the table, as well as the space between the cells themselves.

`COLS=number`

Sets the number of columns in the table. If given, this attribute may speed up processing of tables, especially lengthy ones.

`FRAME=(VOID|ABOVE|BELOW|HSIDES|LHS|RHS|VSIDES|BOX|BORDER)`

Specifies which sides of a frame (outer borders) are displayed. The frame type can be one of these values:

`VOID` removes all outside table borders.

`ABOVE` displays a border on the top of the table frame.

`BELOW` displays a border on the bottom of the table frame.

`HSIDES` displays a border on the top and bottom of the table frame.

`LHS` displays a border on the left side of the table frame.

`RHS` displays a border on the right side of the table frame.

`VSIDES` displays a border on the left and right sides of the table frame.

`BOX` displays a border on all sides of the table frame.

`BORDER` displays a border on all sides of the table frame.

`RULES=(NONE|GROUPS|ROWS|COLS|ALL)`

Specifies which dividing lines (inner borders) are displayed. The rule type can be one of these values:

`NONE` removes all interior table borders.

`GROUPS` displays horizontal borders between all table groups. Groups are specified by the `<THEAD>`, `<TBODY>`, `<TFOOT>`, and `<COLGROUP>` elements.

ROWS displays horizontal borders between all table rows.

COLS displays vertical borders between all table columns.

ALL displays a border on all rows and columns.

WIDTH=(pixels|"%")

Sets the width of the table in pixels or as a percentage of the window. To set a percentage, the number must end with a percent (%) sign.

Context:

<TABLE> ... </TABLE> is legal within the following tags:

<BLOCKQUOTE>, <BODY>, <BUTTON>, <CENTER>, <DD>, <DIV>, <FIELDSET>, <FORM>, <IFRAME>, <LI>, <NOFRAMES>, <NOSCRIPT>, <OBJECT>, <TD>, <TH>

You can use the following tags within <TABLE> ... </TABLE>:

<CAPTION>, <COL>, <COLGROUP>, <TBODY>, <TFOOT>, <THEAD>

Suggested style/usage: Table specifications differ widely, and the browsers that don't support tables can display confusing information when it has been coded into a table. If you use tables, make sure to look at your pages with a text browser, nontables browser, and a tables browser other than the one with which you designed your pages.

Examples: See file /h4d4e/examples/ch06/table.htm.

<TBODY> ... </TBODY> Table body

Definition: Defines the table body. Use this tag to distinguish the rows in the table header or footer from those in the main body of the table.

Attributes: None

Context:

<TBODY> ... </TBODY> is legal within the following tag:

<TABLE>

You can use the following tag within <TBODY> ... </TBODY>:

<TR>

Suggested style/usage: If a table doesn't have a header or footer (<THEAD> or <TFOOT>), the <TBODY> tag is optional; the end tag is always optional. You can use the <TBODY> element more than once in a table, which is useful for dividing lengthy tables into smaller units and in controlling the placement of horizontal rules.

Examples: See file /h4d4e/examples/ch06/tbody.htm.

<TD> ... </TD> Table cell

Definition: Creates a cell in a table.

Attributes:

ALIGN=(LEFT|RIGHT|CENTER|JUSTIFY|CHAR)

> Specifies the horizontal text alignment in the cell. The align type can be one of these values:
>
> LEFT: The text is left aligned. This is the default alignment.
>
> RIGHT: The text is right aligned.
>
> CENTER: The text is centered.
>
> JUSTIFY: The text is double justified.
>
> CHAR: The text is aligned to the character specified by the CHAR attribute.

AXIS="text"

> Provides an abbreviated description of the cell's contents.

AXES="text"

> Using a comma-delineated text, this attribute provides a list of the row and column headers related to the cell's contents.

BGCOLOR=color

> **[Depreciated]** Sets the background color for the cell. The color is a hexadecimal red-green-blue color value, or a predefined color name.

CHAR="text"

> Specifies the character the text will be aligned to when ALIGN=CHAR is used and when the CHAROFF attribute is present.

CHAROFF=number

Defines how far, in pixels, the remainder of text in a line should be offset from the first occurrence of the alignment character specified by CHAR=.

COLSPAN=number

Indicates how many columns the particular cell overlaps.

NOWRAP

[Depreciated] Indicates the contents of the current cell should not be wrapped. You must use <BR> in the cell to force line breaks to prevent the entire cell from showing up as just one line.

ROWSPAN=number

Indicates how many rows the particular cell overlaps.

VALIGN= TOP|MIDDLE|BOTTOM|BASELINE

Specifies the vertical text alignment in the column's cells. The VALIGN type can be one of these values:

TOP: The text is aligned with the top of the cell.

MIDDLE: The text is aligned with the middle of the cell.

BOTTOM: The text is aligned with the bottom of the cell.

BASELINE: The text is aligned with the baseline common to all the cells in the row.

Context:

<TD> ... </TD> is legal within the following tag:

    <TR>

You can use the following tags within <TD> ... </TD>:

    <A>, <ABBR>, <ADDRESS>, <APPLET>, <B>, <BASEFONT>, <BDO>, <BIG>,
    <BLOCKQUOTE>, <BR>, <BUTTON>, <CENTER>, <CITE>, <CODE>, <DFN>,
    <DIR>, <DIV>, <DL>, <EM>, <FIELDSET>, <FONT>, <FORM>, <H*>, <HR>,
    <I>, <IFRAME>, <IMG>, <INPUT>, <ISINDEX>, <KBD>, <LABEL>, <MAP>,
    <MENU>, <NOFRAMES>, <NOSCRIPT>, <OBJECT>, <OL>, <P>, <PRE>, <Q>,
    <S>, <SAMP>, <SCRIPT>, <SELECT>, <SMALL>, <SPAN>, <STRIKE>,
    <STRONG>, <SUB>, <SUP>, <TABLE>, <TEXTAREA>, <TT>, <U>, <UL>, <VAR>

Suggested style/usage: Close each table cell with the </TD> tag; this makes it easier to read. When including a table inside a table cell, close all cells and rows; otherwise, some browsers may render the nested tables incorrectly. Browsers usually render an empty cell different from a cell with white space inside it. When using images in a table cell, be sure to specify the WIDTH and HEIGHT attributes in the <IMG> tag, allowing the browser to start drawing the table before the image is loaded.

Examples: See file /h4d4e/examples/ch06/td.htm.

<TEXTAREA> ... </TEXTAREA> Text input area

Definition: Defines a text input area for an HTML input form, typically for multiple lines of text.

Attributes:

COLS="number"

> Defines the number of columns for any given line of text in the <TEXTAREA> field. Common practice is to limit the number of columns to 72 or less, that being a common limitation for the number of characters a line can hold within the outside page frame of a browser program onscreen (80 is the typical maximum for normal character-mode displays). This is a required attribute, but takes a default of 80.

DISABLED

> Renders the element unusable.

NAME="text"

> Supplies a name for the form field, which will be paired with the value that's ultimately entered for submission to the underlying CGI script or other service program that processes the form. This is a required attribute.

READONLY

> The contents of the text area cannot be modified by the user. Any information contained within the area is automatically submitted with the form.

ROWS="number"

> Defines the number of lines of text the field can accommodate. Typical values for nonnarrative forms range from 2 to 6, but HTML allows large text areas if needed. This is a required attribute, but takes a default of 1.

```
TABINDEX="number"
```

Identifies the element's place in the tabbing order.

Context:

`<TEXTAREA>` ... `</TEXTAREA>` is legal within the following tags:

```
<A>, <ABBR>, <ADDRESS>, <APPLET>, <B>, <BDO>, <BIG>,
<BLOCKQUOTE>, <BODY>, <CAPTION>, <CENTER>, <CITE>, <CODE>, <DD>,
<DEL>, <DFN>, <DIV>, <DT>, <EM>, <FIELDSET>, <FONT>, <FORM>, <H*>,
<I>, <IFRAME>, <INS>, <KBD>, <LABEL>, <LEGEND>, <LI>, <NOFRAMES>,
<NOSCRIPT>, <OBJECT>, <P>, <PRE>, <Q>, <S>, <SAMP>, <SMALL>,
<SPAN>, <STRIKE>, <STRONG>, <SUB>, <SUP>, <TD>, <TH>, <TT>, <U>,
<VAR>
```

Plain text is allowed in the `<TEXTAREA>` tag.

Suggested style/usage: The end tag marks the end of the text used to initialize the field (which can include a default string supplied by the form's author). Thus, even if the field is empty — that is, `<TEXTAREA>` and `</TEXTAREA>` are adjacent to one another — the end tag is essential to indicate a null value for the field. Use `<TEXTAREA>` whenever you have a multiline input field in a form.

Examples: See file /h4d4e/examples/ch06/frameset.htm.

<TFOOT> ... </TFOOT> Table footer

Definition: Defines the table footer. Use this element to distinguish the rows in the table footer from those in the table header or main body.

Attributes: None

Context:

`<TFOOT>` ... `</TFOOT>` is legal within the following tag:

```
<TABLE>
```

You can use the following tag within `<TFOOT>` ... `</TFOOT>`:

```
<TR>
```

Suggested style/usage: The table footer is optional, but if used, only one footer is allowed. The closing tag is optional.

Examples: See file /h4d4e/examples/ch06/foot.htm.

<TH> ... </TH> Table header

Definition: Creates a row or column heading, which is usually displayed in a bold or italic font.

Attributes:

ALIGN=(LEFT|RIGHT|CENTER|JUSTIFY|CHAR)

Specifies the horizontal text alignment in the cell. The align type can be one of these values:

LEFT: The text is left aligned. This is the default alignment.

RIGHT: The text is right aligned.

CENTER: The text is centered.

JUSTIFY: The text is double justified.

CHAR: The text is aligned to the character specified by the CHAR attribute.

AXIS="text"

Provides an abbreviated description of the cell's contents.

AXES="text"

Using a comma-delineated text, this attribute provides a list of the row and column headers related to the cell's contents.

BGCOLOR=color

[Depreciated] Sets the background color for the cell. The color is a hexadecimal red-green-blue color value or a predefined color name.

CHAR="text"

Specifies the character the text will be aligned to when ALIGN=CHAR is used and when the CHAROFF attribute is present.

CHAROFF=number

Defines how far, in pixels, the remainder of text in a line should be offset from the first occurrence of the alignment character specified by CHAR=.

COLSPAN=number

Indicates how many columns the particular cell overlaps.

NOWRAP

[Depreciated] Indicates the contents of the current cell should not be wrapped. You must use ⟨BR⟩ in the cell to force line breaks to prevent the entire cell from showing up as just one line.

ROWSPAN=number

Indicates how many rows the particular cell overlaps.

VALIGN= TOP|MIDDLE|BOTTOM|BASELINE

Specifies the vertical text alignment in the column's cells. The VALIGN type can be one of these values:

TOP: The text is aligned with the top of the cell.

MIDDLE: The text is aligned with the middle of the cell.

BOTTOM: The text is aligned with the bottom of the cell.

BASELINE: The text is aligned with the baseline common to all the cells in the row.

Context:

⟨TH⟩ ... ⟨/TH⟩ is legal within the following tag:

⟨TR⟩

You can use the following tags within ⟨TH⟩ ... ⟨/TH⟩:

⟨A⟩, ⟨ABBR⟩, ⟨ADDRESS⟩, ⟨APPLET⟩, ⟨B⟩, ⟨BASEFONT⟩, ⟨BDO⟩, ⟨BIG⟩, ⟨BLOCKQUOTE⟩, ⟨BR⟩, ⟨BUTTON⟩, ⟨CENTER⟩, ⟨CITE⟩, ⟨CODE⟩, ⟨DFN⟩, ⟨DIR⟩, ⟨DIV⟩, ⟨DL⟩, ⟨EM⟩, ⟨FIELDSET⟩, ⟨FONT⟩, ⟨FORM⟩, ⟨H*⟩, ⟨HR⟩, ⟨I⟩, ⟨IFRAME⟩, ⟨IMG⟩, ⟨INPUT⟩, ⟨ISINDEX⟩, ⟨KBD⟩, ⟨LABEL⟩, ⟨MAP⟩, ⟨MENU⟩, ⟨NOFRAMES⟩, ⟨NOSCRIPT⟩, ⟨OBJECT⟩, ⟨OL⟩, ⟨P⟩, ⟨PRE⟩, ⟨Q⟩, ⟨S⟩, ⟨SAMP⟩, ⟨SCRIPT⟩, ⟨SELECT⟩, ⟨SMALL⟩, ⟨SPAN⟩, ⟨STRIKE⟩, ⟨STRONG⟩, ⟨SUB⟩, ⟨SUP⟩, ⟨TABLE⟩, ⟨TEXTAREA⟩, ⟨TT⟩, ⟨U⟩, ⟨UL⟩, ⟨VAR⟩

Suggested style/usage: ⟨TH⟩ is used for the top of a table column and is usually displayed in a heavier font.

Examples: See file /h4d4e/examples/ch06/th.htm.

<THEAD> ... </THEAD> Table header

Definition: Defines the table header. Use this element to distinguish the rows in the table header from those in the footer or main body of the table.

Attributes: None

Context:

`<THEAD>` ... `</THEAD>` is legal within the following tag:

> `<TABLE>`

You can use the following tag within `<THEAD>` ... `</THEAD>`:

> `<TR>`

Suggested style/usage: The table header is optional, but if used, only one header is allowed. The closing tag is optional.

Examples: See file /h4d4e/examples/ch06/tr.htm.

<TITLE> ... </TITLE> Document title

Definition: Encloses the title of an HTML document, which commonly appears in the title bar in the browser's window. The default title is the HTML filename if a title is not specified.

Attributes: None

Context:

`<TITLE>` ... `</TITLE>` is legal only within `<HEAD>` ... `</HEAD>`.

Only plain text can be used within `<TITLE>` ... `</TITLE>`, as this tag only displays on the title bar of the browser window.

Suggested style/usage: You should come up with a useful title for every HTML document you write. An accurate, descriptive title will help the many Web search engines and tools to find your content.

> `TITLE="text"` can also appear as an attribute for numerous other tags. The text is rendered by browsers in many ways, such as a tool tip.

Examples: See file /h4d4e/examples/ch06/title.htm.

<TR> ... </TR> Table row

Definition: Creates a table header.

Attributes:

ALIGN=(LEFT|RIGHT|CENTER|JUSTIFY|CHAR)

> Specifies the horizontal text alignment in the row's cells. The align type can be one of these values:
>
> LEFT: The text is left aligned. This is the default alignment.
>
> RIGHT: The text is right aligned.
>
> CENTER: The text is centered.
>
> JUSTIFY: The text is double justified.
>
> CHAR: The text is aligned to the character specified by the CHAR attribute.

BGCOLOR=color

> **[Depreciated]** Sets the background color for the row. The color is a hexadecimal red-green-blue color value or a predefined color name.

CHAR="text"

> Specifies the character the text will be aligned to when ALIGN=CHAR is used and when the CHAROFF attribute is present.

CHAROFF=number

> Defines how far, in pixels, the remainder of text in a line should be offset from the first occurrence of the alignment character specified by CHAR=.

VALIGN= TOP|MIDDLE|BOTTOM|BASELINE

> Specifies the vertical text alignment in the row's cells. The VALIGN type can be one of these values:
>
> TOP: The text is aligned with the top of the cell.
>
> MIDDLE: The text is aligned with the middle of the cell.
>
> BOTTOM: The text is aligned with the bottom of the cell.
>
> BASELINE: The text is aligned with the baseline common to all the cells in the row.

Context:

`<TR>` ... `</TR>` is legal within the following tags:

> `<TBODY>`, `<TFOOT>`, `<THEAD>`

You can use the following tags within `<TR>` ... `</TR>`:

> `<TD>`, `<TH>`

Suggested style/usage: Close each table cell because it makes your table easier to read. If you include a table inside a table cell, be sure to close all cells and rows; some browsers get the nested tables wrong and render them incorrectly.

Examples: See file /h4d4e/examples/ch06/tr.htm.

<TT> ... </TT> Teletype text

Definition: Encloses text to be displayed in a monospaced (teletype) font, typically a variety of Courier.

Attributes: None

Context:

`<TT>` ... `</TT>` is legal within the following tags:

> `<A>`, `<ABBR>`, `<ADDRESS>`, `<APPLET>`, `<B>`, `<BDO>`, `<BIG>`,
> `<BLOCKQUOTE>`, `<BODY>`, `<BUTTON>`, `<CAPTION>`, `<CENTER>`, `<CITE>`,
> `<CODE>`, `<DD>`, `<DEL>`, `<DFN>`, `<DIV>`, `<DT>`, `<EM>`, `<FIELDSET>`, `<FONT>`,
> `<FORM>`, `<H*>`, `<I>`, `<IFRAME>`, `<INS>`, `<KBD>`, `<LABEL>`, `<LEGEND>`,
> `<LI>`, `<NOFRAMES>`, `<NOSCRIPT>`, `<OBJECT>`, `<P>`, `<PRE>`, `<Q>`, `<S>`,
> `<SAMP>`, `<SMALL>`, `<SPAN>`, `<STRIKE>`, `<STRONG>`, `<SUB>`, `<SUP>`, `<TD>`,
> `<TH>`, `<TT>`, `<U>`, `<VAR>`

You can use the following tags within `<TT>` ... `</TT>`:

> `<A>`, `<ABBR>`, `<APPLET>`, `<B>`, `<BASEFONT>`, `<BDO>`, `<BIG>`, `<BR>`,
> `<BUTTON>`, `<CITE>`, `<CODE>`, `<DFN>`, `<EM>`, `<FONT>`, `<I>`, `<IFRAME>`,
> `<IMG>`, `<INPUT>`, `<KBD>`, `<LABEL>`, `<MAP>`, `<OBJECT>`, `<Q>`, `<S>`, `<SAMP>`,
> `<SCRIPT>`, `<SELECT>`, `<SMALL>`, `<SPAN>`, `<STRIKE>`, `<STRONG>`, `<SUB>`,
> `<SUP>`, `<TEXTAREA>`, `<TT>`, `<U>`, `<VAR>`

Suggested style/usage: Use for monospaced text, where character position is important, or when trying to imitate the look of line-printer or typewriter output. Teletype is often used to indicate computer output. Two similar display tags of `<KBD>` and `<CODE>` are used to indicate user input or existing text, respectively.

Examples: See file /h4d4e/examples/ch06/tt.htm.

<U> ... </U> Underlined text

Definition: [Depreciated] Enclosed text will be underlined.

Attributes: None

Context:

<U> ... </U> is legal within the following tags:

    <A>, <ABBR>, <ADDRESS>, <APPLET>, <B>, <BDO>, <BIG>,
    <BLOCKQUOTE>, <BODY>, <BUTTON>, <CAPTION>, <CENTER>, <CITE>,
    <CODE>, <DD>, <DEL>, <DFN>, <DIV>, <DT>, <EM>, <FIELDSET>, <FONT>,
    <FORM>, <H*>, <I>, <IFRAME>, <INS>, <KBD>, <LABEL>, <LEGEND>,
    <LI>, <NOFRAMES>, <NOSCRIPT>, <OBJECT>, <P>, <PRE>, <Q>, <S>,
    <SAMP>, <SMALL>, <SPAN>, <STRIKE>, <STRONG>, <SUB>, <SUP>, <TD>,
    <TH>, <TT>, <U>, <VAR>

You can use the following tags within <U> ... </U>:

    <A>, <ABBR>, <APPLET>, <B>, <BASEFONT>, <BDO>, <BIG>, <BR>,
    <BUTTON>, <CITE>, <CODE>, <DFN>, <EM>, <FONT>, <I>, <IFRAME>,
    <IMG>, <INPUT>, <KBD>, <LABEL>, <MAP>, <OBJECT>, <Q>, <S>, <SAMP>,
    <SCRIPT>, <SELECT>, <SMALL>, <SPAN>, <STRIKE>, <STRONG>, <SUB>,
    <SUP>, <TEXTAREA>, <TT>, <U>, <VAR>

Suggested style/usage: This tag has been depreciated in favor of similar style sheet properties. Try to avoid this tag, as most browsers use underlining to indicate hyperlinks. Underlining can confuse your users, making them think they see hyperlinks that do not work. Underlining is an alternative rendering for italic text (for example, on typewriters). Because HTML has an <I> tag for italics, it is better to use that than <U>.

Examples: See file /h4d4e/examples/ch06/u.htm.

<UL> ... </UL> Unordered list

Definition: Produces bulleted lists of items.

Attributes:

COMPACT

> **[Depreciated]** Renders the list as compactly as possible by reducing line leading and spacing.

```
TYPE=(DISC|SQUARE|CIRCLE)
```

The type of bullet can be suggested with the `<TYPE>` attribute. The three styles to choose from are "disc" for a closed bullet, "square" for an open square, and "circle" for an open bullet.

Context:

`<UL>` ... `</UL>` is legal within the following tags:

```
<BLOCKQUOTE>, <BODY>, <BUTTON>, <CENTER>, <DD>, <DIV>,
<FIELDSET>, <FORM>, <IFRAME>, <LI>, <NOFRAMES>, <NOSCRIPT>,
<OBJECT>, <TD>, <TH>
```

You can use the following tag within `<UL>` ... `</UL>`:

```
<LI>
```

Suggested style/usage: To create bulleted lists in which the order of the items is not important or where sequence does not apply. Not all browsers use the `TYPE` attribute, so make sure the information in your list can be conveyed without it.

Examples: See file /h4d4e/examples/ch06/ul.htm.

<VAR> ... </VAR> Variable text

Definition: Highlights variable names or arguments to commands.

Attributes: None

Context:

`<VAR>` ... `</VAR>` is legal within the following tags:

```
<A>, <ABBR>, <ADDRESS>, <APPLET>, <B>, <BDO>, <BIG>,
<BLOCKQUOTE>, <BODY>, <BUTTON>, <CAPTION>, <CENTER>, <CITE>,
<CODE>, <DD>, <DEL>, <DFN>, <DIV>, <DT>, <EM>, <FIELDSET>, <FONT>,
<FORM>, <H*>, <I>, <IFRAME>, <INS>, <KBD>, <LABEL>, <LEGEND>,
<LI>, <NOFRAMES>, <NOSCRIPT>, <OBJECT>, <P>, <PRE>, <Q>, <S>,
<SAMP>, <SMALL>, <SPAN>, <STRIKE>, <STRONG>, <SUB>, <SUP>, <TD>,
<TH>, <TT>, <U>, <VAR>
```

You can use the following tags within `<VAR> ... </VAR>`:

```
<A>, <ABBR>, <APPLET>, <B>, <BASEFONT>, <BDO>, <BIG>, <BR>,
<BUTTON>, <CITE>, <CODE>, <DFN>, <EM>, <FONT>, <I>, <IFRAME>,
<IMG>, <INPUT>, <KBD>, <LABEL>, <MAP>, <OBJECT>, <Q>, <S>, <SAMP>,
<SCRIPT>, <SELECT>, <SMALL>, <SPAN>, <STRIKE>, <STRONG>, <SUB>,
<SUP>, <TEXTAREA>, <TT>, <U>, <VAR>
```

Suggested style/usage: Indicates a placeholder for a value the user supplies when entering text at the keyboard (see example).

Examples: See file /h4d4e/examples/ch06/var.htm.

Whew! That's the facts, Jack. Time for a break or a deep breath, and then take another giant step forward in your budding webmaster career. Now is a good time to join us in Chapter 7, in which you get the rest of the HTML puzzle pieces with an in-depth discussion of entities, both character and numeric.

Chapter 7

Introducing the Unrepresentable: HTML Entities

In This Chapter

▶ Coloring outside the character boundaries

▶ Producing special characters

▶ Inspecting the ISO-Latin-1 character set

*I*f you've seen the panoply of HTML tags and have gone through examples in Chapter 6 that included strange notations like < or °, maybe these odd locutions aren't as cryptic as they first appear. Hopefully, you now realize that they simply instruct the browser to look up these symbols and replace them with equivalent characters as the browser renders a document. The symbol < produces the less-than sign < on your computer screen, and the symbol ° produces the degree symbol °.

Entities Don't Have to Be an Alien Concept

Instructing a browser to look up entities such as the degree symbol with the string &#176 may leave you wondering why these contortions are necessary. Here are three important reasons why:

✔ Entities let a browser represent characters that it may otherwise interpret as markup.

✔ Entities let a browser represent higher-order ASCII characters (those with codes over 127) without having to fully support higher-order ASCII or non-ASCII character types. Also, these codes support some characters that are even outside the ASCII character set altogether (as is the case with non-Roman alphabet character sets and some widely used diacritical marks).

✔ Entities increase portability of SGML documents. Entities are place-holders in the SGML document instance and can be rendered on the fly according to a particular site's requirements. An example is the &COMPANY; entity. One subcontractor could define this entity as *ACME Software,* another as *Alternative Solutions.*

Okay, so now you know what character and numeric entities are for — they let browsers display symbols, not interpret them as markup. These entities also let browsers represent a larger range of characters than is otherwise possible but keep the actual character set as small as possible.

As you travel into the land of HTML character and numeric entities, you encounter strange characters and symbols that you may never use. On the other hand, if your native language isn't English, you can probably find lots of diacritical marks, accents, and other kinds of character modifications that allow you to express yourself much more effectively!

Producing Special Characters

Three characters act as special signals to the browser to let it know that it should look up a string in a character table, instead of just displaying the string on-screen:

✔ **Ampersand (&):** If a string starts with &, it flags the browser that what follows is a character code instead of an ordinary string.

✔ **Pound sign (#):** If the next character after & is #, this tells the browser that what follows next is a number that corresponds to the character code for a symbol to be produced on screen. This kind of code is called a *numeric entity.*

If the next character is anything other than the pound sign, this tells the browser that the string that follows is a symbol's name and must be looked up in a built-in table of equivalent character symbols. This is called a *character entity.*

✔ **Semicolon (;):** When the browser sees a ;, this signals the end of the string that represents a character code. The browser then uses what-ever characters or numbers that follow either the ampersand or the pound sign to perform the right kind of lookup operation and display the requested character symbol. If the browser doesn't recognize the information supplied, most browsers display a question mark (?) instead.

A couple of things about character and numeric entities may differ from your expectations based on what you know about HTML tags and what you may know about computer character sets:

- When reproducing the string of characters for an entity, HTML is case-sensitive. This means that < is different from <, so you need to reproduce character entities exactly as they appear in Tables 7-1 through 7-8. That's one reason we prefer using numeric entities — it's harder to make a mistake.

- Numeric codes for reproducing characters within HTML are not ASCII collating sequences; they come from the ISO-Latin-1 character set codes, as shown later in this chapter in Tables 7-1 through 7-8.

If you concentrate on reproducing characters as they appear in Tables 7-1 through 7-8 or copying the numbers that correspond to the ISO-Latin-1 scheme, you can produce exactly the right effects on your readers' screens.

Nothing Ancient about the ISO-Latin-1 HTML

The name of the character set that HTML uses is ISO-Latin-1. The *ISO* part means that it comes from the International Standards Organization's body of official international standards — in fact, all ISO standards have corresponding numeric tags, so ISO-Latin-1 is also known as ISO8859-1. The *Latin* part means that it comes from the Roman alphabet commonly used worldwide to represent text in many different languages. The number *1* refers to the version number for this standard (in other words, this is the first version of this character set definition).

ISO-Latin-1 distinguishes between two types of entities for characters:

- **Character entities:** Strings of characters that represent other characters; for example, < and È show a string of characters (lt and Egrave) that stand for others (< and È).

- **Numeric entities:** Strings of numbers that represent characters. These are identified by a pound sign (#) that follows the ampersand. For example, < and È show a string of numbers (60 and 200) that stand for characters (< and È).

Table 7-1 illustrates that there are many more numeric entities than character entities. In fact, every character in the ISO-Latin-1 set has a corresponding numeric entity, but this is not true for all character entities.

As the amount and kind of information presented in Web format has grown, the need for a more extensive character entity set has become apparent. HTML 4.0 supports such an extended entity set, which includes:

- Greek characters
- General punctuation
- Letter-like characters
- Arrows
- Mathematical characters
- Miscellaneous technical characters
- Miscellaneous symbol characters

Because the support of these character sets is new to HTML 4.0, only browsers that support a full implementation of HTML 4.0 (Navigator 4.0 and Internet Explorer 4.0 and newer) can render the character entity codes found in these sets correctly.

The remainder of this chapter includes listings of all the character sets supported by HTML 4.0. Tables 7-1 through 7-8 include each character's name, applicable entity and numeric codes, and description. We begin with ISO-Latin-1 because it is fully supported by all current and most older browsers, and then continue with HTML 4.0's new character sets.

Table 7-1		The ISO-Latin-1 Character Set	
Char	*Character*	*Numeric*	*Description*
			Em space, not collapsed
			En space
			Nonbreaking space
		&#00; - &#08;	Unused
		&#09;	Horizontal tab
		&#10;	Line feed or new line
		&#11; - &#31;	Unused
		&#32;	Space
!		&#33;	Exclamation mark
"	&quot;	&#34;	Quotation mark
#		&#35;	Number
$		&#36;	Dollar
%		&#37;	Percent

Char	Character	Numeric	Description
&	&	&	Ampersand
'		'	Apostrophe
(		(	Left parenthesis
)		)	Right parenthesis
*		*	Asterisk
+		+	Plus
,		,	Comma
-		-	Hyphen
.		.	Period (full stop)
/		/	Solidus (slash)
0-9		0 - 9	Digits 0-9
:		:	Colon
;		;	Semicolon
<	<	<	Less than
=		=	Equals
>	>	>	Greater than
?		?	Question mark
@		@	Commercial at
A-Z		A - Z	Letters A-Z (capitals)
[		[	Left square bracket
\		\	Reverse solidus (backslash)
]		]	Right square bracket
^		^	Caret
_		_	Horizontal bar
`		`	Grave accent
a-z		a - z	Letters a-z (lowercase)
{		{	Left curly brace
|		|	Vertical bar
}		}	Right curly brace
~		~	Tilde
		&#127; - Ÿ	Unused
			Nonbreaking space

(continued)

Table 7-1 *(continued)*

Char	Character	Numeric	Description
¡	¡	¡	Inverted exclamation mark
¢	¢	¢	Cent
£	£	£	Pound sterling
¤	¤	¤	General currency
¥	¥	¥	Yen
¦	¦	¦	Broken vertical bar
§	§	§	Section
¨	¨	¨	Umlaut (dieresis)
©	©	©	Copyright
ª	ª	ª	Feminine ordinal
«	«	«	Left angle quote, guillemot left
¬	¬	¬	Not
	­	­	Soft hyphen
®	®	®	Registered trademark
¯	¯	¯	Macron accent
°	°	°	Degree
±	±	±	Plus or minus
²	²	²	Superscript two
³	³	³	Superscript three
´	´	´	Acute accent
µ	µ	µ	Micro
¶	¶	¶	Paragraph
·	·	·	Middle dot
¸	¸	¸	Cedilla
¹	¹	¹	Superscript one
º	º	º	Masculine ordinal
»	»	»	Right angle quote, guillemot right
¼	¼	¼	Fraction one-fourth
½	½	½	Fraction one-half
¾	¾	¾	Fraction three-fourths
¿	¿	¿	Inverted question mark

Char	Character	Numeric	Description
À	À	À	Capital A, grave accent
Á	Á	Á	Capital A, acute accent
Â	Â	Â	Capital A, circumflex accent
Ã	Ã	Ã	Capital A, tilde
Ä	Ä	Ä	Capital A, dieresis or umlaut
Å	Å	Å	Capital A, ring
Æ	Æ	Æ	Capital AE diphthong (ligature)
Ç	Ç	Ç	Capital C, cedilla
È	È	È	Capital E, grave accent
É	É	É	Capital E, acute accent
Ê	Ê	Ê	Capital E, circumflex accent
Ë	Ë	Ë	Capital E, dieresis or umlaut
Ì	Ì	Ì	Capital I, grave accent
Í	Í	Í	Capital I, acute accent
Î	Î	Î	Capital I, circumflex accent
Ï	Ï	Ï	Capital I, dieresis or umlaut
Ð	Ð	Ð	Capital ETH, Icelandic
Ñ	Ñ	Ñ	Capital N, tilde
Ò	Ò	Ò	Capital O, grave accent
Ó	Ó	Ó	Capital O, acute accent
Ô	Ô	Ô	Capital O, circumflex accent
Õ	Õ	Õ	Capital O, tilde
Ö	Ö	Ö	Capital O, dieresis or umlaut
x	×	×	Multiply
Ø	Ø	Ø	Capital O, slash
Ù	Ù	Ù	Capital U, grave accent
Ú	Ú	Ú	Capital U, acute accent
Û	Û	Û	Capital U, circumflex accent
Ü	Ü	Ü	Capital U, dieresis or umlaut
Ý	Ý	Ý	Capital Y, acute accent
þ	Þ	Þ	Capital THORN, Icelandic
ß	ß	ß	Small sharp s, German (sz ligature)

(continued)

Table 7-1 *(continued)*

Char	Character	Numeric	Description
à	à	à	Small a, grave accent
á	á	á	Small a, acute accent
â	â	â	Small a, circumflex accent
ã	ã	ã	Small a, tilde
ä	ä	ä	Small a, dieresis or umlaut
å	å	å	Small a, ring
æ	æ	æ	Small ae diphthong (ligature)
ç	ç	ç	Small c, cedilla
è	è	è	Small e, grave accent
é	é	é	Small e, acute accent
ê	ê	ê	Small e, circumflex accent
ë	ë	ë	Small e, dieresis or umlaut
ì	ì	ì	Small i, grave accent
í	í	í	Small i, acute accent
î	î	î	Small i, circumflex accent
ï	ï	ï	Small i, dieresis or umlaut
ð	ð	ð	Small eth, Icelandic
ñ	ñ	ñ	Small n, tilde
ò	ò	ò	Small o, grave accent
ó	ó	ó	Small o, acute accent
ô	ô	ô	Small o, circumflex accent
õ	õ	õ	Small o, tilde
ö	ö	ö	Small o, dieresis or umlaut
÷	÷	÷	Division
ø	ø	ø	Small o, slash
ù	ù	ù	Small u, grave accent
ú	ú	ú	Small u, acute accent
û	û	û	Small u, circumflex accent
ü	ü	ü	Small u, dieresis or umlaut
ý	ý	ý	Small y, acute accent
þ	þ	þ	Small thorn, Icelandic
ÿ	ÿ	ÿ	Small y, dieresis or umlaut

Table 7-2		The Greek Character Set	
Char	*Character*	*Numeric*	*Description*
A	Α	Α	Capital letter alpha
B	Β	Β	Capital letter beta
Γ	Γ	Γ	Capital letter gamma
Δ	Δ	Δ	Capital letter delta
E	Ε	Ε	Capital letter epsilon
Z	Ζ	Ζ	Capital letter zeta
H	Η	Η	Capital letter eta
Θ	Θ	Θ	Capital letter theta
I	Ι	Ι	Capital letter iota
K	Κ	Κ	Capital letter kappa
Λ	Λ	Λ	Capital letter lambda
M	Μ	Μ	Capital letter mu
N	Ν	Ν	Capital letter nu
Ξ	Ξ	Ξ	Capital letter xi
O	Ο	Ο	Capital letter omicron
Π	Π	Π	Capital letter pi
P	Ρ	Ρ	Capital letter rho
Σ	Σ	Σ	Capital letter sigma
T	Τ	Τ	Capital letter tau
Υ	Υ	Υ	Capital letter upsilon
Φ	Φ	Φ	Capital letter phi
X	Χ	Χ	Capital letter chi
Ψ	Ψ	Ψ	Capital letter psi
Ω	Ω	Ω	Capital letter omega
α	α	α	Small letter alpha
β	β	β	Small letter beta
γ	γ	γ	Small letter gamma
δ	δ	δ	Small letter delta
ε	ε	ε	Small letter epsilon
ζ	ζ	ζ	Small letter zeta
η	η	η	Small letter eta

(continued)

Table 7-2 *(continued)*

Char	Character	Numeric	Description
θ	θ	θ	Small letter theta
ι	ι	ι	Small letter iota
κ	κ	κ	Small letter kappa
λ	λ	λ	Small letter lambda
μ	μ	μ	Small letter mu
ν	ν	ν	Small letter nu
ξ	ξ	ξ	Small letter xi
o	ο	ο	Small letter omicron
π	π	π	Small letter pi
ρ	ρ	ρ	Small letter rho
ς	ς	ς	Small letter final sigma
σ	σ	σ	Small letter sigma
τ	τ	τ	Small letter tau
υ	υ	υ	Small letter upsilon
φ	φ	φ	Small letter phi
χ	χ	χ	Small letter chi
ψ	ψ	ψ	Small letter psi
ω	ω	ω	Small letter omega
υ	ϑ	ϑ	Small letter theta
ϒ	ϒ	ϒ	Upsilon with hook
ϖ	ϖ	ϖ	Pi

Table 7-3   The General Punctuation Character Set

Char	Character	Numeric	Description
•	•	•	Bullet
…	…	…	Horizontal ellipsis
′	′	′	Prime
″	″	″	Double prime
‾	‾	‾	Overline
/	⁄	⁄	Fraction slash

Table 7-4		The Letter-Like Character Set	
Char	*Character*	*Numeric*	*Description*
&weierp;	&weierp;	&#8472;	Script capital P
&image;	&image;	&#8465;	Blackletter capital I
&real;	&real;	&#8476;	Blackletter capital R
™	&trade;	&#8482;	Trademark
ℵ	&alefsym;	&#8501;	Alef

Table 7-5		The Arrows Character Set	
Char	*Character*	*Numeric*	*Description*
←	&larr;	&#8592;	Left arrow
↑	&uarr;	&#8593;	Up arrow
→	&rarr;	&#8594;	Right arrow
↓	&darr;	&#8595;	Down arrow
↔	&harr;	&#8596;	Left-right arrow
↵	&crarr;	&#8629;	Down arrow with corner left
⇐	&lArr;	&#8656;	Left double arrow
⇑	&uArr;	&#8657;	Up double arrow
⇒	&rArr;	&#8658;	Right double arrow
⇓	&dArr;	&#8659;	Down double arrow
⇔	&hArr;	&#8660;	Left-right double arrow

Table 7-6		The Mathematical Character Set	
Char	*Character*	*Numeric*	*Description*
∀	&forall;	&#8704;	For all
∂	&part;	&#8706;	Partial differential
∃	&exist;	&#8707;	There exists
∅	&empty;	&#8709;	Empty set
∇	&nabla;	&#8711;	Nabla
∈	&isin;	&#8712;	Element of
∉	&notin;	&#8713;	Not an element of
∋	&ni;	&#8715;	Contains as member

(continued)

Table 7-6 *(continued)*

Char	Character	Numeric	Description
∏	∏	∏	n-ary product
Σ	∑	∑	n-ary sumation
−	−	−	Minus
∗	∗	∗	Asterisk operator
√	√	√	Square root
∝	∝	∝	Proportional to
∞	∞	∞	Infinity
∠	∠	∠	Angle
∧	∧	⊥	Logical and
∨	∨	⊦	Logical or
∩	∩	∩	Intersection
∪	∪	∪	Union
∫	∫	∫	Integral
∴	∴	∴	Therefore
∼	∼	∼	Tilde operator
≅	≅	≅	Approximately equal to
≈	≈	≈	Almost equal to
≠	≠	≠	Not equal to
≡	≡	≡	Identical to =
≤	≤	≤	Less-than or equal to
≥	≥	≥	Greater-than or equal to
⊂	⊂	⊂	Subset of
⊃	⊃	⊃	Superset of
⊄	⊄	⊄	Not a subset of
⊆	⊆	⊆	Subset of or equal to
⊇	⊇	⊇	Superset of or equal to
⊕	⊕	⊕	Circled plus
⊗	⊗	⊗	Circled times
⊥	⊥	⊥	Up tack
•	⋅	⋅	Dot operator

Table 7-7   The Miscellaneous Technical Character Set

Char	Character	Numeric	Description
⌈	`&lceil;`	`&#8968;`	Left ceiling
⌉	`&rceil;`	`&#8969;`	Right ceiling
⌊	`&lfloor;`	`&#8970;`	Left floor
⌋	`&rfloor;`	`&#8971;`	Right floor
⟨	`&lang;`	`&#9001;`	Left-pointing angle bracket
⟩	`&rang;`	`&#9002;`	Right-pointing angle bracket

Table 7-8   The Miscellaneous Symbols Character Set

Char	Character	Numeric	Description
♠	`&spades;`	`&#9824;`	Black spade suit
♣	`&clubs;`	`&#9827;`	Black club suit
♥	`&hearts;`	`&#9829;`	Black heart suit
♦	`&diams;`	`&#9830;`	Black diamond suit

One thing to note about using this information: If you must frequently work with character or numeric entities in your documents, it's easier to use some kind of HTML editing tool to handle character replacements automatically. Or look for a file-oriented search-and-replace utility that you can use as a post-processing step on your files. For Windows users, check out:

```
ftp://oak.oakland.edu/fdrepl.zip
```

This is a ZIP archive that contains a utility named Find-Replace that works under Windows 3.*x*, 95, and NT.

The Extras portion of the CD-ROM that accompanies this book covers HTML and related tools for a variety of platforms. If you want to be a serious Web developer or often need to use character codes in your pages, please check out the tools available on your favorite platform. Such tools can save you time and effort and make you a happier, more productive webmaster.

Chapter 8

Building Basic HTML Documents

*B*uilding your first Web page is exciting if you keep this thought firmly in mind: You can change anything at any time. Good Web pages always evolve. Nothing is cast in concrete — change is just a keystroke away.

Now that the pressure's off, you can build your own simple, but complete, home page. Think of it as a prototype for future pages. You can always go back and add a variety of bells and whistles to change your home page into any kind of page you want — be it for a business, an academic institution, or a government agency.

The layout, or the way the page looks to the user, creates the first impression of your site. If that first impression doesn't please the user, the first time may also be the last time that the user visits your page. Not to worry, though: Your home page can be pleasing to the eye if you follow the KISS (Keep It Simple, Sweetheart!) approach.

The Web itself is a confusing concept to many users. Everything that you do to keep your page intuitively obvious makes your viewers happy and keeps them coming back for more.

Chapter 3 presents the basic concepts for a good Web page. It emphasizes form and content over HTML and presents the elements of page layout and information flow. You may want to check out Chapter 3 before continuing. If you used Chapter 4 to create a quickie Web page, now is the time to review that Web page and use what you learn in this chapter to improve it.

The basics of good Web page design are content, layout, first impression, and KISS (Keep It Simple, Sweetheart!). Okay, now get on with it.

The Template's the Thing!

Well-constructed Web pages contain the following four elements: title, heading, body, and footer.

If you look at any number of Web pages, you see that most contain these elements in one form or another. You may also notice, as your frustration level increases, that Web pages lacking one or more of these elements are neither pleasing to your eye nor intuitive in their presentation. Don't let that happen to your work — use this basic template for each HTML document you produce:

```
<HTML>
<HEAD><TITLE>Your Title</TITLE>
</HEAD>
<BODY>
<P>
Your headings and wonderful text and graphics go here.
<P>
<ADDRESS>
Your Name<BR>
Phone number<BR>
Standard Mail Address<BR>
E-mail Address
</ADDRESS>
<P>
Copyright  &copy; 1998,  Your Name <BR>
Revised -- Revision Date <BR>
URL: <A HREF = "http://this.page's.url.here">
http://this.page's.url.here</A>
</BODY>
</HTML>
```

Starting down the correct path is really that simple. This template actually works. Figure 8-1 shows what it looks like when viewed with Netscape Navigator.

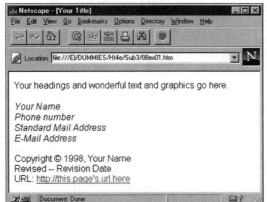

Figure 8-1:
The basic
Web page
template
viewed with
Navigator.

To view local pages with your browser:

✔ Use your browser to open your Web page HTML document file from
your local hard disk.

✔ If you use Navigator, remember to set memory and disk caches to zero
so that Navigator reloads each new version of your file from the disk,
instead of loading from its cache. Other browsers cache pages, too, so
be sure you read what you edited — not some older version!

As you can see, this home page is plain and simple. It won't cause folks to
flock to see it, will it? That's because you need to add your own wonderful
text and graphics. Even though most Web surfers use graphical user interface (GUI) browsers, please follow our advice (from Chapter 2) — put your
energy into high-quality content. With that said, don't worry; in Chapter 10,
we cover how to add graphics to your Web page.

Page Layout: Top to Bottom

Now that you have a basic template, you can start to change it. To begin the
fun, make sure that your first home page doesn't occupy more than a single
screen. This size limit makes a page much easier to edit and test. You can
get more than enough information on a single screen and help your audience avoid unnecessary scrolling.

A *single screen* seems like an easy concept, but is it? A single screen is how
much information a browser can display on a monitor without scrolling.
This amount varies depending upon the users' browsers and their monitors.
You may decide not to design for the lowest common denominator for both

elements, but please understand the following: If you assume that users can see your page the same way that you see it in *your* browser, you're making a mistake! You'll find no easy answer to this problem, but testing your pages at a relatively low resolution (640 x 480 pixels) with several different browsers can help you see your pages through your users' eyes. Getting this view is well worth taking the extra time!

Also, you may find it helpful to sketch your design ideas on paper first or to use a drawing program to create a model of your layout and components. (Figure 8-2 shows an example.) This model shows the spatial relationships on the page and the amounts and locations of the ever-important breathing room that page designers call *white space*. Although you can leave too much white space on a page, most designers err in the other direction and wind up with far too little, which causes a page to appear cluttered.

Title
  Heading

  | Text and/or Main Graphic here. |

  Body

  | Explanation of page purpose. |

  | Information and primary links.
  Most important graphics, but only
  a couple of large or 3-4 small ones. |

  | Secondary links.
  Less important graphics. |

  Footer

  | Author, Date revised, Link to Home
  Page if this isn't, or another page,
  copyright notice if you desire & URL. |

Figure 8-2:
A sketch of basic Web page layout.

Organize your page logically so that viewers can scan it easily. Because everyone is always in a hurry, put the important information near the top, in large type, with plenty of white space surrounding it. Place the remaining items below as you work your way through the less important content.

Remember, you're not trying to stuff as much as possible on a single page — you're trying to cover what's important to the topic at hand. If you have lots of material or more topics to cover, you can easily make more pages and link them to this one. One good rule comes from professional presenters, who say that a single slide should try to convey no more than three to five pieces of related information. We think that the same is true of a single HTML-based screen of information, too!

What's in a Name? Thinking Up Good Titles and Headings

In HTML files, titles provide the most important data that search engines (Yahoo!, Excite, AltaVista, and so on) use to index documents. But once a user enters a Web site, document headings provide visual cues within any page. This happens because HTML styles, or the user's browser settings, determine the font and page size and also control line lengths. With appropriate content and layout, you can make headings on your pages both attractive and informative.

Titles

The title of your page is important. Many Web indexing search engines — the software robots that relentlessly cruise the Web and look for information — use titles to create index records in *their* databases for *your* pages. Also, most browsers use titles in the name fields of their *hotlist* or *bookmark* sections, which collect URLs that users want to revisit. That means they use your titles to figure out what's on your pages.

Because you want people to find and read your pages, make titles as descriptive as possible. Try to limit the length of a title to fit on a single line. Think of a title as the keywords that describe the contents of your page. Understanding how to use titles helps you build titles that work — we hope you get the idea!

One way to create a truly descriptive title is to type a list of the keywords that best describe your page. Then use them in a sentence. Next, delete all conjunctions, adverbs, and unnecessary adjectives. With a little rearranging, what's left should be a pretty good title.

Here's an example of constructing a title:

> ✔ **Words:** George, classical guitar player, bicycle racing.
>
> ✔ **Sentence:** George is a classical guitarist who races bicycles.
>
> ✔ **Title:** George's classical guitar and bike racing page.

This title should fit on one line when viewed by most browsers. Test it with several browsers to see how it looks. If it's too long, shorten it!

Headings

Talking about headings can get confusing, because each Web page needs a heading section after the title, and various paragraph headings within the body of the document. In the print world — for example, in this book — headings are the emphasized text placed before paragraphs. This section explains how to use paragraph headings.

Headings, along with the title, are the most important text in your Web page. They are the first text that users notice. If headings aren't attractive and instantly informative, users may jump to another page with a single click. Well-written headings hook readers and make them want more.

Concentrate on the content of your headings and the consistency of their meaning and usage throughout your pages. Your headings should arise naturally when you analyze your content. They should paraphrase an important concept that you are about to present. If you remove all text from your document (except for the headings), you should be left with a good outline or a detailed table of contents.

If the situation permits, headings may even be humorous. Headings can contain a common theme to help catch users' eyes and their interest. The best approach to writing headings is to use your imagination and keep your audience in mind. We used this approach with the headings in this book; it is a hallmark of the whole ...*For Dummies* series.

As a quick example, Table 8-1 shows some of the headings from this book in their "plain" and "humorous/theme" forms.

Table 8-1	Headings: Plain versus Extra-spicy
Plain	*More Interesting*
Building Better Documents	Building Better Document Bodies
Building Good Paragraphs	Good Bones: Building Strong Paragraphs
Logos and Icons	Eye-Catchers: Logos, Icons, and Other Gems

In your Web pages, you have only a few headings per screen or page, so make the most of them. Keep like headings consistent throughout your pages to help users understand their level of importance. Although most browsers recognize at least four levels of headings, most well-constructed Web pages use no more than three levels, even for long documents.

Two schools of thought exist regarding the use of heading levels. The *information school* says, "Heading tags should be used in increments or decrements of one and always start with ⟨H1⟩." This approach provides an ordered, standardized structure to your content and makes it easy for Web crawlers to pick out headings for their indexes.

The *design school* screams, "BORING!" when the information school mentions this approach. Instead, the design school states, "Use headings to draw attention to content. Putting an ⟨H1⟩ next to an ⟨H3⟩ or an ⟨H4⟩ creates visual interest." As with most design decisions, the choice is yours.

Experiment with heading tags to see what you think looks best. Remember, too much emphasized text diminishes the overall effect. Use it sparingly — emphasis works better when it remains exceptional. If you're a fan of fairy tales, using too many headings is like crying "Wolf!"

Building Better Document Bodies

The body of an HTML document is the core of a Web page. It lies between the header and the footer. Body content depends on the type and amount of information that you want to put online and on the audience you want to reach.

Personal Web pages are generally quite different from business, academic, or government ones in the content and form of their bodies, although the layout for each type may be strikingly similar. The bodies of most personal Web pages contain text for, or pointers to, the following elements:

- **Résumé:** mostly dense text with a picture
- **Personal history:** mostly plain text
- **Favorite sports or hobbies:** text with an occasional picture and links to sports or hobby sites
- **Favorite Web sites:** lists of links to Web sites

The body of a commercial artist's Web pages might contain the following:

- ✔ **Pictures, pictures, pictures:** usually small thumbnail-size pictures that link to much larger versions
- ✔ **Credentials:** a page containing a résumé or a list of shows and exhibits, awards, and other professional activities
- ✔ **Professional references:** links to online samples of work on other pages around the Net

The bodies of many government agency pages contain large amounts of text. Unfortunately, many of these documents are simply HTML reproductions of their long text originals. Some are 100 screens long or more! Fortunately, some government webmasters provide a brief description of their text files along with FTP hyperlinks so you can easily download these monsters without having to read them onscreen.

So, how much text is enough, but not too much, in the body of a Web page? The answer lies in the minds of your viewers. May we suggest, however, that large amounts of scrolling almost always causes them to think, "Too much already!"

Textual sound bites — NOT!

When Web surfers want to read pages and pages of dense text, they buy the book or download the file and print it. For online reading, a large quantity of text isn't much fun, and many users view it as a waste of bandwidth (especially those who dial in with slower connections).

This view doesn't imply that your Web pages should be the textual equivalent of 30-second video bites on TV. It simply indicates that, at the current level of Web development, most users are looking for fast ways to find the information they want. They aren't going to dig deeply into a sea of text to find it. Your job is to make the good information easily available to your readers by using an appropriate page layout and to provide good indexes with hypermedia links within the body of your pages.

Balanced composition

The body on personal Web pages should contain three to five short, well-written paragraphs. If these paragraphs are interspersed with moderately sized headings, enough white space, and small graphics to add visual interest, readers will probably scan them in their entirety.

Good use of separators and numerous links to additional pages are also very much in vogue. Using these techniques should result in a page that's between one and three screens long. Avoid making pages longer than three full screens. Hardly anybody has a 33-inch, high-resolution monitor . . . yet.

Controlling long pages

In general, you should split Web pages composed of more than five screens of text or five screens of URL link lists into multiple pages. If your content insists on being served in long pages, you can increase its readability by linking a table of contents (TOC) to each section and providing a link back to the beginning of the page from each section.

This linking structure has an effect similar to splitting a page into multiple files, but it also lets your readers capture the document as a single file. Also, this structure makes it easier to edit the HTML file. You want to balance your convenience against the penalty of moving a single large chunk of data — moving it takes a long time! Just make sure that you don't overdo the links.

It looks like we've drifted out of the content stream and into the control stream again. These two components tend to blur when discussing the layout of long Web pages. Nevertheless, content remains the most vital concern; but when you have lots of content, make it approachable with effective controls.

The bottom line on bodies

The basic rules for creating great Web page bodies are

- ✔ Keep layouts consistent to provide continuity for users.
- ✔ Provide plenty of white space and headings for easy scanning.
- ✔ Write short paragraphs and use them sparingly.
- ✔ Use meaningful graphics, but only when absolutely necessary.
- ✔ Make liberal use of hypertext links to additional pages, instead of making your audience scroll, scroll, scroll.
- ✔ Vary the placement of hyperlink words to provide more visual contrast on the page.
- ✔ Write meaningful hyperlink text, *not* "Click here."

Good Bones: Building Strong Paragraphs

"Omit needless words!" cried William Strunk, Jr. He also propounds Rule 17 in *The Elements of Style* (cowritten with E. B. White), which states,

> Vigorous writing is concise. A sentence should contain no unnecessary words, a paragraph no unnecessary sentences, for the same reason that a drawing should have no unnecessary lines and a machine no unnecessary parts. This requires not that the writer make all his sentences short, or that he avoid all detail and treat his objects only in outline, but that every word tell.

Rule 13 from the same work reads, "Make the paragraph the unit of composition." Together, these two principles form the essence of writing clear, accurate prose.

Web users demand the clearest and most concise text you can muster. But alas, not everyone on the Web is an English professor. Many have never heard of (much less, read) *The Elements of Style*. Nevertheless, all surfers must read some language, so regardless of that language, clarity promotes accurate communication. To this end, follow these steps to build better paragraphs:

1. **Create an outline for your information.**

2. **Write one paragraph for each significant point, keeping the sentences short, direct, and to the point.**

3. **Edit your text mercilessly, omitting all needless words and sentences.**

4. **Proofread and spell check.**

5. **Ask a few volunteers to evaluate your work.**

6. **Revise your text and edit it again as you revise it.**

7. **Solicit comments when you publish online.**

Listward Ho: Using a List Structure

Chapter 6 presents the different types of HTML lists. Now we can show you an example of the most commonly used list structure, the unordered list.

The *unordered* or *bulleted list* is handy for emphasizing several short lines of information. The following shows HTML markup for an unordered list (displayed with Navigator in Figure 8-3).

```
<UL>
<LI> This is noticed.
<LI> So is this.
<LI> And so is this.
</UL>
```

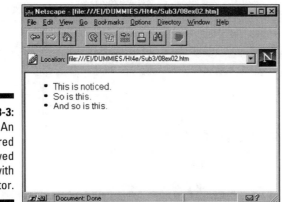

Figure 8-3:
An
unordered
list viewed
with
Navigator.

Although you should keep page layouts simple, you may need to use lists and even nested lists (to produce outline formatting, as we explain in Chapter 11) to display certain information. Use such structures intelligently and sparingly.

The following HTML fragment shows the tags for an unordered list in a Web page body. The list serves to emphasize and separate the text lines.

```
You have reached the <I>HTML for Dummies</I> Web Pages, a
         charming, and hopefully helpful, addition to the
         WWW universe. These pages are designed to aid
         you in three key areas:<BR>
<UL>
<LI> To help you find current information on the Web about
         HTML
<LI> To provide working examples and code for all the Web
         tricks in the book
<LI> To introduce <I>HTML for Dummies</I> - your friendli-
         est resource for HTML material offline!
</UL><P>
```

Figure 8-4 shows how this displays in Internet Explorer. The bulleted list definitely emphasizes the body and adds to the visual appeal of the page.

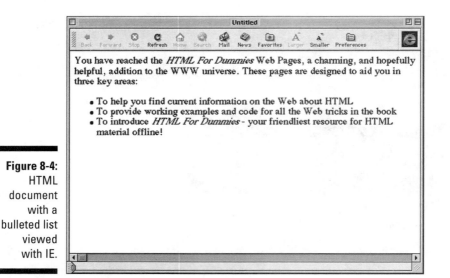

You have reached the *HTML For Dummies* Web Pages, a charming, and hopefully helpful, addition to the WWW universe. These pages are designed to aid you in three key areas:

- To help you find current information on the Web about HTML
- To provide working examples and code for all the Web tricks in the book
- To introduce *HTML For Dummies* - your friendliest resource for HTML material offline!

Figure 8-4:
HTML
document
with a
bulleted list
viewed
with IE.

Hooking Up: Linking Your Pages

Hypermedia links within the body of your pages bring out the power of the Web. To many users, surfing the Web is the ultimate video game. Following links just to see where they go can be interesting and informative.

As a Web page designer and Web weaver, you want users to like your pages well enough to tell others, who tell others, and so on. Therefore, you must provide good links within your own pages and to other Internet resources.

Links to pages within your Web are relative

From previous discussions, you probably know that links come in two flavors: relative and full. You can use a relative link, such as this one:

```
<A HREF="ftpstuff.htm">Click here to jump
straight to the FTP page!</A>
```

You can use the preceding link because the URL referenced is relative to the directory containing the Web page that calls the reference. In this case, the reference is to a file (ftpstuff.htm) in the same directory as the current HTML file (the current URL). The reference is relative to the server's document root plus the path in the file system where the current URL is stored. Got that? Don't worry, you'll understand it better later.

When you create links to HTML documents, you ordinarily use the .html extension. Some Web servers require all four characters in the file extension to recognize the .html extension in your Web document link. If the page resides on a DOS machine, the server ignores the fourth letter (the l). Make sure that you change (to .html) the extensions of the .htm files that you upload from a DOS or Windows computer to a UNIX server (or make sure it recognizes files that end in .htm as valid HTML files). In addition, simple Macintosh text editors (like SimpleText) don't place default .htm or .html extensions after a filename. So, Mac webmasters need to keep a watchful eye on this to maintain PC compatibility.

When you create links to HTML documents, you can use html or htm as extensions as long as you are consistent. Some platforms, servers, and browsers are forgiving when the l is left off; others are not, so be warned. In the past, Web servers required the full four-letter extension for both the filenames and the links that call them. Today, as long as your naming scheme is consistent, you can use either a four- or three-letter extension. But before you take our word for it, ask your webmaster or system administrator about how your server really works; believe us, they know more about your server than we do!

A bit of advice regarding overuse of links: Use them only when they convey needed information and use each specific link only once per page. Users can get irritable when you make a link out of each occurrence of a commonly used word or phrase on a single page.

Links to the world outside of your Web are physical

A physical or full link, such as

```
<A HREF = "http://www.lanw.com/html4dum/html4dum.htm">
```

gives the entire HTTP URL address. You can use physical URLs for all your links without any noticeable difference in speed, even on a local server. But relative links are shorter to type and may improve your overall productivity.

When including physical URLs for links, we strongly recommend that you link to the resource first and capture the URL with your browser. Then, copy and paste this URL into your HTML file to avoid introducing typographical errors.

Whether it's better to use relative or physical links is a debate for the newsgroups or your local UNIX user's group. You are primarily concerned with the content of the links within your Web, their relationships to one another, and their contribution to your overall Web. Chapter 14 contains more advanced information on using Web links.

Choose your hyperlinks with care

Your home page may have links similar to those shown in Figure 8-5 from the *HTML For Dummies* home page. Notice which words in the sentence are included in the hyperlink text (highlighted and/or underlined). You must click on these words to open the link.

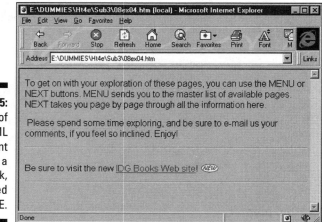

Figure 8-5: Portion of HTML document with a hyperlink, viewed with IE.

The following HTML document fragment shows the tags for the hyperlink in Figure 8-5.

```
To get on with your exploration of these pages, you can use
            the MENU or NEXT buttons. MENU sends you to the
            master list of available pages. NEXT takes you
            page by page through all the information
            here. 
<BR>
<BR> Please spend some time exploring, and
be sure to e-mail us your comments, if you feel
so inclined. Enjoy! 
<HR>
<BR>Be sure to visit the new <A HREF="http://
            www.idgbooks.com/">
IDG Books Web site</A>! 
<IMG SRC="new.gif" HEIGHT=17 WIDTH=32
ALIGN=TOP> 
<HR>
```

Choose your link text and images carefully. Keep the text short and the graphics small. And never, ever use the phrase *click here* by itself for link text. "Why?" you ask. Because your readers may think that you didn't care enough to write text with a meaningful word or phrase for the link.

Well-chosen hyperlinks let your users quickly scan hyperlink text and choose links without reading the surrounding text. Surrounding text is usually included only to provide readers with clarification of the link anyway. Remember, users are in a hurry to scan your pages and quickly pick out the important links from their unique wording or graphics. Make this job easy by using meaningful hyperlinks.

Footers Complete Your Pages

The *Yale C/AIM Web Style Guide* provides a concise statement about the use of footers on your Web pages (`info.med.yale.edu/caim/manual/index.html`):

> Page footers should always carry basic information about the origin and age of the page. Every Web page needs to bear this basic information, but this repetitive and prosaic information often does not deserve the prominence of being placed at the top of the page.

Unlike an HTML header and body, a footer is not a markup. By convention, a footer is the bottom portion of the page body.

Footers contribute greatly to your pages by attributing authorship, contact information, legal status, version/revision information, and a link to your home page. Each footer should contain some or all of the elements listed in Table 8-2.

Table 8-2	Footer Elements
Author's name	Page owner's name
Author's institution or company	Page owner's phone number
Author's phone number	Page owner's e-mail address
Author's e-mail address	Page owner's postal mailing address
Author's postal mailing address	Date of page's last revision
Copyright notice	URL of the page
Legal disclaimer or language designating the page as the official communication of the company or institution	
Official company or institutional seal, logo, or other graphic mark	
Hypertext link(s) to home page or to other pages	
Hypertext link(s) to other sections of this page	

Your basic home page HTML document already contains the minimum suggested footer information for a home page:

```
<ADDRESS>
Your Name<BR>
Phone number<BR>
Standard Mail Address<BR>
E-Mail Address
</ADDRESS><P>
Copyright &copy; 1998, Your Name <BR>
Revised -- Revision Date <BR>
URL: <A HREF = "http://this.page's.url.here">
http://this.page's.url.here</A>
```

Even though it is a home page, it contains a link to itself in the URL line. All other local pages in your Web must also contain a link in the footer to a full home page URL, like the example shown. Why? If a user saves your page as an HTML file and later wants to know its location, there it is on the bottom of the page, both visible and as a link. Don't you wish everyone did this?

The name of your home page file depends on your Web server software. Some servers require a specific name and extension, such as index.html. Check with your ISP to determine the requirements of the server that houses your Web site. Most likely, one of these formats work:

```
<A HREF="http://www.servername.net/yourdirectory">
   <!-- least desirable -->
<A HREF="http://www.servername.net/yourdirectory/">
   <!-- better -->
<A HREF="http://www.servername.net/yourdirectory /
           index.html">
   <!-- most desirable -->
```

Government agencies and other public institutions must include what seems like their entire staff directory and departmental history in their footers. At least they're at the bottom of the page. If you must use a long footer, put a home page link above it so users don't have to scroll as far to find it!

Figure 8-6 illustrates a well-balanced footer for a business style home page, from the LANWrights home page. This footer contains all important footer information (notice the separate contact icon in the upper right of the figure). This footer doesn't contain a phone number or snail-mail address, but you may not want folks calling you or writing letters to you either (the contact page includes all of this information). Anyway, on the Net, e-mail rules!

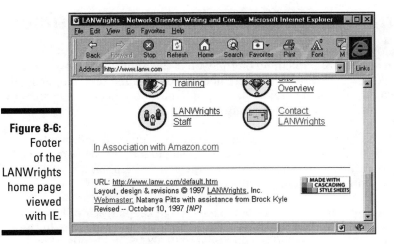

Figure 8-6:
Footer
of the
LANWrights
home page
viewed
with IE.

Use a URL line as part of your page

Notice that the URL appears in the footer. It's a good idea to put the URL for each page in the footer in small type. This helps viewers who print your page but don't add it to their bookmarks to find it again. And adding the URL is a nice finishing touch that tells users that you really do care about them.

Instead of placing all footer information directly in each page, you may want to put some of it in a page of its own and include a link to that information in the footer instead. This works well if your information requires a legal disclaimer or other complex language. Please check with your legal representative concerning the fine points of using disclaimers on the Web.

Copyright

Copyright law hasn't quite caught up with the explosion in electronic publishing on the Web. However, it won't hurt you or your organization to put a copyright notice at the bottom of any Web page that you don't want freely copied without being attributed to you or without your permission.

The copyright notice shown in Figure 8-6 is standard text except for the copyright symbol. Most browsers can display the copyright symbol © if you use the character entity ©. Otherwise, simulate it with (C) or (c).

Counting coup: Versions, dates, and times

Why should you even bother to note when you change your pages? One of the greatest values of publishing on the Web is the ability to change your pages quickly. Not only do your users need to know when this happens, you also need to know which version you're publishing so you can be certain to change old stuff when newer versions are ready.

If it's appropriate, you may want to use version numbers in addition to a revision date. This enables you to refer to a particular page as version 12B, for example, rather than the second revision from December. It's less ambiguous, more direct, and shorter, too!

Placing a revision date in the footer of each page keeps track of its chronology. The format should be January 02, 1999, to avoid confusion. In the United States, this date would be abbreviated 01/02/99. In Europe, this would be read as the 1st of February, 1999. The international ISO 8601 standard date notation is YYYY-MM-DD (year, month, day), which would result in 1999-01-02. Use that format for dates if you want to be globally correct.

If, for some reason, you don't want to show a revision date on the page, you'll be happier in the long run if you use HTML comment tags and hide the revision date inside them.

You may add the time to the date for time-sensitive information. Because users from all over the world can view your information at any time, 24-hour, UTC (Universal Time, which used to be called GMT — Greenwich Mean Time) is the appropriate format, expressed as hh:mm:ss (hour : minute : second). Make sure you note the time as UTC (that is, 18:30:00 UTC or 18:30:00Z for 6:30 p.m.). The *Z* stands for *Zulu* in the NATO radio alphabet and refers to the Zulu or Zero meridian of longitude used for measurement. Now aren't you happy to know that little tidbit for the next time you watch *Jeopardy!*

Pointers to the Author or Owner

You can choose between an e-mail link or a form to obtain feedback. Your choice may depend on which of these options your Web service provider makes available. Of the two, e-mail is simplest, and most generally used on personal home pages. Businesses tend to use custom forms in their attempts to obtain specific information about their users (and to turn them into paying customers). We detail the use of forms in Chapter 12.

A `mailto:` link is a special link that starts an e-mail program on some servers that lets users send e-mail to the page owner. Every well-constructed home page has some way for users to give feedback to a page's developer or owner. The most general approach is to provide an e-mail address in text inside the `<ADDRESS>` ... `</ADDRESS>` tags. Although it isn't supported by all Web server software or browsers, the `mailto:` link is another frequently used method. To use it despite its less-than-universal reach, here's how:

```
E-mail: <A HREF="mailto:html4dum@lanw.com">HTML For Dummies
            at html4dum@lanw.com</A>
```

In this example, the actual hyperlink is `mailto:html4dum@lanw.com` and the second instance of the e-mail address in `HTML For Dummies at html4dum@lanw.com` has been added to highlight the e-mail address on the page for readers who can't use a `mailto:` URL. You can customize the wording to your heart's content, outside the actual address portion (`<A HREF = "mailto:html4dum@lanw.com">` ... `</A>`). You can also put text in front of it as shown by the `E-mail:` in the example taken from our own *HTML For Dummies* Web pages.

Comment Your HTML Documents for Posterity

Do yourself a big favor and comment on your HTML documents liberally. You will thank yourself many times over in the future if you add comments that explain links more fully or state when information needs to be updated.

Comment lines are formatted like this:

```
<! --comment text-- >
```

A comment line starts with `<!--` and ends with `-- >`. Most newer browsers ignore comments inside HTML documents. As a general rule, place comments on a line apart from other HTML text. This way you won't interrupt HTML text because browsers also ignore white space between HTML tags. To be on the safe side, don't use any special characters (<, >, &, !) within comments, either.

The next chapter goes beyond the Web-building that you saw in this chapter. Move "onward, through the fog" to tackle the ins and outs of HTML tables!

Part III
Advanced HTML

The 5th Wave   By Rich Tennant

"Great goulash, Stan. That reminds me, are you still scripting your own Web page?"

In this part . . .

*P*art III takes all the elements covered in Part II and puts them together to help you build commercial-grade HTML documents, a process that includes building complex pages, developing on-screen forms to solicit information and feedback, and creating clickable image maps to let graphics guide your user's on-screen navigation.

Chapter 9

Using HTML Tables Effectively

• •

• •

*I*n HTML, tables are handy to arrange everything from text to images on your pages. Most modern browsers support tables. In fact, if a browser does not support tables, take that as a sure sign it's time for an upgrade.

Since HTML 3.2, tables have become a standard element in the construction of Web documents. With HTML 4.0, proprietary extensions from Netscape and Microsoft have given way to official standards. This chapter introduces HTML 4.0 tables and gives you enough information to use them yourself.

First, Consider the Alternatives

Do you really need to use <TABLE> tags? You can use lists, images, preformatted text, or frames instead of tables. Each of these structures has its own good and bad points.

 ✔ **Lists:** Lists are simple to implement, but they don't give you the formatting capabilities of tables, especially for images.

 ✔ **Images:** You can compose images in grids with borders and colors, but they become static and difficult to change. They also get big and slow!

 ✔ **Preformatted text:** Browsers generally display preformatted text in a nonproportional font that looks terrible. Not recommended.

 ✔ **Frames:** Frames are complex constructs that may offer an additional dimension to your Web site, rather than a replacement for tables.

The preceding caveats notwithstanding, we believe tables are great for many uses, such as presenting financial results, organizing lists of related elements (like dates and birthdays, for instance), and forcing a defined layout of elements.

HTML <TABLE> Overview

The <TABLE> tag provides a formatting method that was sorely missing until its introduction. Because you can put almost any other HTML tag into a table cell, the formatting possibilities that tables afford are virtually limitless.

We strongly recommend that you stick with the basic table elements in your tables, unless you're developing documents for a private Web server where you know your audience is using a particular browser. Sticking to a common denominator (common table elements) is the best way to ensure the widest audience for your work.

If your readership includes users who may be print handicapped or otherwise visually impaired, we strongly recommend you provide an alternative form for your table data. Many browsers that produce Braille or convert text to speech aren't yet able to handle the HTML <TABLE> tag. As a result, many Web sites offer text-only implementations for tables as an alternative. You may want to consider doing the same if appropriate for your audience.

HTML Table Markup

The rest of this chapter shows you the basics and some nifty uses of tables. Be sure you understand how table constructs nest within each other. If you goof up just one nesting order, your information won't display the way you want. A good rule: Every time you add another level to a table, indent the code to offset it from the previous level. Then, when you return to a higher level, decrease your indentation to match previous code at the same level. If this doesn't make sense, examine our examples in this chapter.

Remember, you can put any HTML body element into a table cell. You can even nest multiple tables within a single cell. And you can use formatting tags, such as <CENTER>, on an entire table to position a table on your screen. So if you think that some particular formatting might work for your table, give it a try. Your idea may work better than you think, or it may not work at all — the only way to be sure is to experiment!

The parts of a <TABLE>

The basic parts of a table are the <TABLE> and </TABLE> tags that surround a table, the <TR> and </TR> (table row) tags that define each row, and the <TD> and </TD> (table data) tags that define each cell of a table.

Optional table tags include <CAPTION> and </CAPTION>, which place contained text above or below a table, and <TH> and </TH> (table header), which you can use to label columns and rows in a table. The following simple table illustrates all these tags in the most boring way we could imagine. Hey, we can't jump all the way to the jazzy stuff just yet, ya know!

```
<TABLE>
<CAPTION>The default caption placement.</CAPTION>
  <TR>
    <TH> Header: row 1, column 1</TH>
    <TH> Header: row 1, column 2</TH>
  </TR>
  <TR>
    <TD> Cell: row 2, column 1</TD>
    <TD> Cell: row 2, column 2</TD>
  </TR>
</TABLE>
```

If you put the preceding table code in a Web page, you have a table, but it won't excite users much. That's because the table looks like the one depicted in Figure 9-1 when you view it in your browser. Pretty bland, huh?

Figure 9-1:
A basic
<TABLE>,
complete
with
<CAPTION>
and
headings.

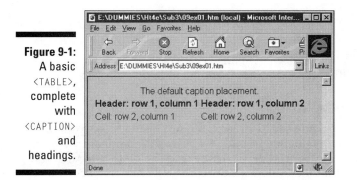

If you understand the basic concepts of table tag layout and the nesting technique shown in this example, you've already mastered the important elements of table building. You can see how easy it is to use table tags to construct a basic table. But now you need to know more about each of these tags. In the next sections, we give you the dirt on the tags and their attributes.

<TABLE> . . . </TABLE>

The `<TABLE>` ... `</TABLE>` tags provide a container for all other table tags. Browsers ignore other table tags if they aren't contained inside `<TABLE>` ... `</TABLE>` tags. The `<TABLE>` tag accepts these attributes: `ALIGN`, `BORDER`, `CELLPADDING`, `CELLSPACING`, and `WIDTH`.

Always include the closing tag for tables; otherwise, your table may not show up at all!

<TR> . . . </TR>

Row tags contain information for all cells within each row of a table. Each set of table row tags represents a single row, regardless of the number of cells in the row. A table row tag can contain both `ALIGN` and `VALIGN` attributes, which, if specified, become the default alignments for all cells in the row. The `<TR>` tag accepts these attributes: `ALIGN` and `VALIGN`.

<TD> . . . </TD>

Each cell in the table is defined by the table data tags (`<TD>` ... `</TD>`), which you must nest within table row tags. Here are some good tidbits to know about table data tags and how they work:

✔ You needn't worry about making each row contain the same number of cells, because short rows are padded with blank cells on the right.

✔ A cell can contain any HTML tag normally used within the body of an HTML document.

The `<TD>` tag accepts these attributes: `ALIGN`, `COLSPAN`, `HEIGHT`, `NOWRAP`, `ROWSPAN`, `VALIGN`, and `WIDTH`.

<TH> . . . </TH>

Table header tags (`<TH>` ... `</TH>`) display text in `BOLD` with a default `ALIGN="center"`. Otherwise, they are identical to table data tags.

<CAPTION> . . . </CAPTION>

Place `<CAPTION>` tags inside `<TABLE>` tags, but not inside table rows or cells. Like table cells, any document body HTML tag can appear in a caption. Captions are horizontally centered with respect to the table, and their lines are wrapped to fit within the table's width. The `<CAPTION>` tag accepts the `ALIGN` attribute.

Basic table attributes

You can use several attributes with table tags. Innovative use of attributes is key to making tables good-looking or, at least, visually interesting. Here's a quick overview of these attributes; next, we show you how to use them.

ALIGN=[top\bottom] / [left\center\right]

When you use the ALIGN attribute with the <CAPTION> tag, specify ALIGN="top" or ALIGN="bottom" to control whether a caption appears above or below a table. The default alignment for a caption is top alignment.

When you use ALIGN inside a <TABLE>, <TR>, <TH>, or <TD> tag, ALIGN accepts any of these values: left, center, or right to control horizontal placement of text within cells. The default is left alignment.

BORDER[=number]

You use the BORDER attribute in a <TABLE> tag to instruct the browser to display borders around the table and all cells. Space is reserved for borders around tables, so table width does not change when borders appear. If no value is specified, BORDER defaults to a width of one (1) pixel.

CELLPADDING=number

When used within a <TABLE>, CELLPADDING determines the amount of space between a cell's borders and its contents. The default is one (1) pixel. Setting cell padding to zero on a table with borders causes text to touch the border. Padding cells can enhance the visual impact of tables, especially when you combine cell padding with cell spacing and border sizing.

CELLSPACING=number

Use the CELLSPACING attribute within the <TABLE> tag to determine the amount of space inserted between individual cells. The default value is two pixels between cells. Couple this with the CELLPADDING attribute and you can really make interesting-looking tables.

WIDTH=[number\"percent%"]

Use the WIDTH attribute inside the <TABLE> tag to set the width of a table in absolute terms, measured in pixels, or as a percentage of a browser's display area. When you use the WIDTH attribute in the <TH> or <TD> tag, you set the width of a cell as an absolute number of pixels or as a percentage of the table's overall width.

VALIGN=[top|middle|bottom|baseline]

The VALIGN (vertical alignment) attribute is used inside a <TR>, <TH>, or <TD> tag to control placement of the cell's contents at the top, middle, or bottom of the cell or to align all elements with a common baseline.

NOWRAP

When you use NOWRAP in a table cell (<TH> or <TD>), this attribute forces browsers to display all the text for that particular cell on a single line. Using this attribute can create extremely wide cells, so be careful!

COLSPAN=number

Use COLSPAN in any table cell (<TH> or <TD>) to specify how many columns of the table the cell should span if you want it to span more than a single cell (which is the ordinary default).

ROWSPAN=number

Use ROWSPAN in any table cell (<TH> or <TD>) to specify how many rows of a table a cell should span if you want it to span more than a single cell (which is the ordinary default).

Build Your Own Tables

Building tables by hand is time consuming, repetitive work, so be sure that a tabular form enhances your content. You can simplify your work, however, by carefully planning the layout of your tabular data and by making use of search, replace, copy, and paste functions in your HTML/text editor. Here are some elements to consider before tagging up to any tabular data.

Laying out tabular data for easy display

First, make a sketch of how you want your table to look. Then create a small HTML table with only a few rows of data to test your layout and to see if the table appears the way you envisioned it. If you're using multicolumn and multirow spanning heads, you may need to make some adjustments to space them properly to fit your data. Finally, test your tables with several browsers to see how they look on each one. This will help you finalize your design, before you add all the data you wish the table to contain.

Multirow and Multicolumn

Remember to build your tables by rows. If you use ROWSPAN="3" in one table row (<TR>), you must account for the extra two rows in the next two <TR>. The idea is to leave out a cell in each row or column that will be assumed — or "spanned into," if you prefer — by the ROWSPAN or COLSPAN cell (see Figure 9-2). For example:

```
<TABLE BORDER>
    <TR><TD ROWSPAN=3>Letters</TD><TD>A</TD></TR>
    <TR>                          <TD>B</TD></TR>
    <TR>                          <TD>C</TD></TR>
</TABLE>
```

Figure 9-2:
The <ROWSPAN> tag, applied to Letters, creates a single left-hand column to match all three rows for A, B, and C.

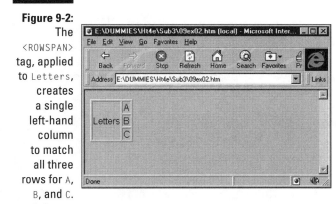

Mixing graphics and tables makes for interesting pages

Tables provide an effective way to present text in a visually pleasing and well-ordered manner, so that you don't frighten off your readers with a screen full of dense and impenetrable information. Something about a long, unbroken list of numbers quickly drives away all but the truly masochistic. But putting those numbers into an attractive table, or better yet several tables interspersed with a few well-chosen images, does wonders for a page's attractiveness and readability. Here are some tips for "effective mixing" of elements (and even tables) within tables:

Nesting

Nesting is an important concept when building tables. This method relies on nesting one set of tags within another set — hence the term. You can easily get lost and confused when building complex tables. To keep confusion to a minimum, always type both the opening and closing tags of a pair before adding attributes or content. This ensures that you always close your tags. This helps prevent the "disappearing table" phenomenon — sometimes, when you forget to close table tags, a browser will be unable to display the table's contents and will therefore skip the whole thing!

Another good habit is to code each element of a table on a separate line in your HTML source files. Every <TD> tag pair needs to appear on its own line, indented to offset it from other levels of table markup. If you're unsure about this, please reexamine the HTML example that goes with Figure 9-1 to see what we're talking about.

Graphics

Within individual table cells, you can position graphics quite precisely. The key to successful incorporation of graphics within a table is to

✔ Select images that are similar in size and look.

✔ Measure the images to determine their heights and widths in terms of pixels (shareware programs like Paint Shop Pro and GraphicConverter do this automatically).

✔ Use HTML markup to position these images within table cells.

By sizing rows or columns of cells that contain images to accommodate the largest graphic, and centering all graphics in each cell (vertically and horizontally), you can create a consistent, coherent image layout. Check out the Dilbert Zone later in this chapter for a good example of this approach.

Tools automate tedious markup

Most decent HTML editors (which we cover in Extras 5 through 9 on the CD-ROM that comes with this book) will build tables for you. Likewise, Microsoft Excel now offers a Save as HTML option in the File⇨Save menu. You can use either of these approaches to handle data entry for tables, and then convert them into HTML to paste into your Web documents.

Why then did we make you learn all the details about HTML table markup? Because none of these tools fully automates the details needed to create borders, cell padding, cell spacing, and so on. None of them really understands how to position graphics as precisely as a human designer can, either. Since you're going to have to tweak such tables by hand anyway, we figured the best way to get started was with a little "manual labor."

Some Stunning Table Examples

Rather than print out pages and pages of complex table markup from real-world Web sites, we provide a list of sites that make excellent use of tables in their layout and design. After you load these documents into your Web browser, take a look at each one's HTML source code (probably View⇨ Source from your menu bar). You see how complex the markup is (and often how poorly that markup is arranged — but then, they didn't ask us).

Well, what are you waiting for? Pull up one of these pages:

- ✔ CNET — This entire site uses tables for all the complex layout. Notice how they often use tables within tables within tables: `www.cnet.com`.

- ✔ Yahoo! — The most popular search engine on the Web used tables to display their front page and all of the navigation items on all results pages: `www.yahoo.com`.

- ✔ Dilbert Zone — The only engineer on the planet to publicly disparage his boss and still keep his job. This daily dose of Dilbert is completely presented by using tables: `www.unitedmedia.com/comics/dilbert/`.

As we mentioned earlier in this chapter, tables can be simple and elegant or complex and astonishing. We aim to give you just enough information to make you hanker to create your own elegant tables, as well as tease you to want to find out how to create astonishing tables. For more about tables, you either need to figure them out on your own or get our companion volume, *MORE HTML For Dummies*.

So now you know the basics about tables. Hey, you're smart! You bought this book, didn't you? Now you know how to make use of the table tags and attributes to make your Web site all the more inviting to potential users. In the next chapter, we go beyond the basics of page construction and move into more sophisticated forms of HTML page design.

Chapter 10

Beyond Basics: Adding Flair and Impact to Your Pages

In This Chapter

▶ Adding logos, icons, and other little gems

▶ Building high-impact graphic pages

▶ Putting your best footer forward

▶ Copyrighting your copy

▶ Including version information

*E*veryone needs influences and role models when it comes to creating original content. When you see a Web page with a layout that you especially like, view the HTML source to examine its formatting techniques. You can use your browser's Save As feature to save any HTML source to your own hard disk for later study, or you can print it.

At the same time, you can add the page to your bookmark file so that you can find it again. Most browsers also let you save the images associated with a page to files on your hard disk. However, before you include somebody else's work on your pages, be aware of copyright — always get the author's permission in writing. (If you're in doubt whether it's okay to reuse something, the safest course of action is not to do it!)

Borrowing Can Lead to Sorrow

Imitation may be the sincerest form of flattery, but stealing other authors' work to use on your Web pages (as if it were your own) is illegal in most countries. However, discovering new techniques from the work of others is the way most Web weavers expand their horizons.

Use these techniques to build your own pages, with your own content, in your own unique manner. You can always e-mail another Web author and request permission to use something in your page. Many independent Web authors are happy to help because others helped them in their quests for new Web tools and techniques. Most corporate Web sites are completely copyrighted, and they take a dim view toward anyone who uses things from their site without permission, which they probably won't grant. The Web is becoming highly commercialized and competitive, so you need to know and respect the legal limitations for others' property.

Eye-Catchers: Logos, Icons, and Other Little Gems

Graphics add impact and interest to Web pages for users with GUI browsers. Unless the primary focus of your Web pages is computer graphics, use small graphics only where they add extra value to your pages. Again, remember that the only speed acceptable to computer users is instantaneous. The larger a graphic, the slower it loads. That's why small is beautiful!

Speaking of small, fast-loading graphics, it's time for you to add some sparkle to your plain-Jane home page. So far, the page has nice-looking headings and simple black bullets next to the list lines (see Figure 8-4). Because the basic layout is well-established, all you need is a few splashes of color in appropriate locations to really spice things up.

Adding an image to your HTML document is as simple as inserting a line using the <IMG> tag:

```
<IMG SRC="graphics/dotred.gif">
```

This line contains the mandatory source reference (URL) to a .GIF file named dotred.gif. It is a relative reference to a file that the Web server expects to find in a subdirectory named graphics directly beneath the directory where the current page resides (that is, the page from which the link is called). For the example shown, using this relative URL for the red dot would cause the server to look for

```
http://www.lanw.com/html4dum/graphics/dotred.gif
```

Alternatively, you may use the following image tag with the full URL for the red dot:

```
<IMG SRC="http://www.lanw.com/html4dum/graphics/dotred.gif">
```

If you want to link to an image file of a red dot (`dotred.gif`) located on another Web site, you must use a full URL (sometimes called an absolute URL) in the `<IMG>` tag like this:

```
<IMG SRC="http://www.someothersite.net/icons/dotred.gif">
```

If you use a full URL in a link, each time the user's browser loads the image, that browser actually links to a remote location. This increases the time needed for the browser to load the file. If the remote location is not online, the browser can't load the image. Therefore, it usually works better if you keep your graphics in the same place on your own server.

A couple of exceptions are when you include an image from another location that changes over time (weather map, clock, and so on), or a large image. In the first case, the other site maintains a changing image and your users see it directly from their site, but included in your page. In the second case, you save on server disk space by pointing to a remote location for a multimegabyte picture.

The rest of this section discusses several small graphic elements as they are used to navigate the LANWrights Web site, as displayed in Figure 10-1. This portion of the document uses nine different small graphic elements built as navigation icons throughout the site. Each of these graphics is less than 1K in size, so they download and display quickly.

Figure 10-1:
A view of the LANWrights navigation icons.

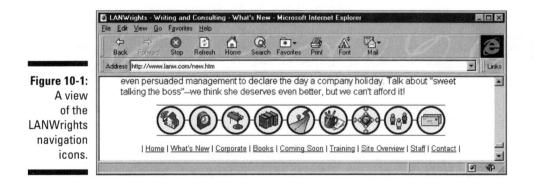

Reusing the same graphics on a single Web page doesn't add significant time or disk storage requirements when a user's browser *caches* them (or stores previously viewed images in memory). Therefore, using the same graphical elements repeatedly helps keep load and display times for these images to a minimum. Recycling images makes as much sense for Web pages as it does for the environment!

Horizontal rules — but rainbow lines bring smiles

Separating sections with a rainbow line graphic can add an additional touch of color to a page. You could accomplish this separation using a simple HTML horizontal rule tag `<HR>`. However, because `<HR>`'s only display is as a 3-D line (gray, black, and white to give the 3-D effect), you don't get the same visual impact that a brightly colored rainbow line provides. This baby changes from red, to violet, blue, green, yellow, orange, and back to red for a nice look.

Using a rainbow line to bracket an announcement just above footer information sets it apart from surrounding text, thereby drawing the user's attention. When used this way, colored ruler lines are perfect for segmenting pages into eye-pleasing information blocks. You can make these lines with most "paint" programs in any length, thickness, and color combination imaginable. You can also find many on public access graphic Web sites where they are available for your use, generally with no strings attached. In fact, feel free to use ours any way you like! You'll find the rainbow image on the CD in the /html4dum/graphics directory, named rainbow.gif.

Rather than list any of the thousands of sites with .GIFs and .JPEGs available for download here, we suggest that you search for `GIF archives` or `JPEG archives` on one of the many Web search engines such as `www.altavista.com`, `www.excite.com`, or `www.yahoo.com`.

Just a couple of thoughts about using colored line images in place of the `<HR>`. It may be quicker and easier to click the HTML editor button that inserts the `<HR>` into your document than to type the link to the colored line image, especially if you have more than a few of them over many pages. Also, some Web searching spiders or agents use the `<HR>` to distinguish breaks in text for their indexes. They won't necessarily recognize the colored line image as a replacement for the `<HR>` tag.

Colored dots beat list dots

Instead of using an unordered list structure, which places black dots (bullets) to the left its elements by default, you can use small graphical elements for heightened visual appeal, such as the redball.gif image in the /html4dum/graphics directory on the CD. This graphic is not just a colored dot. It contains highlights and shadows that make it resemble a three-dimensional ball. If you alternate them in red, white, and blue or other colors, you increase their eye-catching effects and differentiate each line from the lines above and below (look for files named whiball.gif and bluball.gif in the same directory).

One word of caution about replacing lists with colored dots: The HTML standard includes unordered or bulleted lists for a reason — that is, to list items in a nonsequential order and set them off by preceding each one with a symbol. Style attributes in the HTML 4.0 DTD lets you set the way you want numbers or bullets to display in your lists. Every browser that adheres to the HTML 4.0 standard should display these bullets in a similar fashion. This can't be said about individual images of colored dots. Thus, if you use your own images to create snappy lists, the standard HTML list structure won't be reflected in your document. This may not matter to you though, so try it both ways and see which you like best. We generally reserve these special effects for home pages and other documents where looks are most important.

Just as with <HR> versus colored lines, an active spider or agent looking at your page can deduce that an object following an <LI> tag is part of the list it just entered and can organize its gleanings accordingly, but a spider or agent cannot recognize an imitation list that uses colored dots. If you're presenting a true list of items, use HTML list tags. However, if you are more interested in adding some life to your page with colored dots next to some lines, go for it.

Using colored dots and other small icons within lines of text is as simple as inserting a tagged URL in the text at the point where you want it to appear. In the line below, the red dot is created by <IMG SRC="graphics/ dotred.gif"> and displayed before To help you... Notice the space between the > and the To. Although browsers generally ignore spaces, Netscape Navigator, Internet Explorer, and others may recognize a single space before or after text to help you format sentences properly and keep images from crowding text.

```
<IMG SRC="graphics/dotred.gif"> To help
you find current information on the Web about HTML<BR>
```

Many browsers ignore multiple spaces when they render text, but when you're working in and around HTML tags, careful placement of spaces while writing the code can prevent painstaking reformatting work later on.

Icons

We use the term *icon* here to describe any small graphic image that you can substitute for a unit of text. A few well-designed and carefully located icons can help your users quickly find their way around your Web pages.

Icons stored as .GIF files are usually small and load quickly. In most instances, an icon is simply added as a standard image-tagged URL in the position where you want it to appear.

Most icons are so small that you don't need to align text next to them, but for larger images, we discuss alignment later in this chapter. The default for most browsers is to align the text with the bottom of an image.

For example, a set of navigation icons appears in a navigation bar on the right-hand side of the pages for a Web site management class we built to teach a class. These icons are designed to let users jump easily among the modules of the class or to a set of navigation instructions. We added these icons to the HTML document via the lines shown below:

```
<HTML>
<BODY BGCOLOR="#ffffff">
<A HREF="navigate.htm">
<IMG VSPACE=1 ALIGN="CENTER" BORDER="0"
SRC="graphics/nav.gif" ALT="Navigation"></A><P>
<A HREF="isp.htm"><IMG VSPACE=1 ALIGN="CENTER"
BORDER="0" SRC="graphics/isp.gif" ALT="ISP"></A><P>
<A HREF="track.htm"><IMG VSPACE=1 ALIGN="CENTER"
BORDER="0" SRC="graphics/track.gif" ALT="Tracking">
</A><P>
<A HREF="search.htm"><IMG VSPACE=1 ALIGN="CENTER"
BORDER="0" SRC="graphics/search.gif"
ALT="Searching"></A><P>
</BODY>
</HTML>
```

Here, we make each icon a hyperlink that can transport users to the right HTML document, as soon as it's clicked. This creates a compact, simple navigation technique that's easy for users with graphical browsers to use. A full-blown implementation also includes an equivalent set of text-based hyperlinks, so that visually impaired users or those with graphics turned off can also navigate as well. The navigation bar appears on the right-hand side of Figure 10-2.

Logos and graphics as hyperlinks

Logos are special-use graphics. They vary from icon size to much larger, sometimes too large. Remember KISS (Keep It Simple, Sweetheart)? Complex logos that take too long to load are nugatory on any Web page.

Use logos to identify your business or institution in a pleasing, eye-catching manner. Don't use them to overpower the page or to irritate the users. A moderately sized logo at the top of the home page is generally acceptable. Using icon-sized logos in the footer of each Web page is equally acceptable. Remember that text-only browsers and GUI browsers with image loading turned off (for faster page loading) won't display your fantastic logos, anyway.

Figure 10-2:
The icons on the right-hand side of the page provide a constant source of navigation in this example site (available at www. lanw.com/ training/ myw/).

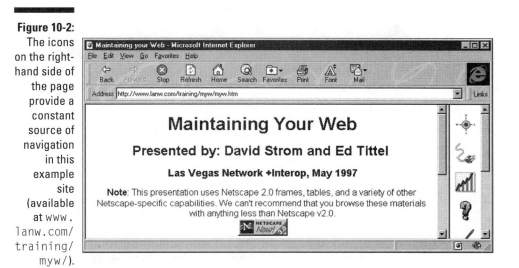

Figures 10-3 and 10-4 illustrate the visual effects of using a moderately sized logo .GIF at the top of a page. The LANWrights logo file is only 4,930 bytes, so it loads in a few seconds. On the home page shown in Figure 10-3, the logo is used by itself; on the subsidiary pages, the logo is combined with an associated navigation icon to create a visual link between the topic and its related image, as shown in Figure 10-4. This second image, despite the increase in size, is still only 7,342 bytes.

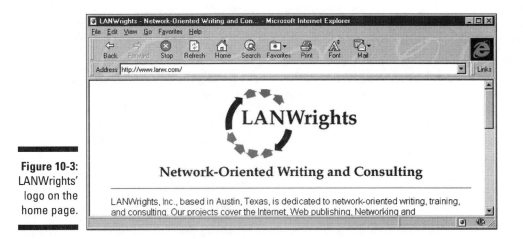

Figure 10-3:
LANWrights' logo on the home page.

Figure 10-4:
LANWrights'
logo is
integrated
with
navigation
icons on
other
pages.

Figure 10-5:
LANWrights
uses
navigation
graphics as
hyperlinks.

A table of navigation icons under the LANWrights Logo at the top of the home page (shown in Figure 10-5) illustrates the use of tabular graphics as hyperlinks. The following lines from the HTML document that produced the views illustrate how you can nest an icon image within link reference tags (between <A HREF> and </A>) to make each icon act as a hyperlink:

```
<P><CENTER><TABLE WIDTH="90%" BORDER="0"
CELLSPACING="4" CELLPADDING="2">
<TR>
<TD WIDTH="10%"></TD>
<TD WIDTH="15%" HEIGHT="23"><P><CENTER>
<A HREF="new.htm"><IMG SRC="graphics/new.gif"
ALIGN="BOTTOM" WIDTH="51" HEIGHT="51" BORDER="0"
ALT="What's New!"></A></CENTER></TD>
```

```
<TD WIDTH="30%"><A HREF="new.htm">What's New</A></TD>
<TD WIDTH="15%"><P><CENTER><A HREF="corporat.htm">
<IMG SRC="graphics/corporat.gif" WIDTH="51"
HEIGHT="51" ALIGN="BOTTOM" ALT="Coporate Services"
BORDER="0"></A></CENTER></TD>
<TD WIDTH="30%"><A HREF="corporat.htm">Corporate
Overview</A></TD></TR>
<TR>
<TD></TD>
<TD HEIGHT="23"><P><CENTER><A HREF="books.htm">
<IMG SRC="graphics/books.gif" WIDTH="51" HEIGHT="51"
ALIGN="BOTTOM" ALT="Books in Print"
BORDER="0"></A></CENTER></TD>
<TD><A HREF="books.htm">Books in Print</A></TD>
<TD><P><CENTER><A HREF="topress.htm">
<IMG SRC="graphics/comisoon.gif" WIDTH="51"
HEIGHT="51" ALIGN="BOTTOM" ALT="Coming Soon"
BORDER="0"></A></CENTER></TD>
<TD><A HREF="topress.htm">Coming Soon</A></TD></TR>
<TR>
<TD></TD>
<TD HEIGHT="23"><P><CENTER><A HREF="training.htm">
<IMG SRC="graphics/training.gif" WIDTH="51"
HEIGHT="51" ALIGN="BOTTOM" BORDER="0"
ALT="Training"></A></CENTER></TD>
<TD><A HREF="training.htm">Training</A></TD>
<TD><P><CENTER><A HREF="overview.htm">
<IMG SRC="graphics/wayfind.gif" WIDTH="51"
HEIGHT="51" ALIGN="BOTTOM" ALT="Wayfinder"
BORDER="0"></A></CENTER></TD>
<TD><A HREF="overview.htm">Site Overview</A></TD></TR>
<TR>
<TD></TD>
<TD HEIGHT="23"><P><CENTER><A HREF="lanwstaf.htm">
<IMG SRC="graphics/staff.gif" WIDTH="51" HEIGHT="51"
ALIGN="BOTTOM" ALT="Staff" BORDER="0"></A></CENTER></TD>
<TD><A HREF="lanwstaf.htm">LANWrights Staff</A></TD>
<TD><P><CENTER><A HREF="lanwcmmt.htm">
<IMG SRC="graphics/contact.gif" WIDTH="51" HEIGHT="51"
ALIGN="BOTTOM" ALT="Contact" BORDER="0"></A></CENTER></TD>
<TD><A HREF="lanwcmmt.htm">Contact LANWrights</A></TD></TR>
</TABLE>
</CENTER></P>
```

Notice also the use of the alternate text attribute, ALT="text" that appears within each image tag. Text-only browsers display associated "text" as a hyperlink instead of the icon. Some graphic browsers display an image-holder icon and alternate text when their image display function is turned off. Either way, this leaves the graphically challenged users who visit your site with some way to use the navigation you've so painstakingly defined. For better looks, we added explicit text definitions in the tables cells next to each icon, too.

Creative use of the icon images as hyperlinks to other pages within the LANWrights Web site adds visual interest to the home page as well as providing users with direct links to other parts of the site. If you use a few well-selected icons in this manner, your Web pages stand out and are remembered, in addition to being easier to navigate.

Building Graphic Page Layouts

As you should now thoroughly understand, the graphic layout of the Web pages you see in this chapter did not occur by accident. These page layouts were drawn with the best locations for graphics noted. The graphics were carefully chosen and sized to fit the layout and purpose of each page.

As you can see by viewing the LANWrights Web site at www.lanw.com, we added graphics sparingly to brighten and enhance the visual contrast within our pages. Upon first viewing the home page, the user sees the company logo and icons that link to different sections of the site. This setup is good because its primary purpose is to focus on LANWrights services, books, and capabilities.

As the user scans down the page, horizontal rules and highlighted hyperlinks focus attention on the page's important parts. The overall layout is conservative yet far more interesting than it would be without graphics.

The top portion of the pages, shown in Figures 10-3 and 10-4, illustrates the additional thought that goes into the design and layout of pages that use larger graphics. These pages work well for text-only browsers, yet they show interesting graphics to users of GUI browsers. If you experiment with the various tags available in HTML and follow the suggestions in this book, you can do the same — and much more — on your Web pages.

Working with graphics files

You must work with graphics on two distinct levels to arrive at a good page layout and optimum functionality. First, consider the size of the graphics on the screen and their impact on the complexity of your document's layout. Second, consider the size of the image files (in bytes) and how long it takes users to download them.

The original logo file shown in Figure 10-3 was built in Adobe Illustrator and was over 1MB in size, filling the entire screen. Careful cropping, resizing, and resampling (using fewer pixels per inch) resulted in a file under 5,000 bytes in size. These changes resulted in a dramatic improvement in load time — it's not unusual for a megabyte of data to require several minutes to load over a slow link, but a 5,000-byte file moves in seconds, even over a slow modem.

To produce high-quality images for your Web pages, you don't have to become an expert at using the old standby graphics manipulation programs, such as Paint Shop Pro, GraphicConverter, Photo Styler, Graphics Workshop, Wingif, LView Pro, or some of the newer programs that seem to pop up weekly on the Web. However, if you plan to work with images regularly, you should try to become fairly adept at one of these programs, or a commercial equivalent.

Search for GIF EDITOR on your favorite search engine and you can find links to many useful sites for freeware and shareware tools.

.GIF and .JPEG file formats

Although you can use many different types of graphic files on the Web, virtually all GUI browsers have internal display capabilities for .GIF and .JPEG formats. Browsers use external helper applications to display other file types. Also, compressed .GIF and .JPEG files are the smallest and, therefore, the fastest to load of all the commonly used file types.

Most good shareware image-manipulation programs, such as those mentioned above, can load and save .GIF and .JPEG format files. These programs also support GIF87a and transparent and/or interlaced GIF89a formats. If you work on a Macintosh, use GifConverter for interlaced .GIFs.

Whenever you build GIF89a graphics, be sure to test any interlaced images on multiple browsers. Some color depths lend themselves better to interlacing (and transparency, too) than others. Unfortunately, this seems to be a trial-and-error process and not an exact science; that's why testing your images across multiple browsers on multiple platforms is a must!

Seeing through the graphic to the background

The GIF89 format also introduced the *transparent background* feature. This feature "turns off" one of the colors in an image — when displayed by a browser — and allows whatever is behind the image to show through at every point where the color is transparent. Usually, this is a background color, but you can lay images over other images or text as well. To users, your image appears to float on the browser's background, instead of atop a square of some other color around the image.

Programs such as giftrans for UNIX and DOS and Transparency for the Macintosh create images with transparent backgrounds for browsers that support the GIF89 format. For Windows users, LView for Windows is also worth checking out. Transparent images really add to the impact and drama of a Web page.

A new pic's resolution . . .

One last technical aspect of dealing with images involves the number of bits per pixel stored in their files. Although reducing bits per pixel reduces the resolution (and therefore, the quality) of images as rendered by a browser, try storing images with 7 or even 5 bits per pixel if you need to show a large image as quickly as possible. Alternatively, you can reduce the number of colors in a picture to lower its overall image size. Check your graphics program for more information on either of these techniques.

A standard .GIF image requires 8 bits per pixel, which results in 256 colors. Seven bits of information per pixel produces 128 colors, 5 bits 32 colors, etc. Some programs, such as Paint Shop Pro (shareware) and Adobe Photoshop (commercial) allow a specific number of colors to be selected. For example, setting the number of colors to 43 results in 7 bits per pixel, but the remaining 85 empty color definitions are set at 0,0,0 (or undefined), which results in a smaller (and faster) graphic than one set to 7 bits per pixel alone. Most of these programs also tell you how many unique colors appear in an image and let you manipulate the number of colors until you can achieve the best compromise between size and fidelity.

Slice up your graphics for better response time!

"What is an *interlaced .GIF*," you ask? Well, an interlaced .GIF stores graphics information in a .GIF file so that a browser can load a low-resolution image on the first of multiple passes, then fill in to the normal resolution on subsequent passes. This method gives images a "Venetian blind" look as your browser draws them.

The load time for images remains the same whether images are interlaced or not, but some browsers load the text of the page with the first pass of the images. This lets users begin scrolling and reading while the browser completes additional image passes. Therefore, users get to your information faster, which generally results in happier users!

Rules for using graphics

Keep these rules in mind while you design your Web pages:

- ✔ Sketch your layout with and without graphics.
- ✔ Focus on overall page look and content.
- ✔ KISS your images . . . small and simple.
- ✔ Use compressed, interlaced .GIFs or .JPEGs.
- ✔ Link thumbnail versions of images to larger files instead of dumping megabyte-sized files on your unsuspecting users.
- ✔ Include the size of image files in the text that describes large images.
- ✔ Use graphics sparingly for maximum effect.
- ✔ Use images or graphics to enhance text information.

If you understand and can implement all the topics discussed in this chapter, congratulations — you're not an HTML ignoramus. You know enough to design and create well-balanced, attractive, user-friendly Web pages. Keep right on going to find out even more fun things to add to your Web pages. In the next chapter, you find out how to master the intricacies of complex Web pages, with élan and panache.

Chapter 11

Going High-Rise: Building Complex Pages

- -

In This Chapter

▶ Expanding your home page into a Web

▶ Moving around inside your documents and local Web

▶ Jumping to remote sites

▶ Nesting lists

▶ Analyzing sophisticated Web pages

▶ Animating .GIFs

- -

*Y*ou're probably not satisfied with your nice, but simple, single-screen home page. Because of all the wonderful stuff you've seen out there on the Web, you really want to make a Web of pages with all sorts of great material in them, right? That's pretty natural, and it doesn't compromise the KISS (Keep It Simple, Sweetheart) principle, either. After all, simple is a relative term.

You may recall that we suggested that you'd want to make more pages as you expanded your Web. But the more pages you add, the harder it becomes for your users to find their way around. While you're growing a Web, your most important job is to make your users' journey through it as enjoyable as possible. In fact, you've already discovered the necessary methods and techniques in previous chapters. Now it's time to put them to use.

This chapter covers creating complex Webs. After an initial discussion, we comment on the elements and layout of a few advanced Web sites.

There's No Place Like Home

Home isn't only your home page; it's your own Web, a local constellation of planets orbiting your home page. It's your turf in cyberspace, where Web surfers can find information that you think is important. But even if your site is fantastic and beautiful, you can put off users if they have trouble navigating around your site. That's why you need a clear mental picture of its fully developed organization *before* you start expanding things.

Organization

If you listen closely to your content, it can tell you the organizational style that it needs — or, rather, demands. Hierarchical style, linear style, and interlinked combinations of these two styles are the standard organizational structures used in most Webs. These Web structures are illustrated in Figures 11-1, 11-2, and 11-3.

It's straightforward to "Web-ify" a linear document, but the converse is untrue: Organizing a random collection of ideas and concepts into a linear document is very difficult. When designing and using links within or among Web documents, you need to be clear about the organization and interconnectedness of their content.

The hierarchical, or tree, structure is used as the basis of most Web designs (see Figure 11-1). It is logical and has a familiar look to most computer users (think hard-disk file trees or GUI help systems). This organization is easy for users to navigate, especially when you include links back to the home page on each page.

Figure 11-1:
A hierarchical structure looks like a family tree.

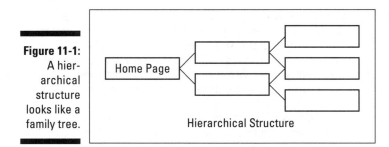

Home Page

Hierarchical Structure

When using a hierarchy, your information should progress from the most general (root) level, or a table of contents on your home page, to the most detailed content in the outermost leaves. Your content dictates the divisions of the tree, but you can include interesting links between seemingly unrelated branches to better inform your users. Also, try providing multiple links to individual pages. In this way, the structure includes aspects of the index of a book, as well as its table of contents.

Keep in mind that readers can enter your Web space from somewhere other than your home page, so make sure that you provide navigational clues for *jumped-in* users. You want them to find your home page or other relevant pages easily. It's frustrating to land on a page whose URL you obtained by e-mail from some cohort who says, "Check out this page," only to be forced to blunder around because you can't find home! Preventing users from experiencing this frustration is an excellent reason to provide navigational clues on each Web page you create. For an example of good style (even if we do say so ourselves), check out this URL: www.lanw.com/html4dum/.

Simple, book-like, but also *rigid* and *confining,* are common descriptions of the linear structure (see Figure 11-2). If your information presents a series of steps or follows a process from start to finish, linear structure is a fitting choice for your document's organization. A linear structure keeps users on track and out of trouble. Here, you can make good use of links to "next page," "previous page," and "top or start page."

Figure 11-2:
Linear
structure
goes from
start to
finish, one
step at a
time.

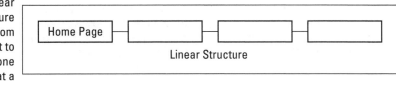

Be sure to put links to your home page (or a starting point) on each page in a linear structure. Without such links, users who drop into the middle of your site can only use their browser's controls to bail out. If you trap them like this, they'll talk about your site on the Net, but the talk won't be flattering!

The WWW itself is a Web structure (see Figure 11-3). It's a great example of the fantastic freedom of movement and free-flowing design that are implicit in such a loosely linked environment. Providing structure without constraining users' freedom to explore your space is the goal of any well-designed Web structure.

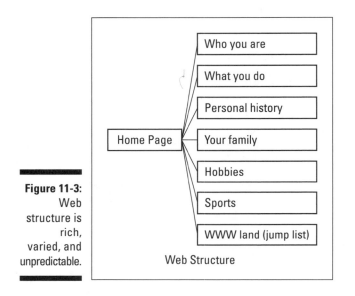

Figure 11-3: Web structure is rich, varied, and unpredictable.

Web Structure: Home Page links to Who you are, What you do, Personal history, Your family, Hobbies, Sports, WWW land (jump list)

If your information on related subjects is extensive, put hyperlinks within the text to specific paragraphs in other pages where users can see more detailed information about the content. Be careful how you do this, though. Too much linkage can be just as bad as not enough! Hypertext linking is the most time-consuming part of HTML document development. Do it well, and your users will love you forever. We discuss this further later in this chapter.

When you build a complex Web structure, always, always, always put a link to your home page on each page. It's also a great idea to reproduce the URL for each page in its footer in small type. If you provide this data, users can return to any specific page in your Web by using that URL later on, even if they didn't add it to their bookmarks.

It's story (board) time, boys and girls!

If you read Chapter 8 before now and you sketched your home page, it's time to lay your hands on pencil and paper again. For this exercise, you get to draw your Web site's structure. For a personal Web site, pencil and paper should do nicely. For larger, more complex sites, you may require additional tools. Read on for the details!

First Things First: List 'em Out

Make a list of the major pieces of information that you want to include in your Web site. These major points will probably turn into links on your home page and may be similar to the following:

- ✔ Who you are
- ✔ What you do
- ✔ Personal history
- ✔ Your family
- ✔ Hobbies
- ✔ Sports
- ✔ WWW land (jump list)

Sketch the Web

In the preceding example, you have relatively few topics to consider, so a combination Web/hierarchical structure looks appropriate. This structure should look familiar, because it's probably similar to the way your hard disk's directories are organized.

By using this sketch to analyze your home page, you can see some links that aren't readily apparent from looking at the HTML. These links exist between the "Who you are" page and the "What you do," "Personal history," and "Sports" pages, as well as between the "Your family" and the "Hobbies" and "Sports" pages. Of course, you also need to link all these secondary pages directly to the "Home Page."

Board the whole story

Whatever simple sketch you create to represent your Web site at first can't provide enough information for you to fully visualize a site. What you really need to do now is to prepare a storyboard for your pages — that is, unless you can mentally picture the elements and links on each of all eight separate pages.

Every movie, TV show, and comic book gets storyboarded before any production takes place. Producing a set of Web pages is a lot like making a TV show, especially if you think of each Web page as a separate scene. Over time, an entire collection of Web documents and associated materials evolves from your work, making it resemble a whole season's worth of TV episodes instead of a single show.

To prepare a storyboard, simply prepare a sketch of the layout of each Web page with the URLs for links written on each one. For small Webs, some Web authors use a white marker board with colored pens. The colors are handy for showing different types of links, forms, or other HTML elements.

For more complex Webs, many authors use a sheet of paper for each Web page, some string, some push pins, and a large bulletin board (cork type, not BBS). This method allows complex arrangements that you can change easily. Also, the storyboard method is invaluable for identifying potential hypertext links, if you attach the text of each Web page to its layout sheet. Whenever you create a Web of more than a handful of pages, do a storyboard. This saves you much more time than it takes initially, and after you finish, you appreciate its value.

On the other hand, some Web authors turn to software to help them when things start getting more complicated. If you investigate further (and Extras 5 through 9 on the CD are some great places to start), you find that Web site management tools abound, and that some of them work well during design and storyboarding, as well as during maintenance and update phases after a site has been fully realized. Products like FrontPage 98 and SiteMill often receive favorable mention in this category of tools.

Anchors Away: Jumping Around Your Documents

We did say that it wasn't too terrible to create Web pages spanning up to three screens, if your information demands extra room and if you put the most important information on the first screen. You may even expand your home page to more than one screen if you carefully drop your anchors and don't go overboard on images.

You can use two different anchor tag attributes for movement within your pages. To provide viewers with links to specific parts within a Web page (called intradocument linking), use the `NAME="text"` anchor to provide the destination of an `HREF="#label"` tag. Use the standard `HREF="URL"` (called interdocument linking) to let users jump from page to page. Or to jump to a specific location within another page, you can combine both approaches and use `HREF="URL#label"`.

When following links inside a browser, you must note the important distinction between interdocument linking and intradocument linking. With *interdocument* linking (between documents), most browsers land the reader on the first line of a target document. On the other hand, *intradocument* linking (within the same document) takes you to a place other than the default top of page, unless you put a named anchor at the top of the page and the URL calls this anchor out.

Here's another interesting quirk about browsers — namely, their behavior with named anchors that occur near the bottom of a document. If an anchor appears near or at the very bottom of a document, most browsers do *not* bring the named anchor to the first line on the screen. This is because the browser usually renders a full screen of text; thus, if the anchor is near the bottom of a document, the link may take you to a point toward the bottom of the screen, rather than the absolute bottom of the document itself.

Linking to text in another page

The LANWrights Corporate Overview page provides an example of how you might use the NAME="text" attribute in anchor tags. An HTML line in this document that looks much like the following recurs in four locations, before each of that document's major headings, to speed users' transitions among those headings:

```
<CENTER><A HREF="#History">Corp History</A> 
| <A HREF="#Svcs">Services/Capabilities</A> 
| <A HREF="#Rate">Rates</A></CENTER><P>
```

This HTML code creates an intradocument text navigation bar and provides selections for other major headings that aren't showing at various locations on the page. If the browser can't find a named anchor, you get the default instead, which is the top of the document.

For example, selecting the text that reads Services/Capabilities on the page results in jumping to the "LANWrights Services/Statement of Capabilities" heading. This may seem a bit abstract, but you'll catch on if you remember this: The anchor with the NAME="text" attribute is the destination for a link. As the author, you can control how your information is displayed and how your document is linked. If you think users may find a heading within a specific page relevant or important, then give it a name with the NAME attribute and create a link to it. This internal navigation bar is shown in Figure 11-4, just beneath the top-of-page logo image.

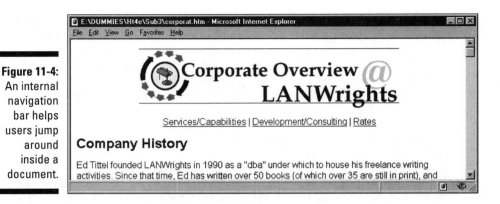

Figure 11-4:
An internal
navigation
bar helps
users jump
around
inside a
document.

Linking to text within a page: Table of Contents links

You can use the NAME="text" attribute to create a really jumping table of contents (TOC) for long documents. Providing a linked TOC takes a little more time, but it's a great way to impress your users. Remember to provide a link back to the TOC after each block of text in the destination document.

The following HTML code illustrates how to use the TOC links within a large document:

```
<!-- Make this an anchor for return jumps.-->
<A NAME="TOC">Table of Contents</A><P>
<!-- This is the link to the section 1. below.-->
<A HREF="#SEC1">Section 1.</A><BR>
<A HREF="#SEC2">Section 2.</A><BR>
<A HREF="#SEC3">Section 3.</A><BR>
<!-- This is a named anchor called "SEC1".-->
<A NAME="SEC1"><H2> CFR Section 1.</H2></A>
<P> Text of section 1 is here.<BR>
<!-- This is a link back to the TOC at the top of the page-->
<A HREF="#TOC">(TOC)</A> <P>
<A NAME="SEC2"><H2> CFR Section 2.</H2></A>
<P> Text of section 2 is here.<BR>
<A HREF="#TOC">(TOC)</A><P>
<A NAME="SEC3"><H2> CFR Section 3.</H2></A>
<P> Text of section 3 is here.<BR>
<A HREF="#TOC">(TOC)</A><P>
```

Seeing the (TOC) after each text section may seem strange at first, but your users quickly become accustomed to this method of intradocument linking (see Figure 11-5). We recommend using this approach for longer, more complex documents or for a collection of related documents, but not for shorter pieces. A ubiquitous TOC in a short document may seem obtrusive to your users.

You can use this same general method for links to anything within a single HTML document. It may look strange as HTML, but this is the way you create hypertext links within a paragraph. Only use the "text" in each NAME="text" once per document, though, to keep the browser from becoming terminally confused. Otherwise, your users may wind up at the top of page (which is the default for all unrecognized text anchors)!

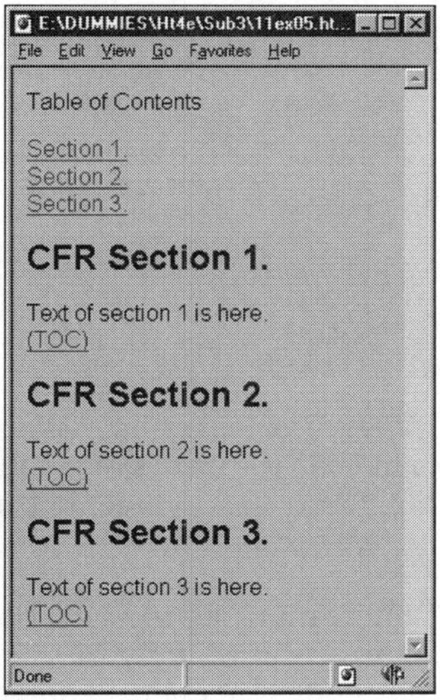

Figure 11-5:
Table of
Contents
and text
links.

complex documents browser window showing:

```
E:\DUMMIES\Ht4e\Sub3\11ex05.ht...
File  Edit  View  Go  Favorites  Help

Table of Contents

Section 1.
Section 2.
Section 3.

CFR Section 1.

Text of section 1 is here.
(TOC)

CFR Section 2.

Text of section 2 is here.
(TOC)

CFR Section 3.

Text of section 3 is here.
(TOC)

Done
```

You should name named anchors with text starting with a character from the set {a-z, A-Z}. They should never be exclusively numeric, like <A NAME="12">blah</A>. Make sure to give anchors unique names within any single document. Anchor names are case sensitive, so NAME="Three Stooges" is not the same as NAME="ThreeStooges" is not the same as NAME="THREESTOOGES". You get the idea. . . .

Jumping to Remote Pages

Hypermedia links from text in your pages directly to other Web sites amazes and amuses your users. Although you can't create NAME="text" anchors in text at remote sites, you may be able to use anchors already in place there.

If you find a linked TOC at another site, you can reference the same links that it uses. Remember, if you can link to it by using your browser, you can copy the link into the text of your Web pages. Just make sure you include the full URL in the `HREF="URL"`.

Hypertext links to outside resources

Links to Web sites outside of your own Web require fully qualified URLs, such as

```
<BR>
URL: <A HREF="http://www.lanw.com/html4dum/html4dum.htm">
http://www.lanw.com/html4dum/html4dum.htm</A> 
<BR>Text - Copyright &copy; 1995-1998 Ed Tittel &amp;
Stephen N. James. 
<BR>Dummies Design and Art - Copyright &copy; 1995-1998
IDG Books Worldwide, Inc. 
<BR>Web Layout - Copyright &copy; 1995, 1996, 1997
<A HREF="http://www.lanw.com/">LANWrights</A> 
<BR>Revised - October 17th, 1997 [ERT] 
```

The two links (`HREF`) connect the *HTML For Dummies* home page to itself and to the LANWrights Web site. Why include the page's own URL as a link? It not only shows the user the URL, but it also allows direct linking if users save this page's HTML source to their own computers.

All these tags and links make for difficult reading of the actual HTML code unless you view them through a browser, as shown in Figure 11-6. Through the browser, hypertext words appear in a different color, underlined, or both, depending on your browser's preference settings.

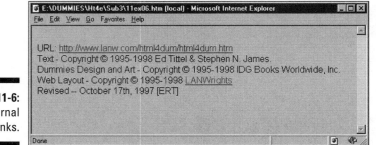

Figure 11-6:
External
links.

Jump pages

The term *jump page* refers to a Web page that contains a list of URLs to other Web pages, usually remote sites. HTML list tags are invaluable when creating visually pleasing and easily understood lists of links. Jump pages, also known as *hotlists,* differ from basic Web pages only because they contain primarily hyperlinks. This arrangement is appropriate for quick scanning, but not for general reading.

Use icon images and spacer lines to visually separate sections of a hotlist. Carefully choose the words you use for each hyperlink, keeping in mind the main point of the information to which the link refers. When entering URLs for links, we strongly recommend that you first link to the destination URLs by using your browser. Then highlight, copy, and paste the URLs directly into your HTML file to cut down on typos and syntax errors.

A special <LINK>

The <LINK> tag provides information that links the current Web page to other Web pages or to other URL resources. When you want to be sure that your Web pages tell browsers and other software about themselves, put a <LINK> in the <HEAD> ... </HEAD> section.

Chapter 6 shows several attributes that you may use in the <LINK> tag. If you start using one of the advanced HTML-generating programs, it may insert several <LINK> tags of various types within the head section of each page. The programs use these links to keep track of the pages themselves.

Perhaps the most commonly used is NAME="text" to provide an anchor from other locations. You use this named anchor for reference access from other locations or documents. Your HTML code should look like this:

```
<HTML>
<HEAD>
<TITLE> The Title of Your Page </TITLE>
<LINK NAME="My Home Page">
</HEAD>
<BODY>
<H1> The Heading of Your Page That Users See </H1>
and so on...
</BODY></HTML>
```

The Nesting Instinct: Lists Within Lists

When you create longer Web pages, you want to keep visual diversity high by using text formatting. If you are preparing your Web site for the newer browser versions, you can work with tables and frames (Chapters 9 and 10) to format your text. However, older versions of GUI browsers and text-only browsers understand the more basic HTML formatting: headings, emphasized text (bold, strong, font size), and indented lists. Lists within lists create the old, familiar outline form when displayed by most browsers. Here's how a list within a list looks:

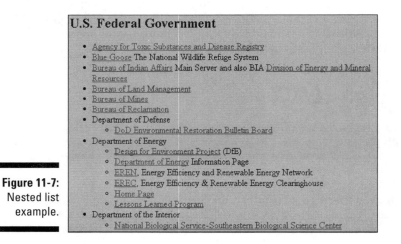

Figure 11-7:
Nested list
example.

The following HTML code created the browser display in Figure 11-7. As you look through this HTML markup, remember that you see only a fragment, not the whole thing:

```
<p><h2>U.S. Federal Government</h2>
<ul>
<li><a href="http://atsdr1.atsdr.cdc.gov:8080/
        atsdrhome.html">Agency for Toxic Substances and
        Disease Registry</a>
<li><A HREF="http://bluegoose.arw.r9.fws.gov/">Blue Goose</
        A> The National Wildlife Refuge System
<li><A HREF="http://info.er.usgs.gov/doi/bureau-indian-
        affairs.html">Bureau of Indian Affairs</a> Main
        Server and also BIA <A HREF="http://
        snake2.cr.usgs.gov/">Division of Energy and
        Mineral Resources</a>
<li><A
```

```
HREF="http://info.er.usgs.gov/doi/bureau-land-
          management.html">Bureau of Land Management</a>
<li><A HREF="http://www.usbm.gov/">Bureau of Mines</a>
<li><A HREF="http://info.er.usgs.gov/doi/bureau-of-
          reclamation.html">Bureau of Reclamation</a>
<li>Department of Defense
<ul> <li><a href="http://www.dtic.dla.mil/envirodod/
          envirodod.html">
DoD Environmental Restoration Bulletin Board</a>
</ul>
<li>Department of Energy
<ul>
<li><a href=http://w3.pnl.gov:2080/DFE/home.html>Design for
          Environment  Project</a> (DfE)
<li><A HREF="http://web.fie.com/web/fed/doe/">Department of
          Energy</A> Information Page
<li><a href="http://www.eren.doe.gov/ee/ee.html">EREN</a>,
          Energy Efficiency and Renewable Energy Network
<li><a href="http://www.nciinc.com/~erec">EREC</a>, Energy
          Efficiency & Renewable Energy Clearinghouse
<li><a href="http://www.doe.gov">Home Page</a>
<li><a href=http://venus.hyperk.com/trl/11/11.html>Lessons
          Learned Program</a>
</ul>
<li>Department of the Interior
<ul>
<li><a href="http://www.nfrcg.gov/">National Biological
          Service-Southeastern
Biological Science Center</a>
</ul>
</ul>
```

Carefully track the list start (<UL>) and end (</UL>) tags. Directly under the U.S. Federal Government heading you see a start tag, and at the bottom of the listing you see its end tag. This placement of the tags indents and bullets all items that fall between them and are marked with the <LI> tags. This is a normal unordered list. What about all items that are indented a second time and preceded by a box rather than a bullet, you ask?

Each of these sections is contained within another pair of list tags. For example, the second level list start tag appears immediately under the Department of Defense heading, and its end tag occurs immediately before the Department of Energy heading. The text between them, "DoD Environmental Restoration Bulletin Board," is marked with an <LI> tag, which causes the browser to indent it farther and place a box in front of it (in Netscape Navigator).

Some HTML 4.0-aware browsers keep track of the number of nests you use and change the bullets for each successive nesting to blocks or other symbols. You can also use the style tag to specify a symbol for each level in your list. It may be easier to visualize nested lists without the <LI> lines:

```
<UL> Start level 1.
     <UL> Start level 2.
          <UL> Start level 3.
          </UL> End level 3.
     </UL> End level 2.
</UL> End level 1.
```

Nested lists are a good way to instruct a browser to indent certain lines of text without using the <PRE> ... </PRE> or <BLOCKQUOTE> ... </BLOCKQUOTE> tags. Along with indentations, your users must cope with bullets or numbers, but that's fine for lists, as in the earlier example.

Check your favorite browser developer's Web site to determine if they have a version that understands the use of style tags in lists for changing the bullets and numbering. Who knows what they'll think of next?

Analyzing Sophisticated Pages

Now it's time for a quick look at a complex Web page. We also encourage you to surf the Web for pages that strike your fancy. When you find one, view its source to see how the author worked the underlying magic. The Web is one of the few places where you can easily look behind the curtain to see how an illusion is created, so take full advantage of this opportunity.

...For Dummies home page

IDG Books' own ...*For Dummies* home page illustrates what you can accomplish if you use HTML 4.0 tags (without frames) and your imagination. It's eye-catching but not overdone (see Figure 11-8). Its information is arranged nicely and gives users multiple avenues of access. The graphics (logo and link images, or the client-side or CGI image maps) have neighboring text commands to make the site easy to navigate quickly, both graphically and textually. Users who want to "scan the site" can use the menu selections in the right-hand column to explore the site systematically. The right-hand column even includes a "search" function to let users find anything contained in the site and jump directly there.

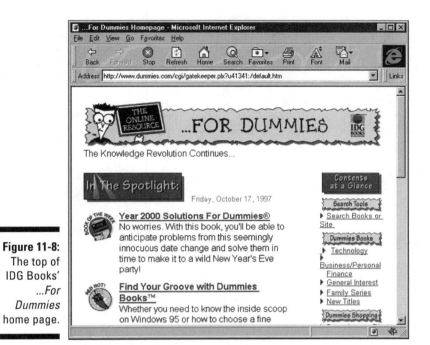

Figure 11-8:
The top of
IDG Books'
*...For
Dummies*
home page.

The entire home page is less than two screens long. It makes liberal use of color and blank space to keep the text readable. The graphics load quickly, because each has been designed with only a few colors (under 16, in fact) and simple graphics components. Each link image or image map is repeated in text immediately to the right for users who don't have GUI browsers.

The footer contains much of the requisite information — but not the page's URL, however — and makes much of the legal copyright notice that publishers must hold so near to their hearts.

The HTML code for the *...For Dummies* home pages is HTML 4.0 compliant. It shows some interesting tricks that you may find useful. Its use of ALT text with images ensures navigation even for non-GUI browsers. It also plays some interesting games with tables to arrange graphics and text elements, and to build the right-hand column of menu selections.

```
<head>
<!-- For brevity, we skipped lots of HTML in the head -->
<title>...For Dummies Homepage</title>
</head>
```

(continued)

(continued)

```
<body bgcolor="#FFFFFF">
<div align="center"><center>

<table border="0" width="544" height="124">
    <tr>
        <td colspan="2">
<img src="http://www.dummies.com//images/mastb.gif"
align="top" width="56" height="83"><img
src="http://www.dummies.com//images/mast.side.b.gif"
align="top" width="477" height="83"><br>
The Knowledge Revolution Continues...
        </td>
    </tr>

</table>
</center></div><div align="center"><center>

<table border="0" cellpadding="0" cellspacing="0"
width="540">
    <tr>
        <td valign="top" colspan="2">
<img  src="http://www.dummies.com//images/spot1.gif"
alt="In the Spotlight:" width="179" height="51"><font
        color="#808080" size="2">  Friday,
        October 17, 1997  </font> </td>
        <td valign="top" width="60"> </td>
        <td valign="top" rowspan="8" width="120">
<img src="http://www.dummies.com//images/cag.bkg.gif"
alt="Contents at a Glance" width="113" height="38">
<a href="http://www.dummies.com/cgi/gatekeeper.plx:/
search.html"  ><font
        size="2"></font></a><font size="2">
        <br>
        </font><a  href="http://www.dummies.com/cgi/
            gatekeeper.plx:/
search.html"  ><font size="2"><img
src="http://www.dummies.com//images/cag_search.gif"
alt="search" border="0" width="113"
height="31"></font></a><font size="2"> </font>
<a href="http://www.dummies.com/cgi/gatekeeper.plx:/
search.html"  ><font size="2">
```

```
<img src="http://www.dummies.com//images/blue-bullet.gif"
border="0" width="7" height="10"> Search Books or Site
</font></a>
<a href="http://www.dummies.com/cgi/gatekeeper.plx:/
dummies_books/" ><font size="2">
<img src="http://www.dummies.com//images/cag_books.A.gif"
alt="books" border="0" width="113" height="31">
</font></a><font size="2">
<img src="http://www.dummies.com//images/blue-bullet.gif"
width="7" height="10"> </font>
<a href="/cgi/dblookup.plx" ><font
        size="2">Technology</font></a><font size="2"><br>
        <img src="http://www.dummies.com//images/blue-
            bullet.gif" width="7" height="10"></font>
        <a href="/cgi/dblookup.plx" >
        <font size="2"> Business/Personal</font></a>
        <font size="2"> <br>
        <!-- and so on... -->
```

As you can see, the HTML arranges the "In The Spotlight" elements in the left-hand column and the "Contents at a Glance" elements in the right-hand column. Note the repeated use of the font tag to control type size, and the consistent use of ALT text to permit words to stand in for graphics where necessary. All of these are elements of good design.

Animating .GIFs

One of the hidden capabilities of the GIF89a standard is that it supports the inclusion of multiple images in a single shared file. It's also possible to embed instructions in such a file's header to describe how its contents should be sequenced. This permits multiple images to act like the individual frames in a frame-by-frame animation and delivers a crude, but effective, technique for building simple animations on your Web pages.

In fact, if you visit the ...*For Dummies* Web site and look closely at the "In The Spotlight" graphic, you immediately realize it's an animated .GIF. It uses three versions of the same graphic, each with differently positioned light beams from a spotlight above the upper left-hand corner of the graphic, creating the illusion of spotlights tracking across the image.

You can find a bevy of tools to assist in constructing animated .GIFs, including shareware and commercial software. Brian Hovis's Gif Animation page includes pointers to the vast majority of such tools, as well as an excellent tutorial that covers the details of constructing .GIF animations. You can get to all this material though this URL:

```
www.bendnet.com/users/brianhovis/anime.htm
```

In its most basic form, the process of creating an animated .GIF works like this:

1. **Create each of the graphics for the sequence as a separate .GIF file.**

2. **Determine the sequence of images.**

3. **Establish the startup delay, delay between images, and decide if the animated .GIF should cycle through the sequence once or keep cycling (as the "In The Spotlight" image does on the ...*For Dummies* page).**

4. **Tell your software tool which images to grab, in which order, set delays, and define cycling behavior.**

5. **Let the tool create the animated .GIF for your page(s).**

Be aware that an animated .GIF will be slightly larger than the sum of all the images that go into the animation sequence (to include the header information, of course). That's why animated .GIFs should work with small, compact images, with only a few colors and as little complexity as possible — otherwise, these files may grow too large to appeal to users who must download them over slow connections!

Other sophisticated Web sites

We strongly urge you to explore the Web and view HTML source code for the many exciting sites that abound in Web space. You need to look not only at HTML source for a site's primary page, but also at HTML source for each frame on those sites that use HTML frames. Try right-clicking on a frame and see what your browser lets you do. You may be surprised — newer browsers should show you the HTML source code for the frame you selected.

Also, some webmasters hide their code so you can't view it. They have their right to privacy, so you just have to look at other, more accessible sites and try new things on your own Web documents.

Chapter 12

Strictly Pro Forma: Using Forms for Feedback

. . . .

In This Chapter
▶ Discovering what forms are for

▶ Dealing with browser and server limitations

▶ Finding out about form tags

▶ Using form tags

▶ Forming good attitudes

▶ Formulating good layouts

. . . .

*W*hen all the pieces come together properly, it's easy to see how the Web brings people and organizations together. At first glance, the Web might look pretty much like a one-way street — that is, an environment where webmasters communicate aplenty with Web users, with not much interaction coming back from users at all. But it doesn't have to be that way.

What HTML Forms Are For

The essence of serving up useful information is relevancy and immediacy. But the best judge of the quality of your information is your audience. Wouldn't it be wonderful if your readers could give you feedback on your Web pages? Then, they could tell you what parts they like, what they don't like, and what other things they'd like to see included in your site.

Getting feedback is where HTML forms come into play. Up to this point in the book, we've talked about all the basics — and even a few advanced techniques — for communicating with an audience. In this chapter, you find out how to turn the tables and create HTML that lets your audience communicate with you!

As it turns out, HTML supports a rich variety of input capabilities to let you solicit feedback. In the pages that follow, you discover the tags to use, the controls and inputs they enable, along with some layout considerations for building forms. You also get to see some interesting example forms to help you understand what HTML forms look like and how they behave.

Living within Your Forms Limitations

HTML forms were established way back in the HTML 2.0 days — ancient history on the Web, but only a few years in how we measure time. With HTML 4.0, forms have gained some new capabilities and a bit of a face-lift, too. But even though forms give users the ability to communicate with Web authors and developers, you still find some important limitations in using them. You must be keenly aware of their abilities and limitations before you deploy forms on your site.

Beware of browser!

Most new browsers — Netscape Navigator or Communicator 4.0 (and higher) and Microsoft Internet Explorer (Windows 95 version 3.0.3 and higher), plus NCSA Mosaic and its variants — already include HTML 4.0-level forms support, but other browsers do not. In fact, you won't know how well your favorite browser handles HTML 4.0 forms until you test your forms with it. If you follow our suggestions and test your pages against multiple browsers, you'll immediately observe different levels of robustness and capability when it comes to forms implementations.

The bottom line is that not all browsers support forms equally, but that support is pretty commonplace. Current or modern browser versions have no problem interacting with most form constructs. But don't be surprised if on older browsers forms don't work that well or not at all.

Assuming that the information your form solicits is important to you, consider adding an FTP URL to your page to let users download a file containing a text-only version of the form's content. Then they can download this file and complete with any text editor. If you include an e-mail address inside the form itself, they can e-mail it back to you and you get feedback, even from users who can't deal with forms. That way nobody gets left out!

Sorry, servers . . .

Because the Web is a client/server environment, be aware that just because your browser supports forms doesn't automatically imply that the server installed at your site handles them. Unfortunately, keeping up with HTML advancements means that Web servers have to change right along with clients. In other words, your server may not support the input-handling programs necessary to process a form's input when it gets delivered. Or you may not be able to access the right input-handling programs on the server without help from an administrator, even if everything you need is already in place.

However, you'll find a silver lining in this potentially dark cloud: The most common implementations of the *httpd* server (the *http daemon* — the Web server software that handles requests for Web services, including forms, and responds as needed) come from NCSA and the W3C and run in the UNIX environment, among other platforms. Both of these industry groups have standardized forms-handling technology and offer useful, robust forms-handling capabilities.

These implementations are so common, in fact, that we assume your Web server works the same way that they do. This means that you may have to alter some of the approaches to CGI scripting and other programming that you might use to handle forms on your server, if our assumption is incorrect. If you're not using UNIX and the NCSA or CERN implementations of httpd, you'll want to investigate the particulars that your server's implementation requires and alter our instructions accordingly. This statement is particularly true for Windows NT, in which Perl is not a common language in the standard arsenal of server capabilities, and in which equivalent input-handling is available in a variety of alternate guises.

By this point in the evolution of the Web, you probably won't run into a Web server that does not offer some sort of support for forms, either through CGI, server-side includes, some native scripting language, or some other proprietary solution (like Microsoft Active Server Pages or its Internet Information Server API, also known as ISAPI).

What's in a Form?

When adding forms support to a Web page, you must include special tags to solicit input from users. You surround these tags with text to prompt user responses. You also include tags to gather input and ship it to your Web server, or to other servers that may offer services — like Gopher or Archie — that your form knows how to query. Here's how this works:

✔ On a particular Web page, you include tags to set up a form and solicit input from users. Some users work their way through this material and provide the information that you want. This essentially amounts to filling out the form that you supply.

✔ After users fill out your form, they can then direct their input to the program running on the Web server that delivered the form. In most cases, they select a particular control, called SUBMIT, to gather the data and send it to a specific input-handling program on your Web server.

✔ Assuming that the program is available (installed and running properly, that is), it accepts the input information. Then the program decodes and interprets the contents to guide its further actions.

✔ After the input is received and interpreted, the program can do pretty much anything it wants. In practice, this boils down to recognizing key elements in a form's content and custom-building an HTML document in response. Building a document isn't required, but is a pretty common capability within the majority of forms-handling programs.

✔ This custom-built document is delivered to the user in response to the form's content. At this point, additional interaction can occur (if the "return page" includes another form), requested information can be delivered (in response to requests on the form), a simple acknowledgment issued, or so forth.

The information collected from a form can be

✔ Written to a file

✔ Submitted to a database, such as Informix or Oracle

✔ E-mailed to someone in particular

Forms can also allow users to participate in building an evolving Web document, such as the Web site called WaxWeb, that allows users to dictate how a story plays out; in this case, the users collectively determine the outcome.

Thus, forms not only provide communication from users to servers, but also provide ongoing interaction between users and servers. This interaction is pretty powerful stuff and can add a lot of value to your Web pages.

Forms involve two-way communication

Most input-catching programs on the Web server rely on an interface between Web browsers and servers called the *Common Gateway Interface* (CGI). This interface codifies how browsers send information back to servers. It codifies formatting for user-supplied input, so that forms-handling programs know what to expect and how to deal with what they receive.

The ACTION attribute in a <FORM> tag specifies a URL that indicates a specific CGI script or program that collects the form data that a user entered. Likewise, the METHOD attribute describes the way in which input data is delivered to such a forms-handling program.

In this chapter, we concentrate on the input side of HTML forms — that is, you find out how to build forms. This is a pure exercise in building the front end of a form — or the part that users see. You find out a little about how to build the back end — the CGI or equivalent programs that your server uses to deal with forms input — in Extra 2 on the CD-ROM. Not to worry — you have plenty of interesting front-end material to understand here!

Tag! You're a form . . .

HTML includes several different classes of forms tags (for the details on syntax and usage, please consult Chapter 6). To begin with, all HTML forms occur within the <FORM> . . . </FORM> tags. The <FORM> tag also includes attributes that specify where and how to deliver input to the appropriate Web server.

All other forms-related tags and text must appear within the <FORM> . . . </FORM> tags. These tags include methods for

- ✔ Specifying input (the <INPUT> tag and its many attributes).

- ✔ Grouping related sets of form controls and fields using the <FIELDSET> . . . </FIELDSET> tags.

- ✔ Employing <BUTTON> . . . </BUTTON> tags to create forms controls. (Usually, this markup surrounds graphics of buttons, with alternate text defined by the value of the button's NAME attribute for non-GUI viewers.)

- ✔ Using <LABEL> . . . </LABEL> tags to identify form controls and fields.

- ✔ Using <LEGEND> . . . </LEGEND> tags to create captions for sets of related form controls (field sets, in other words).

- ✔ Setting up text input areas (the <TEXTAREA> . . . </TEXTAREA> tags).

- ✔ Selecting values from a predefined set of possible inputs (the <SELECT> . . . </SELECT> tags).

- ✔ Managing the form's content (using the SUBMIT attribute for INPUT to deliver the content to the server, or the RESET attribute to clear its contents, and start over).

Forms-input tags support multiple ways to interact with users, including

- ✔ Creating text input fields, called *text areas*, where users can type in whatever they want. Designers can choose either single- or multiline text input fields, and can govern how much text displays on screen and how much text can be entered into any text area.

- ✔ Generating pull-down menus, often called *pick lists* because they require making one or more selections from a set of predefined choices.

- ✔ Creating custom buttons and graphical controls for incorporation into forms.

- ✔ Assigning all kinds of labels and captions to individual fields or buttons, or to groups of fields or buttons, as needed.

- ✔ Creating labeled check boxes or radio buttons on screen, which users can select to indicate choices. Check boxes allow multiple selections and radio buttons allow just one selection.

This may not sound like much, but when you combine these capabilities with the ability to prompt users for input using surrounding text and graphics, forms provide a surprisingly powerful way to ask for information on a Web page. Thus, the real answer to the question at the head of this section, "What's in a form?" has to be, "Almost anything you want!"

The remainder of this chapter takes you through all the details of building a form, so you can use the capabilities we just described.

Using Form Tags

To start out, you want to set up your <FORM> environment to build a form within a Web page. It's okay to add a form to an existing HTML document or to build a separate one just to contain your form. We recommend that you add shorter forms (half a screen or less) to existing documents, but that you create new files for forms that are longer than half a screen.

Setting the <FORM> environment

The two key attributes within the <FORM> tag are METHOD and ACTION. Together, these attributes control how your browser sends information to the Web server and which input-handling program receives the form's contents.

A *METHOD* to our madness

METHOD indicates how your browser sends information to the server when you submit the form. METHOD takes one of two possible values: POST or GET.

Of these two methods, we prefer POST because it causes a form's contents to be parsed one element at a time. GET, on the other hand, joins all field names and their associated values into one long string. Because UNIX (and most systems) have a limit on how long a single string can be (for UNIX it's 255 characters), it's not hard to imagine that some information might get lost when its excess length is truncated.

For this reason, we use POST as our only METHOD for submitting forms in this book. That's also why you should do the same, unless you're dead certain that the number of characters in a form will never, ever exceed 255.

Lights, camera . . . *ACTION*

ACTION supplies the URL for the CGI script or other input-handling program on the server that receives a form's input. This URL can be a full specification (absolute) or simply a relative reference. Either way, you need to make sure it points to the right program, in the right location, to do the job you expect. You also need to make sure that the CGI script or program is executable and that it behaves properly. You find a lot more about this in Extra 3 on the CD-ROM, which goes into the ins and outs of testing HTML documents and related CGI programs.

Let's make an assumption . . .

Because you won't have to worry about handling input until Extra 2 on the CD-ROM, we follow two conventions for all forms syntax in this chapter:

- In every <FORM> tag, METHOD="POST".

- For every ACTION, URL="/cgi-bin/form-name" where we replace the placeholder *form-name* with the name of the form under discussion (that is, for the form named *get-inf.html*, URL="/cgi-bin/get-inf").

These conventions make it easy to create sample HTML files to implement the forms in this chapter. (You can also find these examples on the CD-ROM that accompanies this book.)

Knowing what's (in)coming: the <INPUT> tags

The <INPUT> tag defines a basic form element. This tag takes at least two attributes — namely TYPE and NAME. TYPE indicates what kind of element should appear on the form. NAME assigns a name to go with the input field or value that corresponds to the <INPUT> tag.

You use NAME to identify the contents of a field in the form information that is ultimately uploaded to the input-handling Web server. In fact, what the server receives is a series of name/value pairs. The name that identifies the value is the string supplied in the NAME="string" attribute, and the value is what the user enters or selects for that particular field. Read on — the section titled "A TEXT-oriented <INPUT> example" contains an example that makes all this clear!

TYPE-casting still works!

The TYPE attribute can take any of the following values:

- BUTTON: Creates a button that has no specific use, except to call a script upon selection.

- CHECKBOX: Produces an on-screen check box for users to make multiple selections.

- FILE: Allows users to upload a file, but for this to work, you must provide a list of acceptable file types using the ACCEPT attribute.

- HIDDEN: Produces no visible input area; use this to pass data needed for other uses through the form. For example, this might be an ongoing series of forms based on an earlier interaction during which the user identifies himself or herself — a HIDDEN field contains the name-value pair for that data but doesn't show it on the current form. (Some browsers display these fields at the bottom of a form, and each field has no accompanying label.)

- IMAGE: Designates a graphic as a selectable item in a form. You can use this to include icons or other graphical symbols.

- PASSWORD: Same as the TEXT type, but characters display as asterisks ("****") or some other masking character, to keep passwords from showing in clear text.

- RADIO: Creates a radio button for a range of selections, from which the user may select only one.

- RESET: Creates a button labeled "reset" in your form. Include this so that users can clear a form's contents and start over. Be sure to place it well away from other controls — you don't want them to clear the form by accident!

- SUBMIT: Creates a button labeled "submit" (by default, or whatever name you supply for the VALUE attribute for SUBMIT) in your form. The type SUBMIT tells the browser to bundle the form data and pass it all to the CGI script indicated by the ACTION attribute. In plain English (remember that?) SUBMIT is the button readers use to send in the filled-out form, so a form is useless without an <INPUT> field of type SUBMIT.

- TEXT: Provides a one-line area for text entry. Use this for short fields only (as in the example that follows). For longer text fields, use the <TEXTAREA> ... </TEXTAREA> tags instead.

These TYPE attribute values provide a wide range of input displays and data types for form input. As you look at HTML forms on the Web and in this book with a new (and more trained) eye, you can see how effectively you can use these types.

Other <INPUT> attributes

Most remaining attributes exist to modify or qualify the <INPUT> attribute with TEXT type as the default. Here's a quick review of what we covered in Chapter 6, in alphabetical order for easy reference:

- ALIGN=(TOP|MIDDLE|BOTTOM|LEFT|RIGHT): For IMAGE elements, determines how the graphic is aligned on the form, vis-à-vis the accompanying text.

- CHECKED: Makes sure that a certain radio button or check box is checked when the form is either visited for the first time or when it is reset. You can control default settings with the CHECKED attribute of <INPUT>.

- DISABLED: Renders an input element unusable (but it will still display on screen).

- MAXLENGTH="number": Sets the maximum number of characters that a value in a TEXT element can contain.

- READONLY: Neither the contents of the control, nor the control itself, may be modified by the user. Any information already present in this control will be automatically submitted with the form. If combined with HIDDEN, provides a way to pass "invisible" data along with other form input.

- SIZE="number": Sets the number of characters that a TEXT element can display without scrolling.

- SRC="URL": Provides a pointer to the graphic for an IMAGE.

- TABINDEX="number": Specifies an element's position in the tabbing order, so that field-to-field transitions when the user strikes the tab key can be explicitly controlled (default is by order of appearance).

- USEMAP="*filename*": Identifies a client-side image map to be used to solicit user input.

- VALUE="value": Supplies a default value for a TEXT or HIDDEN element or supplies the corresponding value for a radio button or check box selection. You can use this to determine the label of a submit or a reset button, like VALUE="Submit to Admin" for a submit or VALUE="Clear Form" for a reset.

A TEXT-oriented <INPUT> example

That's it for the <INPUT> tag. Here's a look at a relatively simple survey form:

```
<HTML>
<HEAD>
<TITLE>Reader Contact Information</TITLE>
<!-- the name of this form is usr-inf.html -->
</HEAD>
<BODY>
<H3>Reader Contact Information</H3>
<P>Please fill out this form, so we'll know how to get in
touch with you. Thanks!
<FORM METHOD="POST" ACTION="/cgi-bin/usr-inf">
<P>Please enter your name:
<P>First name: <INPUT NAME="first" TYPE="TEXT" SIZE="12"
          MAXLENGTH="20">
MI: <INPUT NAME ="MI" TYPE="TEXT" SIZE="3" MAXLENGTH="3">
Surname(last name): <INPUT NAME="surname" TYPE="TEXT"
          SIZE="15" MAXLENGTH="25">
<P>
<P>Please give us your mailing address:
<P>Address 1: <INPUT NAME="adr1" TYPE="TEXT" SIZE="30"
          MAXLENGTH="45">
<P>Address 2: <INPUT NAME="adr2" TYPE="TEXT" SIZE="30"
          MAXLENGTH="45">
<P>City: <INPUT NAME="city" TYPE="TEXT" SIZE="15"
          MAXLENGTH="30">
<P>State: <INPUT NAME="state" TYPE="TEXT" SIZE="15"
          MAXLENGTH="15">
   ZIP&#47;Postal Code: <INPUT NAME="zip" TYPE="TEXT"
          SIZE="10" MAXLENGTH="10">
<P>Country: <INPUT NAME="country" TYPE="TEXT" SIZE="15"
          MAXLENGTH="15">
<P>
<P>Thank you! <INPUT TYPE="SUBMIT"> <INPUT TYPE="RESET">
</FORM>
<ADDRESS>
Sample form for <I>HTML for Dummies</I> Version 3.1<BR>10/
          16/97 http://www.noplace.com/HTML4D/usr-inf.html
</ADDRESS>
</BODY></HTML>
```

Figure 12-1 shows this HTML form on display. Note the positions of the one-line text boxes immediately after field names and the ability to set these boxes on individual lines (as with Address1 and Address2) or together — as with First name, Middle initial (MI), and Last name (Surname). These options makes it easy to build simple, usable forms.

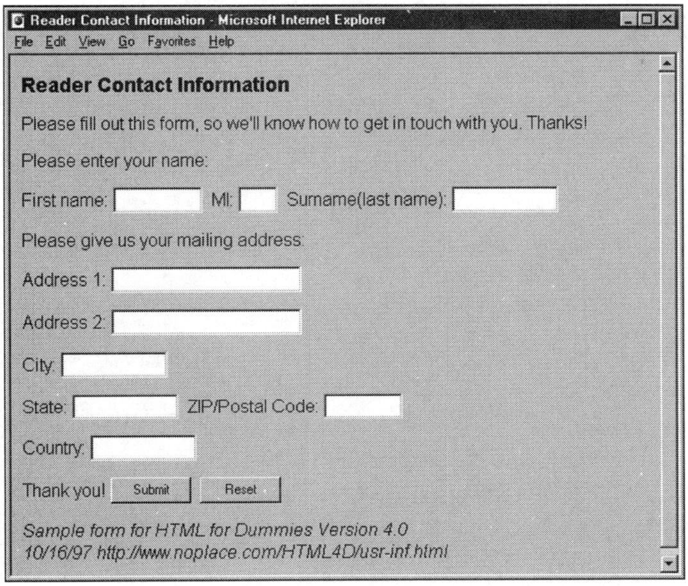

Reader Contact Information - Microsoft Internet Explorer

File Edit View Go Favorites Help

Reader Contact Information

Please fill out this form, so we'll know how to get in touch with you. Thanks!

Please enter your name:

First name: [   ] MI: [   ] Surname(last name): [   ]

Please give us your mailing address:

Address 1: [   ]

Address 2: [   ]

City: [   ]

State: [   ] ZIP/Postal Code: [   ]

Country: [   ]

Thank you! [Submit] [Reset]

Sample form for HTML for Dummies Version 4.0
10/16/97 http://www.noplace.com/HTML4D/usr-inf.html

Figure 12-1:
The
"Reader
Contact
Information"
form on
screen.

Being <SELECT>ive

The `<SELECT>` ... `</SELECT>` pair works much like a list style, except that it builds a selectable list of `<OPTION>` elements, instead of the `<LI>` list items. Within the `<SELECT>` tag, the following attributes can occur:

- `DISABLED`: Renders an element unusable, but still viewable.

- `TABINDEX="number"`: Identifies an element's position in the tabbing order defined for the page, so that field-to-field transitions when the user strikes the tab key can be explicitly controlled (default is by order of appearance).

- `NAME="text"`: Provides the name that is passed to the server as the identifying portion of the `name-value` pair for this element.

- `SIZE="number"`: Controls the number of elements that the pick list displays; even though you can still define more than this many elements, it keeps the size of the list more manageable on screen.

- `MULTIPLE`: Indicates that multiple selections from a list are possible; if this flag isn't present in a `<SELECT>` statement, your users can select only a single element from the pick list.

Building a `<SELECT>` field for your form doesn't take much work. In the following example, you see how easy it is to construct a list of spices from which a user can select and order:

```
<HTML>
<HEAD>
<TITLE>&lt;SELECT&gt; Spices</TITLE>
   <!-- the name of this form is sel-spi.html -->
   </HEAD>
   <BODY>
   <H3>This Month's Spicy Selections!</H3>
<P>Spice up your life.  Order from this month's special
         selections.
<BR> All items include 2 oz. of the finest condiments,
         packed in tinted glass bottles for best storage.
<HR>
   <FORM METHOD="POST" ACTION="/cgi/sel-spi">
<P>
   <FIELDSET>
   <LEGEND>Pepper Selections:</LEGEND>
   <SELECT NAME="pepper" SIZE="4" MULTIPLE>
   <OPTION>Plain-black
   <OPTION>Malabar
   <OPTION>Telicherry
   <OPTION>Green-dried
   <OPTION>Green-pickled
   <OPTION>Red
   <OPTION>White
   </SELECT>
   <P>Please pick a button to indicate how the pepper<BR>
         should be delivered:
   <BR>Ground <INPUT TYPE="RADIO" NAME="grind"
         VALUE="ground">
   <BR>Whole <INPUT TYPE="RADIO" NAME="grind"
         VALUE="whole">
   <BR></FIELDSET>
   <P>
   <HR>
   <P>Imported and Domestic Oregano:
   <SELECT NAME="oregano" SIZE="4" MULTIPLE>
   <OPTION> Italian-whole
   <OPTION> Italian-crumbled
   <OPTION> Greek-whole
   <OPTION> Indian
   <OPTION> Mexican
   <OPTION> Organic-California
   </SELECT>
   <P>Thanks for your order! <INPUT TYPE="SUBMIT"
         VALUE="Send Order">
```

```
<INPUT TYPE="RESET">
   </FORM>
<ADDRESS>
Sample form for <I>HTML for Dummies</I> Version 3.1<BR>
3/17/97 http://www.noplace.com/HTML4D/spc-ord.html
</ADDRESS></BODY></HTML>
```

Figure 15-2 shows what nice results you can get from using <SELECT> elements to provide options for your users to pick from. Also, notice the radio buttons to specify whether they want whole or ground pepper. By giving both radio buttons the same NAME, we indicate that only one option can be chosen.

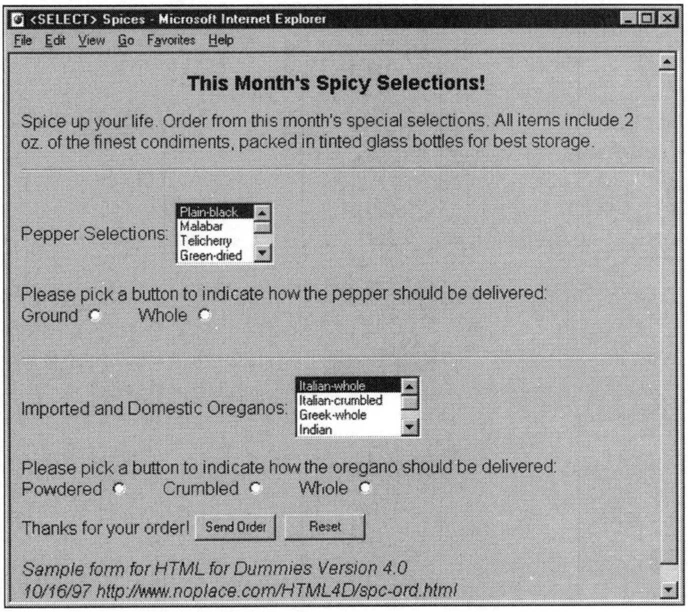

Figure 15-2:
<SELECT>
creates
scrolling
pick lists of
choices for
users to
select.

<TEXTAREA> lets users wax eloquent . . . or profane!

The <TEXTAREA> ... </TEXTAREA> tags let you create input elements of more or less arbitrary size on a form. Any text that appears between the opening and closing tags is displayed within the text area on screen (and if left unaltered, the text area supplies the default value delivered by the form).

`<TEXTAREA>` takes these attributes:

- ✔ `COLS="number"`: Specifies the number of characters that can fit onto any one row of the text area; this value also sets the width of the text area on screen.

- ✔ `DISABLED`: Makes the element unusable, even though it still displays.

- ✔ `NAME="text"`: Provides the identifier part of the all-important `name-value` pair delivered to the server.

- ✔ `READONLY`: When set, this value prevents users from modifying the text area; any information contained therein will automatically be submitted with the form.

- ✔ `ROWS="number"`: Specifies the number of lines of text that the text area will contain.

- ✔ `TABINDEX="number"`: Identifies this element's position in the tabbing order defined for fields on the page, so that field-to-field transitions when the user strikes the tab key can be explicitly controlled (default is by order of appearance).

The example that follows shows how you can use a text area to provide space for free-form feedback or information as part of a survey-style form:

```
<HTML>
<HEAD>
<TITLE>&lt;TEXTAREA&gt; On Display</TITLE>
    <!-- the name of this form is txt-ara.html -->
</HEAD>
    <BODY>
    <H3>The Widget Waffle Iron Survey</H3>
<P>Please fill out the following information so that we
    can register your new Widget Waffle Iron.
<HR>
    <FORM METHOD="POST" ACTION="/cgi/txt-ara">
<FIELDSET><LEGEND>Model Number</LEGEND>
    <SELECT NAME="mod-num" SIZE="3">
    <OPTION>102 (Single Belgian)
    <OPTION>103 (Double Belgian)
    <OPTION>104 (Single Heart-shaped)
    <OPTION>105 (Double Heart-shaped)
    <OPTION>204 (Restaurant Waffler)
    <OPTION>297 (Cone Waffler)
    </SELECT>
</FIELDSET>
    <HR>
    <B>Please complete the following purchase information:
        </B><BR>
```

```
<P>Serial number: <INPUT NAME="snum" TYPE="TEXT" SIZE="10"
   MAXLENGTH="10">
   <P>Purchase Price: <INPUT NAME="price" TYPE="TEXT"
         SIZE="6"
   MAXLENGTH="10">
   <P>Location: <INPUT NAME="location" TYPE="TEXT"
         SIZE="15"
   MAXLENGTH="30">
   <HR>
   <B>Please tell us about yourself:</B>

<P>Male <INPUT NAME="sex" TYPE="CHECKBOX" VALUE="male">
   Female <INPUT NAME="sex" TYPE="CHECKBOX" VALUE="female">
   <P>Age:
   under 25 <INPUT NAME="age" TYPE="CHECKBOX" VALUE="lo">
   25-50 <INPUT NAME="age" TYPE="CHECKBOX" VALUE="med">
   over 50 <INPUT NAME="age" TYPE="CHECKBOX" VALUE="hi">
<P>
<HR>
   Please share your favorite waffle recipe with us. If we
like it, we'll include it in our next Widget Waffler cook
book! Here's an example to inspire you.
<P><TEXTAREA NAME="recipe" ROWS="10" COLS="65">
   Banana Waffles
   Ingredients:
   2 c. waffle batter (see Widget Waffler cookbook for
         recipe)
   2 ripe bananas, peeled, sliced 1/4" thick
   1 tsp. cinnamon
   Preparation:
   Mix ingredients together.
   Preheat Widget Waffler (wait 'til light goes off).
   Pour 1/2 c. batter in Waffler (wait 'til light goes
         off).
   Keep browned waffles warm in oven until ready to serve.
   </TEXTAREA>
<P>Thank you! <INPUT TYPE="SUBMIT" VALUE="Register now">
<INPUT TYPE="RESET">
</FORM>
<ADDRESS>
Sample form for <I>HTML for Dummies</I> Version 3.1<BR>
3/17/97 http://www.noplace.com/HTML4D/wfl-srvy.html
</ADDRESS></BODY></HTML>
```

The screen that results from this HTML document appears in part in
Figure 12-3. Notice the use of check boxes for survey information, coupled
with the text input area for recipes. Makes us wonder "What time's breakfast?"

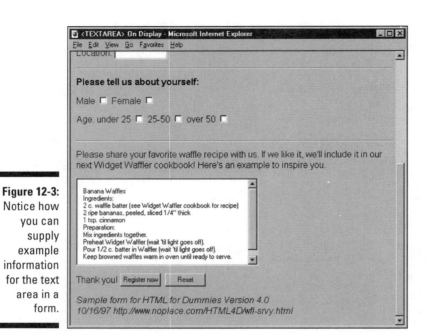

Figure 12-3:
Notice how
you can
supply
example
information
for the text
area in a
form.

If you've read this whole section, you've seen most of the nifty little tricks — we like to call them *widgets* — that work within forms, but you can't really appreciate what forms can do until you've browsed the Web to look at what's out there. Our examples barely scratch the surface, so there's a lot more to see!

Formulating Good Attitudes

Whenever you create an HTML form, it's especially important to test it against as many browsers as you possibly can. Don't forget to work with character-mode browsers, like Lynx, as well as more exciting graphical browsers.

Ultimately, the HTML rules regarding layout versus content apply to forms: If you can create a clear, readable layout and make a form interesting to your users, you'll probably be a lot happier with the information returned than if you spend extra hours tuning and tweaking graphics elements and precise placement of type, widgets, and fields. Remember, too, that a form's just the front end for your user interaction or data collection. In Extra 2, you pick up the back end of the forms business as you tackle the demanding, but rewarding, task of building CGI scripts and other input-handling programs for your server. If you need more details on this subject, don't forget to check out our other books:

- *CGI Bible* by Ed Tittel, Mark Gaither, Sebastian Hassinger, and Mike Erwin. IDG Books Worldwide, Inc., Indianapolis, IN, 1997. ISBN 0-7645-8016-7.

- *Web Programming Secrets With HTML, CGI, and Perl,* by Ed Tittel, Mark Gaither, Sebastian Hassinger, and Mike Erwin, IDG Books Worldwide, Inc., Indianapolis, IN, 1996. ISBN 156884-848-X.

In Extra 2, we talk about a few tools you can use to automate the form and background CGI script creation process. Then in our companion book, *More HTML For Dummies,* 2nd Edition (IDG Books Worldwide, Inc.), we discuss Forms, CGI, and Web page authoring automation in much greater detail.

Chapter 13

For HTML, Style Is Its Own Reward!

S tyle sheets represent one of the most exciting new additions to HTML 4.0 and the Web. Style sheets allow authors to specify layout and design elements — such as fonts, colors, indentation, and precise control over how elements appear on a Web page — for an entire Web site. Neither users' whims — nor misconfigured browsers — can mangle the display of style-dependent Web documents.

A style sheet's specification combines with users' personal settings to make sure an HTML document displays "properly." You must understand that the term *properly* is determined by a document's creator, not its viewer — if you don't believe us, ask any artist how she feels about her work!

Style sheets are important enough that the W3C has devoted an entire section of its Web site to this topic. You can find style-sheet information there, plus a collection of links for further study. Look them up at www.w3.org/pub/WWW/Style/.

Before you dive into this chapter expecting to find out how to create and use style sheets, please understand that we don't to tell you how to make style sheets of your own in this book! Style sheets are more than complex; they're quite advanced and difficult to wrap your brain around. Not that we think you can't tackle them successfully, it's just that creating style sheets isn't for beginners. The real reason we don't cover them in depth here is that we'd have to write a whole book on the subject to do them complete justice. In fact, we've done just that — it's called *The HTML Style Sheets Design Guide,* by Natanya Pitts, Ed Tittel, and Stephen N. James (Coriolis Group Books).

Instead, we give an introduction to the concept of style, describe Cascading Style Sheets (CSS), and show you an example style sheet, complete with comments, so you can get a taste of what style sheets are and how they work. We hope our introduction to this new Web technology gives you an idea of what style sheets can do and shows you what direction your site can follow after you master the fundamentals of HTML style.

Of Styles and Style Sheets

If you've worked with desktop publishing applications, you should be familiar with the concept of a style sheet or template. If not, the idea isn't that complicated, so bear with us. (If you belong to the cognoscenti on this subject, see the sidebar "Background investigation reveals. . . .")

A style sheet defines design and layout information for documents. Usually, style sheets also specify fonts, colors, indentation, kerning, leading, margins, and even page dimensions for any document that invokes them.

In the publishing world, style sheets are indispensable. Style sheets enable numerous people to collaborate. All participants can work at their own systems, independently of other team members. When the pieces of a project are brought together, the final product derives a consistent look and feel (or design and layout, if you prefer "typographically correct" language), because a common template — what style sheets are often called in the print industry — ensures a common definition for the resulting final document.

Consistency is a highly desirable characteristic in final products for both print and electronic (online) documents. The W3C has therefore made a gallant effort to incorporate such consistency on the Web by introducing style sheets. With the use of Web style sheets, an entire site can look nearly the same on every platform, within any browser that supports style sheets. For Web authors who want to create consistent documents, this promises a vast improvement over the current, somewhat more chaotic, status quo.

A second issue that arises out of proprietary non-SGML-compliant HTML extensions is *browser envy*. Since Netscape introduced proprietary markup in 1994, other vendors — such as Microsoft and NCSA — introduced gimmicks and flashy additions to their own browsers. All this work has been expended in hopes that those browsers that can display proprietary Web documents correctly will draw the largest customer bases. This conflict has spawned some exciting and eye-catching HTML, but it has caused more harm than good. Incompatible HTML, stifled competition, and narrow-minded browser development is just some of the fallout from this battle.

Background investigation reveals. . . .

As you no doubt know, HTML is both a subset and a superset of SGML. If you don't know what this means, take a quick look online at `www.w3.org/pub/WWW/MarkUp/`.

Scroll down to the SGML link in the Related Resources section (or read the introductory chapters in this book). The Document Type Definitions (DTDs) that define how HTML works are written using a Backus-Naur Format (BNF) grammar notation. For more information, please visit

```
cuiwww.unige.ch/db-research/
Enseignement/analyseinfo/
AboutBNF.html
```

These original DTDs were designed to keep HTML within the confines of SGML. But recently, HTML's DTDs have been modified to allow non-SGML functionality. For many standards-obedient programmers and designers, this violates proper programming and design. For those interested in extending HTML's capabilities, it's a breath of fresh air (and function).

Web-based style sheets offer a promising solution to this situation. Style sheets allow proper separation of a document's structure and content from its form and appearance. With the implementation of style sheets, HTML can return to handling document structure and content (and get back to being proper SGML); style sheets can handle document form and appearance.

The separation of form and content allows authors and users to influence the presentation of documents without losing software or device independence. It also lessens the need for new HTML tags, either proprietary and standard, to support more sophisticated layout or appearance controls. Every possible layout or design element in a document can be defined by an attached — that is, linked — style sheet. This reduces the pressure to add tags and controls directly to HTML, when this capability becomes a matter of style.

Cascading Style Sheets (CSS1)

Today, the first version of the CSS standard, known as CSS1, is not quite an official standard, but it is so nearly complete that any forthcoming changes promise to be minor and cosmetic, rather than sweeping or major. Rather than explore its details completely, we discuss its key concepts to help you appreciate its capabilities. We also use a style sheet in the sample Web site included on our CD-ROM to heighten your appreciation of their use.

One of CSS1's fundamental features is its assumption that multiple, related style sheets can *cascade,* which means that authors can attach preferred style sheets to Web documents, yet readers can associate their own personal style sheets to those same documents, to correct for human or technological handicaps. Thus, a print-handicapped reader could override an author's type distinctions between 10 and 12 point sizes, accommodating that reader's need for 40-point type. Likewise, local limitations on resolution or display area might override original layouts and type styles.

Basically, CSS contains a set of rules to resolve style conflicts that arise when applying multiple style sheets to the same document. Because conflicts are bound to arise, some method of resolution is essential to make the content of a document appear properly on a user's display.

The specifics of these rules depend on the assignment of a numeric weight to represent the relative importance of each style item. You accomplish this by assigning a value between 1 (least important) and 100 (most important) for a particular style element when it's referenced in a style sheet.

To prevent users' preferences from being completely overridden by a document's author, never set style-item weights to the maximum setting of 100. Keeping the settings low enables users to override settings at will, which is especially helpful for visually handicapped users who may require all characters to be at least 36 point, or who may demand special text-to-speech settings.

After all the referenced style sheets and their alterations are loaded into memory, the browser resolved conflicts by applying the definition with the greatest weight and ignoring other definitions.

For example, assume that a document's author creates a style for a level-1 heading, <H1>, using the color red and assigns that rule a weight of 75. Further assume that the reader has defined a style for <H1>, colored blue with a weight of 55. In that case, a CSS-enabled browser uses the author's definition, because it has the greater weight.

You can incorporate CSS into a Web document using one or more of four methods. The following code fragment illustrates all four of these methods:

```
<HEAD>
  <TITLE>title</TITLE>
  <LINK REL=STYLESHEET TYPE="text/css"
    HREF="http://www.style.org/cool" TITLE="Cool">
  <STYLE TYPE="text/css">
    @import "http://www.style.org/basic"
```

```
      H1 { color: blue }
    </STYLE>
</HEAD>
<BODY>
   <H1>Headline is blue</H1>
   <P STYLE="color: green">While the paragraph is green.
</BODY>
```

You see all four CSS implementation methods:

- ✔ Using the <LINK> tag to link an external style sheet (line 3 of the preceding listing).
- ✔ Using <STYLE> inside the <HEAD> section (lines 5 through 8).
- ✔ Importing a style sheet using the CSS @import notation (line 6).
- ✔ Using the STYLE attribute in an element inside the <BODY> section (line 12).

Other benefits of the CSS implementation of style sheets include

- ✔ **Grouping:** You can group multiple style elements or definitions together as follows:

  ```
  H1 {font-size: 12pt; line-height: 14pt; font-family:
         Helvetica}
  ```

- ✔ **Inheritance:** Any nested tags inherit the style-sheet definitions assigned to the parent tag, unless you explicitly redefine the same elements. For example, in the HTML line

  ```
  <H1>The headline <EM>is</EM> important!</H1>
  ```

  if you define <H1> to display in red, then the text enclosed by <EM> also displays in red, unless you specifically assign <EM> another color.

- ✔ **Alternative Selectors:** Post-HTML 2.0 includes CLASS and ID attributes for most HTML tags. You can use these to define subsets or alternative sets of tags defined by a style sheet. For example:

  ```
  <HEAD>
    <TITLE>Title</TITLE>
    <STYLE TYPE="text/css">
      H1.punk { color: #00FF00 }
    </STYLE>
  </HEAD>
  <BODY>
   <H1>Not green</H1>
   <H1 CLASS=punk>Way too green</H1>
  </BODY>
  ```

✔ **Context-Sensitive Selectors:** CSS also supports context-based style definition. This is best described using an example:

```
<STYLE>
  UL UL LI    { font-size: small }
  UL UL UL LI { font-size: x-small }
</STYLE>
```

Following this notation, the second and third nested unnumbered lists (`<UL>`) use increasingly smaller font sizes.

✔ **Comments:** You can add comments inside a style sheet using the common C language syntax: `/* comment */`.

Style's Got Pros and Cons

The CSS1 standard includes some amazing features and capabilities, most of which mean little until you see them in action. Not every aspect of CSS1 is perfect, but to incline you further toward a positive outlook on style sheets, consider these other benefits of CSS1:

✔ The viewer can turn style sheets on and off.

✔ Style element definitions replace nonstandard tags.

✔ You can hide most complicated presentation markup within style sheets, instead of embedding it in documents, which results in cleaner HTML markup.

✔ You can use one style sheet for multiple HTML documents, making it easier to create consistent styles across a collection of pages.

✔ Both authors and readers can create new, previously impossible Web layouts.

Before you get too excited, though, we feel compelled to bring you back to earth by pointing out that CSS lacks a few items that you may consider important:

✔ **No absolute enforcement.** Any user has the option to turn off styles or use a style sheet with higher weights. Authors do not have absolute control over the display of their creations on other systems.

✔ **No multiple columns or overlapping frames.** Styles cannot define overlapping `<FRAME>`s, or assign the number of columns in a `<TABLE>` layout. In other words, such definitions must still be hard-coded in HTML documents and cannot be tweaked in a style sheet.

✔ **No query language.** Users have no way to figure out what a style looks or acts like by asking for a definition from some kind of all-knowing style-sheet facility. Inspection is the only way to get that information.

A Bit of Speculation

You may find these other stylish things of interest. The W3C's goal is to create a platform-independent method to control the appearance of a Web document. With CSS1, the W3C took a big step in that direction, but other issues remain unresolved.

✔ Some parties have voiced interest in creating a public style-sheet server, where standard, general-use style sheets can reside. Doing so would encourage users to use widely accepted and broadly compatible style sheets. Although creating a core set of style sheets as a basis for most Web creations is a good idea, this kind of forced conformity can provoke a style-sheet standards battle among industry leaders (think Beta versus VHS). Also, the load placed on a "worldwide style-sheet server" could be overwhelming, even with lots of mirror sites — further diminishing bandwidth available on the Internet.

✔ A second, often-discussed issue is the extra lag or transfer time associated with long, complex style sheets. It's not hard to imagine a style sheet (`<LINK>`ed or included in the `<HEAD>`) as big as 50K, especially if an author is "layout happy." Although authors should practice restraint, using common style sheets or the same style sheet over an entire Web site shouldn't significantly increase the time needed to transfer and view Web pages. After a `<LINK>`ed or `@imported` style sheet is cached, it can be quickly recalled whenever needed.

✔ A third and extremely important issue is media-specific style sheets. Most Web content is designed for presentation through a graphical browser viewed on a computer monitor. The influences of the Web are quickly expanding beyond pixel-based displays, however. Print, fax, Braille, audio, and other media must also be considered for Web content.

Ideas for implementing media-specific style sheets include on-the-fly style cascades, standardized formats available on Web servers, and native browser support for alternate media. These areas of style-sheet standardization are sure to attract a lot of attention in upcoming months.

CSS1 has made a significant impact on the Web, even before the standard has become final. Stay tuned to your favorite Web developer or Internet news provider for the latest updates and implementations. As always, for the latest style-sheet specification information, turn to the W3C's style-sheet pages at `www.w3.org/Style`.

Chapter 14

The Map's the Thing!

*I*f you're interested in this chapter, you already know how to insert graphics into your HTML documents using the `<IMG>` tag. And you probably have seen examples of using graphics as hypertext links within anchor tags (`<A HREF=...><IMG SRC=...></A>`). In this chapter, we show you how to take the next logical step and treat a graphic as a collection of selectable regions, each of which points to a different hypertext link or resource.

Where Are You? (Using Clickable Maps)

Geographically speaking, a map takes a land mass and divides it up along boundaries into named regions: Typically, these regions might be countries, counties, or other territories. When it comes to using graphics this way on the Web, the boundaries should be obvious in the displayed graphic, where users simply select whatever portion of the graphic attracts their interest. Users familiar with graphical interfaces have no trouble interacting with buttons, icons, and other kinds of interface controls. Graphical maps add this capability to a single image displayed on a Web page.

In Web-speak, such graphical maps are usually called *image maps* or *clickable maps*. We prefer the latter term, because it emphasizes the important aspects of this graphical element:

✔ Clickable maps break a graphic into discrete regions that function as a collection of individual hyperlinks.

✔ Users can select regions by putting the cursor inside the desired region and clicking the mouse.

You should already have a clue about the fundamental limitation inherent in a clickable map: It absolutely requires a GUI browser. The image that represents the map and drives the selection process isn't visible in a character-mode browser. Therefore, if you use clickable maps, you must implement alternate navigation methods for users with text-only browsers.

An example of a clickable map should lend some reality to this concept. Figure 14-1 shows the home page graphic for the third edition of *HTML For Dummies* (it appears in the file named ht4menum.gif in the /graphics subdirectory on the CD-ROM). This graphic features a set of buttons at the bottom, where each button contains a major access category for that set of *HTML For Dummies* pages. As part of a set of Web pages for the third edition of this book, it acts as the gateway to a page, or set of pages, for each category or topic mentioned.

Figure 14-1:
The *HTML For Dummies* home page (server version) includes a row of buttons on the bottom.

In this chapter, you see how to set up an image as a clickable map and how to use it to drive page navigation. Please note: The approach that we used to build the identical graphic for the pages on the CD-ROM breaks the image into pieces. The top part of the graphic represents one piece (ht4logoi.gif), and each button has its own associated icon file. We did this because a local HTML file cannot use a server-side image map. This restriction exists because there's no server in the background to map the user's selection coordinates into a corresponding URL. Instead, each button's icon is directly linked to a URL, and clicking a graphical element automatically selects the right link.

Cosmic Cartography: What It Takes to Present Maps on the Web

Building a clickable map requires three ingredients:

- ✔ **Creating (or selecting) a usable image:** This image can be an existing graphic or a custom-built one. Our *HTML For Dummies* button bar uses five custom-built icons, one for each button.

- ✔ **Creating the *map file:*** This requires a step-by-step investigation of the image file inside a graphics program that gives you the pixel addresses (coordinates) of each point on the boundary of the regions you want to create (or use of a map-building utility, like the one we mention later in this chapter).

  Our icons are all about the same size, so working through this process is easy: The image starts in the upper-left corner of the button bar (at vertical location 142, or about the middle of this 285-pixel-high image) and is consistently 143 pixels high. The individual buttons vary slightly in width, producing the following set of coordinates:

  ```
  ( 0,142)---( 99,142)------(199,142)------(299,142)-----(399,142)---(499,142)
  |          |              |              |             |            |
  |  button 1 |   button 2   |   button 3   |   button 4  |  button 5  |
  |          |              |              |             |            |
  ( 0,285)---( 99,285)------(199,285)------(299,285)-----(399,285)---(499,285)
  ```

  Unfortunately, the only way to produce this collection of numbers is to view the graphic inside a graphics program that shows pixel coordinates (we used Paint Shop Pro 4.12, a widely available shareware graphics program for Windows), or to use an image-map construction program.

  If you use an image-map tool, it generates a map after you tell it what kind of shapes you're outlining. One example is Tom Boutell's excellent program, called Mapedit, which builds map files at your command. It's available for Mac, DOS/Windows, and UNIX. To find a suitable version, use "Mapedit" as a search string in your favorite Web search engine (a quick jump to Yahoo! turned up more than 40 sites that offer one or more versions of this program).

- ✔ **Establishing the right HTML information in your page:** You must link an image, its map file, and a CGI script to decode map coordinates and use that information to select an appropriate link to follow.

Here, we take you through the concepts of making this work in your HTML document. Later, we show you how to build a complete back-end CGI script to translate the pixel coordinates for a user's map selection into a corresponding HTML link. In this chapter, we only cover the techniques and generalities needed to construct the image map and to create links between map regions and hypertext documents or resources.

By obtaining the information for the images and map files and establishing a convention to call the script that handles coordinate-to-link translation, you have most of what you need to know to set up a clickable map.

We suggest that you use the same name for the image map as for its related script: Thus, if the image is named `ht4menum.gif`, the script would be called `ht4menum.map`, or simply `ht4menum`. If your scripts reside in a CGI directory one level down from your HTML files, the URL for this script would then be `/cgi-bin/ht4menum.map`.

Warning: Different maps for different servers

Unfortunately, the two most popular httpd servers — NCSA and CERN — differ on clickable map formats. You find differences when defining image maps for one kind of server versus the other. You also find Web servers that won't support either format, especially if they're not UNIX-based. (Windows NT supports more than 20 Web servers. Some Web servers use their own proprietary image-map formats. The leading Macintosh Web server — WebSTAR — supports NCSA format.)

To make a clickable map work, stick within the requirements of the server where the map resides. If you don't know those requirements, contact your local webmaster — or at least, the system administrator for your Web server. The administrator should be able to set you straight right away and can probably help you find some useful information about how to build clickable maps for your system, above and beyond what we tell you here.

Throughout this chapter, where differences between CERN and NCSA requirements exist, we fill you in. If you're not using an httpd server of either variety, you may want to investigate your server's requirements immediately and adjust our examples and recommendations to meet those requirements!

Dealing with shapes in maps

You can use various ways to identify boundaries when assembling coordinates to build a clickable map. Both CERN and NCSA image-map definitions recognize the following regions:

- ✔ **Circle:** (Specified by the coordinates for a point at the center and the number of pixels for the radius.) Use this to select a circular (or nearly circular) region within an image.

- ✔ **Rectangle:** (Specified by the coordinates for the upper-left and lower-right corners.) Use this to select a square or rectangular region in your image. (This is the one we use in our button-bar map.)

- ✔ **Polygon:** (Specified by the coordinates for the point at the vertex of each edge.) Use this to outline the boundaries of regularly or irregularly shaped regions that aren't circular or rectangular. Although it takes more effort, the more points you pick to define the outline, the more the region behaves as the user expects it to when clicking.

- ✔ **Point:** (Specified by its x and y coordinates.) Use this only when a specific point is easy to select. (A point is usually too small a region on screen and requires exact control to select — we recommend surrounding a point with a small circle or square so users can be a little sloppy.) We've never actually used a point reference in an image map, except as the vertices for a polygon, rectangle, or center of a circle.

Selecting boundaries for map regions determines the selection of the related links. Even though users see a nicely shaped graphic to click, what really drives selection is the areas you outline on top of that graphic.

The better a map's regions fit an image, the more the map behaves as users expect! The moral of the story is: Take your time and, when in doubt, pick more points to outline something, rather than less. Even better, use a tool that follows your cursor movement to build the map for you. We mentioned Tom Boutell's Mapedit program earlier; other alternatives galore abound on the Web.

For example, an image-map tool called MapMaker is available at

```
icg.stwing.upenn.edu/~mengwong/mapmaker.html
```

If you provide the tool with a URL for a graphic you want to map, the tool can guide you through the rest of the process using your very own Web browser!

Building and Linking to CERN Map Files

Map files for CERN httpd servers take a form that looks like this:

```
circle (x,y) r URL
rectangle (x1,y1) (x2,y2) URL
polygon (x1,y1) (x2, y2) (x3,y3) ... (xn,yn) URL
point (x,y) URL
default URL
```

The shapes are pretty much self-evident, except for the polygon, which represents an attempt to trace a region's outline by connecting a series of points. If this sounds like connect-the-dots, you've got the concept!

Don't forget to close your polygons; make sure that the last segment fills the gap between your last point and your first.

Another entry that might seem mysterious is the default URL: Define a default so that if users click an undefined location in the map, they choose a fail-safe. A default can be a script that sends a message back that says, "Click within the lines!" or "You have selected an area of the image that is not defined. Please try again."

The menu bar map file

Thus, for our menu bar example, the CERN map is

```
rectangle (0,142) (98,285) http://www.domain.com/html4dum/
          ftpstuff.htm
rectangle (99,142) (198,285) http://www.domain.com/
          html4dum/contents.htm
rectangle (199,142) (298,285) http://www.domain.com/
          html4dum/search4d.htm
rectangle (299,142) (398,285) http://www.domain.com/
          html4dum/contact.htm
rectangle (399,142) (499,285) http://www.domain.com/
          html4dum/whatsnew.htm
default http://www.domain.com/html4dum/contents.htm
```

Because the button bar is a collection of rectangles, defining its coordinates is easy. (Why do you think we picked this example?) Then we provide a default link to a contents page if somebody insists on staying outside the boxes that we gave them to play in! Notice, too, that we use absolute URLs. Absolute URLs make maps easier to debug and relocate.

Using map files

To use a map file with the CERN httpd, your system must already have a program that handles image maps. The name of this program, which is included with the CERN httpd materials, is *htimage*. You must have htimage installed if you plan to use image maps on your system. After it's available, you must also know how to invoke it. For the purposes of this example, we assume it lives on the directory path `/cgi-bin/`.

Building and Linking to NCSA Map Files

Map files for NCSA servers, look much like those for CERN servers, but there are some differences. NCSA map files take a form that looks like this:

```
circle URL x,y r
rect URL x1,y1 x2,y2
poly URL x1,y1 x2,y2 x3,y3 ... xn,yn
point URL x,y
default URL
```

The shapes are the same as the CERN varieties and the same kinds of coordinates define them. But names are shorter, and URLs come first (instead of last) in the list of attributes. Here again, defaults work the same way: to provide a handler for people who click outside the image frame.

The button-bar map file

For the *HTML For Dummies* graphic, the NCSA map is

```
rect http://www.domain.com/html4dum/ftpstuff.htm (0,142)
          (98,285)
rect http://www.domain.com/html4dum/contents.htm (99,142)
          (198,285)
rect http://www.domain.com/html4dum/search4d.htm (199,142)
          (298,285)
rect http://www.domain.com/html4dum/contact.htm (299,142)
          (398,285)
rect http://www.domain.com/html4dum/whatsnew.htm (399,142)
          (499,285)
default http://www.domain.com/html4dum/contents.htm
```

Except for a change in the shape's name (rect instead of rectangle) and reordering the arguments (URLs first, then coordinates), the map is identical to the CERN variety.

Using map files

Like CERN, to use a map file with the NCSA httpd, a system must already have a program that handles image maps. The name of this program, which comes with the NCSA httpd materials, is *mapper*. If it's not installed, you must have the program installed to use image maps on your system.

Also, check that you have the latest version. Version information appears at

```
hoohoo.ncsa.uiuc.edu/docs/setup/admin/imagemap.txt
```

If the file date is more recent at NCSA, download the new file, rename it to `imagemag.c`, and recompile. Use the new version instead of the old one.

After you have imagemap available, you must then invoke it on the server. For our example, we assume it lives in the `/cgi-bin/` directory.

Final Touches

No matter which type of Web server you use to host your image maps, they all have a few things in common.

Creating and storing map files

You can create a map file with any plain text editor. Store the map file on the server in a special directory for your map definition files. Contact your system administrator or your webmaster to find out where this is and if you have *write* permission. If you don't, you must enlist the administrator's help to get those files installed. For our examples, we use the name, `ht4menum.map`, and store it in the `http://www.domain.com/cgi-bin/` directory, with our other scripts.

Defining a clickable map in your HTML document

After you define a map and store it in the right location, you must bring all three elements together in an HTML file. Here's how:

```
<A HREF="http://www.lanw.com/cgi-bin/ht4menum.map">
<IMG SRC="graphics/ht4menum.gif" ISMAP>
</A>
```

Here's what's going on in this series of statements:

✔ The opening anchor tag combines the htimage location, which handles the coordinate-to-URL translation, with a full URL for the map file. Even though you see no space between the name of the program (htimage) and the file specification, the server still knows what to do.

✔ The IMG tag points to the button-bar graphic, but adds an ISMAP attribute to indicate that it's a clickable map.

✔ The closing anchor tag </A> indicates that the graphic specified by IMG is the target for the map file specified in the opening anchor tag.

There you are! After you make sure that all the right pieces are in place on your CERN server, you can try this, too.

"The Map Is Not the Territory"

Although Alfred Korzybski didn't know about clickable images when he uttered this section's title (in *Manhood of Humanity: The Science and Art of Human Engineering,* in case the question ever shows up on *Jeopardy!*), it's still a point worth pondering. Because not all users can see an image map, be prepared to show the same set of selections in text that GUI users get in visual form. How might you do this?

Because what you provide in an image map is a set of choices, you can also add an equivalent set of text-based links near the image. Here's what the HTML for this looks like:

```
<A HREF="http://www.lanw.com/cgi-bin/html4dum.map">
<IMG BORDER=0 ALIGN=TOP SRC="graphics/ht4menum.gif"
  ALT="Navigation Bar" ISMAP></A><P>
<IMG ALIGN=MIDDLE WIDTH=130 HEIGHT=0 SRC=graphics/space.gif
  ALT=" ">
<B><A HREF="ftpstuff.htm">FILES</A> &#32;&#124;
<A HREF="contents.htm">CONTENTS</A> &#32;&#124;
<A HREF="search4d.htm">SEARCH</A> &#32;&#124;
<A HREF="contact.htm">CONTACT</A> &#32;&#124;
<A HREF="whatsnew.htm">NEW</A><BR>
<IMG ALIGN=MIDDLE WIDTH=240 HEIGHT=0 SRC=graphics/space.gif
  ALT=" ">
<A HREF="navigate.htm">HOW TO NAVIGATE</A></B><P>
<A HREF="html4du2.htm">Click here for a non-imagemap
          version</A>
```

As shown in Figure 14-2, this creates a text bar (right beneath the graphic) that offers the same choices. Users with graphical browsers won't suffer from this redundancy, and character-mode browsers get a reasonable facsimile of what the graphically advantaged see in living color. We call this *mastering the art of compromise!*

Figure 14-2:
A text-based bar combined with a button bar keeps everybody in the know.

Of Clickable Maps and URLs

Image links can sometimes play hob with relative URLs within HTML documents. One unforeseen side effect of following links through a map-reading script — to the map and back to the target page — can be a complete mangling of the context within which URLs are addressed. In English, this means it's a really, really, really good idea to use full URLs, instead of relative references, in documents that include clickable maps.

You would be wise to be cagey when using relative URL references in documents with clickable maps. You must test this practice thoroughly to make sure everything works as it should, or use the <BASE> tag. Avoiding trouble is, in general, the best way to cure the URL relative reference blues!

Client-Side Image Maps!

A client-side image map is a graphical navigation tool that runs within the users' browsers and requires neither a server nor a CGI map file to operate. Both Netscape's and Microsoft's Web browsers support client-side image maps. Creating one is as easy as building a server-side image map.

Building a client-side image map involves

▶ Defining the hot spot areas of the image.

▶ Embedding the coordinates in an HTML document.

Possible area definitions include

▶ **Point** — `<AREA SHAPE="point" COORDS="x,y" HREF="URL1">`

▶ **Circle** — `<AREA SHAPE="circle" COORDS="x,y,x2,y2" HREF="URL2">`

▶ **Rectangle** — `<AREA SHAPE="rect" COORDS="x,y,x2,y2" HREF="URL3">`

▶ **Polygon** — `<AREA SHAPE="poly" COORDS="x,y,x2,y2,x3,y3,…" HREF="URL4">`

▶ **Default** — `<AREA SHAPE="default" HREF="URL5">`

You probably recognize all of these types except for circle. A circle's area is defined by a central point and a point on the circle's edge (which defines its radius). Coordinates are grouped together, separated by commas.

Slam a set of AREA tags inside a MAP tag associated with a properly labeled IMG tag, and you've built a client-side image map. Notice that we name a client-side image map using the NAME attribute of the MAP tag and reference it with the USEMAP attribute in the IMG tag. Here's an example:

```
<IMG SRC="HT4MEMU.GIF" USEMAP="#h4dmap">
<MAP NAME="h4dmap">
  <AREA SHAPE="rect" COORDS="0,142,98,285" HREF="http://
        www.domain.com/html4dum/ftpstuff.htm">
  <AREA SHAPE="rect" COORDS="99,142,198,285" HREF="http://
        www.domain.com/html4dum/contents.htm">
  <AREA SHAPE="rect" COORDS="199,142,298,285" HREF="http://
        www.domain.com/html4dum/search4d.htm">
  <AREA SHAPE="rect" COORDS="299,142,398,285" HREF="http://
        www.domain.com/html4dum/contact.htm">
  <AREA SHAPE="rect" COORDS="399,142,499,285" HREF="http://
        www.domain.com/html4dum/whatsnew.htm">
  <AREA SHAPE="default" HREF="http://www.domain.com/
        html4dum/contents.htm">
</MAP>
```

If you can master the art of cut and paste, you can use such simple map constructs in your own documents. Remember, client-side image maps don't need a map file (that information is included in the HTML) or a server (the client handles all map processing). If you want to see one in action, load up the front page of the example Web site from the book's CD-ROM and select "client-side image map version."

Note for Internet Explorer 3 for Macintosh users

You may find that HTML4DUM.HTM, which is on the CD-ROM, opens with graphics that appear cropped — that is, cut so that only a part of the title graphics appears at the top of the page. To resolve this, choose the client-side version of the page by clicking the client-side link in the loaded HTML4DUM.HTM file, or open the file HTML4DU2.HTM.

Given this flexibility, why use server-side image maps at all? Only one reason: Not all browsers support client-side image maps. But any graphical browser that can call a CGI can use a server-side image map. So be wary when switching to the client-side.

Remember, too, that character-mode browsers (or GUI browsers with graphics turned off) can handle image maps of any kind. So, even if you do take the plunge into client-side image maps, always provide a text alternative just as you would with a server-side equivalent. Either way, there has to be another way for the graphically disadvantaged to compensate!

In Chapter 15, we roll up our sleeves and start taking Web page navigation seriously — because traveling around a Web site is the name of this game, so you'd better buckle up!

Chapter 15
Navigation Aids

● ●

In This Chapter

▶ Searching for Web satisfaction

▶ Staying out of the maze

▶ Providing added document structure

▶ Doing things the database way

▶ Avoiding diminished returns

▶ Leading the search for good information

● ●

*I*f you think forms are where the fun is in HTML, prepare to enjoy yourself further. In this chapter, you discover additional techniques to make your documents searchable and your sites easier to surf, so that users can find what they want quickly and easily. Some of this is overkill for basic home pages, but wonderful for larger, more complex sites. In fact, without searchable versions of the HTML DTDs (Document Type Definitions), we couldn't have written this book.

You must help your potential readers find your Web site, and then help them move around easily within the site. While there are many ways to do this job, some of the best methods include

🖝 Improving the information that search engines gather about your site (using the `<META>` tag)

🖝 Working with intelligent robots (also called *Web spiders*)

🖝 Adding a search engine to your site

🖝 Adding a menu, a list of pages, an index, or a site map

🖝 Creating a *Wayfinding Toolkit*

🖝 Providing consistent navigation tools

You find out more about each of these techniques in the sections that follow.

The <META> Tag

The <META> tag is an HTML markup element that appears within the head of a document to define what's contained therein. That really sounds like a mouthful, but it's true. A <META> tag identifies meta-information or data about the content of a document. If you don't understand what we mean, take a peek at the examples in this section: They should clarify this concept.

The <META> tag is often used by browsers and Web automata (spiders, worms, wanderers, and so on) to gather information about Web sites. Browsers use this information to alter their displays, gather statistics, or even associate activities with commands. More commonly, however, search engine robots read <META> information and add it to their databases. When users perform searches with queries that match such <META> information, the results returned are more likely to be accurate and informative. In other words, when you use <META> tags, you improve the odds that search engine users find relevant information at your site.

Now that you know the <META> secret, you may want to add <META> tags to your documents. As a rule, place <META> tags in entry-point documents (that is, in documents where most users — or robots — enter your site).

The NAME and HTTP-EQUIV values are not predetermined by HTML DTDs and can be fully customized, which means that every search engine can define its own unique sets of metadata to collect and catalog. Nevertheless, we don't recommended that end users like you (yep — as a webmaster, you're just an end user compared to those who manage search engines and Web-tool sites) create any new or unused values for the <META> tag. In fact, you'd just be wasting your time since most search engines or other Web tools ignore items they don't recognize.

In the examples that follow, we show the most common NAME and HTTP-EQUIV values. We recommend that you stick with these. If you discover that a specific search engine or Web tool supports other strings, feel free to add those to your collection.

Rather than simply repeating the tag definition for <META> that appeared in Chapter 6, we skip the formalities and show you a few examples you can put to use in your own documents. Remember, a <META> tag must appear within the <HEAD> tag pair.

✔ Use this construction to indicate the creation date of the document:

```
<META NAME="creation_date"
CONTENT="DDD, DD MMM YYYY HH:MM:SS GMT">
```

✔ Use this construction to indicate the date the content expires, which tells a search engine when to remove stale documents from its database and to refresh this information:

```
<META HTTP-EQUIV="expires"
CONTENT="DDD, DD MMM YYYY HH:MM:SS GMT">
```

✔ Use this construction to supply keywords to search engines in addition to those found automatically by robots within the document itself:

```
<META NAME="keywords"
CONTENT="keyword1 keyword2 keyword3">
```

✔ Use this construction to supply an e-mail address for the author or individual responsible for the document:

```
<META HTTP-EQUIV="reply-to"
CONTENT="username@email.domain.name">
```

✔ Use this construction to indicate the author's name:

```
<META NAME="author" CONTENT="Name">
```

✔ Use this construction to indicate the document's resource type (common values include document, catalog, bibliography, and news release):

```
<META HTTP-EQUIV="resource-type" CONTENT="document">
```

✔ Use this construction to define a description to be used by search engines that support this tag:

```
<META NAME="description" CONTENT="text">
```

✔ Use this construction to indicate the scope or range of a document's distribution or application (common values include global, domestic, local, or private):

```
<META HTTP-EQUIV="distribution" CONTENT="scope">
```

✔ Use this construction to indicate the program used to generate a document, such as the name of the HTML editor used:

```
<META NAME="generator" CONTENT="program name">
```

✔ Use this construction to indicate a document's copyright holder and date:

```
<META HTTP-EQUIV="copyright" CONTENT="name @hy date">
```

✔ Use this construction to force a document to reload or a new document to load after a specific number of seconds:

```
<META HTTP-EQUIV="REFRESH" CONTENT="value[; URL]">
```

Tada! That's the `<META>` tag in a nutshell. Go ahead and use it!

There's a Spider on the Web!

If you think of the Web as a vast, gossamer skein of interconnected documents around the world, you're close to visualizing its basic topology. But knowing how the strands are arranged is only half the picture. You must also understand about the denizens that inhabit this cyberspace realm.

Webcrawlers and search engines

In addition to the vast multitude of users happily browsing their way through a myriad of links, cyberbeasts frolic through the Web as well. Some are computer programs called *robots* or *spiders* that do nothing but follow links around the Web — to see where they lead — and catalog and categorize what they find along the way.

The best known spiders lurk behind popular search engine sites at

- Yahoo!: Guide to the WWW: www.yahoo.com
- Infoseek Net Search: www.infoseek.com
- AltaVista: www.altavista.com

We mention search engines several times in this book, most notably in Chapter 14. No matter whether you call them spiders, robots, Webcrawlers, or "Hey, you!" these tireless, automatic searchers use <META> tag information, document titles, headings, and the first paragraph of text within the documents they visit to catalog and report on what they find. Search engines compile and manage the information that these spiders report. Then, humans use engines to search these catalogs when seeking Web sites of interest.

If your Web site appears in all major Web search databases, you're more likely to attract a large number of users. Because the number of Web sites surpassed 10 million in 1997, users have lots of variety to choose from! If yours is listed at a search site, this often increases the number of visitors, because your site is more visible to the public.

Don't wait for the spider to come to you — register!

Most Web search engines offer methods to register your site, or at least to supply them with its URL. Make sure that you register or list your site at all possible locations. Such listings shouldn't cost anything, and they don't take much time or effort, either. You may elect to pay for listings at numerous online *malls* if you like their exposure and can afford their charges. These malls aren't used nearly as much as free search engines, but if you're in a specialized niche, one or more of them may be right up your alley (find them by searching for "mall" or "market place" with any of the free search engines).

Keeping Bugs Away

Just because spiders can find every document on the Web doesn't mean they should. All too often, automated robots on the Internet find their way into areas of Web sites that the owners would rather not have indexed or accessed from outside. In such cases, the only way to prevent robots from finding hidden treasures is to tell them to stay away. Fortunately, you have two ways to do this: First, use a special `<META>` tag to discourage robots; or second, create a `robots.txt` file to control robot activities at your site.

We encourage you to find out how to put these conventions into practice. Complete details on both of these methods appear on the Web Robots Pages at

```
info.webcrawler.com/mak/projects/robots/robots.html
```

<META> content

The `<META>` tag markup defines how robots should deal with any specific document. For example, the following markup prevents robots from indexing or analyzing links that might appear therein:

```
<META NAME="ROBOTS" CONTENT="NOINDEX, NOFOLLOW">
```

Using various `CONTENT` values, you can specify a different level of activity for each document:

- ✔ `INDEX` — index the document
- ✔ `NOINDEX` — do not index the document
- ✔ `FOLLOW` — analyze the links in the document
- ✔ `NOFOLLOW` — do not analyze the links in the document
- ✔ `ALL` — `INDEX, FOLLOW`
- ✔ `NONE` — `NOINDEX, NOFOLLOW`

Note that such values pertain only to documents they appear in. Adding a `<META>` tag to one document does not affect the activity of the robot for other documents. Note also that the `<META>` tag is not as widely supported as the Robot Exclusion Protocol covered in the next section.

Robots go home!

The `robots.txt` file uses a scripting language called the Robots Exclusion Protocol. This protocol allows you to restrict all, or part, of your Web site from all robots, or merely from specific robots. For example, a `robots.txt` file that contains the following code restricts all robots from visiting the `CGI-BIN` and `TMP` directories:

```
User-agent: *
Disallow: /cgi-bin/
Disallow: /tmp/
```

This next example restricts all but one robot:

```
User-agent: WebCrawler
Disallow:
User-agent: *
Disallow: /
```

As you can see, if you take the time to learn the syntax of the Robots Exclusion Protocol, it offers a simple solution to the issues of robot control. Most robots are programmed to recognize and follow this protocol. We recommend using this technique to control their activities on your Web site.

Searching Documents for Details . . .

The latest versions of Web robots and crawlers don't delve deeply into the contents of every document they find. In computer lingo, they search broadly (go everywhere and grab one or a few items from each site) but not deeply (they don't catalog the entire contents for every site). They'll probably find your site, but consider yourself lucky if you get more than your home page indexed and listed in their search engines. If your site contains large, complex documents, you might need to install a different kind of search tool locally to make it easier for serious researchers to find what they seek.

The functionality required is the electronic equivalent of an index for a book: a list of key words, topics, or phrases with pointers to their locations within documents at your site. Fortunately for you, this technology is easy to deploy, because your documents are already in electronic format and merely require a bit of extra massaging to accommodate such use.

As a budding Web author, you may wonder what you have to do to add this kind of capability to your documents. We can give you two kinds of answers to this question. (And you can also see our discussion of CGI programs in Extra 2 on the CD-ROM.)

✔ **In nontechnical terms:** You have to create an index to your document and then figure out how to link that index to the actual content.

✔ **In technical terms:** You must do the following:

1. **Add** <ISINDEX> **to your document's** <HEAD> ... </HEAD> **section.**

2. **Use a database or some similar program to build an index of keywords and phrases for your document.**

3. **Identify all the index words as anchors for hypertext links in your document (so that the index can take you to those words and phrases).**

4. **Establish the anchors in your document.**

5. **Create a CGI program to handle user requests for keywords or phrases; the program should build a list of links for each corresponding instance in the document.**

Basically, the way this works is that you turn on search capability in a user's browser (where available) by including an <ISINDEX> tag in a document's head section. Then, provide a URL for an input-handling CGI program that builds search responses for users with specific requests. This program uses the electronic equivalent of an index — a list of keywords and phrases with pointers to their locations in the document's text — to respond to queries. These responses consist of HTML documents, with links to URLs in your document set where the requested keywords or phrases reside.

As programming problems go, this one is not too bad. You do have to locate or build an indexing tool to prepare the data files that you search in response to user queries. These data files usually consist of alphabetized (or ASCII-collated) lists of the keywords and phrases that your index recognizes. If you build your program so that it returns information for unsuccessful searches ("String not found" is good; a list of near-matches is even better), you can field some of the weird nonsequiturs that bored users may sometimes be tempted to try on your indexing program.

Then you can use the CGI program that searches the list to build an HTML document that lists *hits* in order of occurrence, with links to various URLs for documents where matches were found. This creates a hotlist of such locations that your users can select to find the information they seek.

We also suggest pulling some surrounding text from each part of the document where a hit occurs and writing that to your *return page* with your CGI program as well. Including surrounding text lets users understand some of the context in which a hit occurs and helps them to decide which links they really want to follow.

For an outstanding example of what a well-organized index offers, please investigate the searchable version of the HTML 2.0 specification available at the following URL:

```
hopf.math.nwu.edu:80/html2.0/dosearch.html
```

This document is the work of the HTML working group, an Internet Engineering Task Force (IETF) group focused on packaging HTML DTDs and specifications into Internet RFCs.

The Bigger Things Get, The Easier It Is to Get Lost!

Why are indexing tools worthwhile? Because finding your way around complex collections of information — like the HTML specifications and related DTDs — can get hairy without computer-aided help. Here's a good rule for deciding whether you need indexing: If your site has more than 30 documents, start thinking about indexing!

Indexing is also valuable for sites containing large documents that cover government rules or regulations. By their very nature, these documents are best displayed in single files, even though they may be hundreds of screens long. Readers of large documents greatly appreciate searchable indexes!

If you're worried about how much work is involved, don't be. If you ask, "Do I have to get into heavy database programming and implement all the functionality mentioned in the preceding section, just to make my document searchable?" the answer (fortunately) is "No."

In fact, using the first type of search engine we mentioned at the beginning of this chapter — the kind that looks for documents based on titles — we came up with a number of pointers to help you get started on this kind of effort for your own materials. Using the following search query to the Yahoo! search engine,

```
search.yahoo.com/bin/search?p=indexing
```

we came up with a number of tools and locations that we can recommend for further investigation.

✔ Indexmaker is a Perl script that produces an index for a virtual document consisting of a number of HTML files in a single directory. (This is the tool used to build the searchable HTML DTD's that helped us write this book.)

```
hopf.math.nwu.edu/docs/utility.html#indexmaker
```

✔ For inclusion in an online searchable index at the MIT Artificial Intelligence Laboratory, try this URL.

```
www.cs.indiana.edu/item-index/intro.html
```

✔ For local indexing and related services, please consult this URL.

```
www.ai.mit.edu/tools/site-index.html
```

✔ Finally, here's the URL for a whole page of information about indexing and related tools.

```
union.ncsa.uiuc.edu/HyperNews/get/www/indexing.html
```

Rest assured that somewhere in the haystack of information we've just shared with you is the needle you may be seeking. Plus, it's no accident that the tool we admired most shows up first on the list! The Yahoo! search engine is a great magnet for finding that needling program in the cyberhaystack!

Documentary Integuments: Indexes, Jump Tables, and Internal Links

You've already heard this before, but we're compelled to remind you that as documents get bigger and more complicated, more structure is needed. That's one reason why we think indexes are a great idea. But it's also why you should make liberal and extensive use of internal links in documents, to help your readers navigate without having to scroll, scroll, scroll.

Starting off a long document with a hyperlinked table of contents is a really good idea; it acts like a "jump table" to provide an immediate way to get your users from a list of topics to the real thing with the click of the mouse. Also, breaking long blocks of text into regular screenfuls of information, coupled with navigation controls (which range from navigation bars to full-blown clickable image maps with nice-looking 3-D buttons) really helps users keep from getting lost in your Web. Explicit document navigation controls should never be more than a screenful of information away. (Even better is keeping a control always in sight.)

Searchable indexes can help readers in search of specific information, which is why they naturally complement our recommended frequency of navigation controls. Searchable indexes are more difficult to implement, but if your content is appropriate, that's life. Users will show their appreciation by returning time and again to your site, and they will bring their friends.

Doing Things the Database Way

For long and complex documents (governmental regulations, tax codes, how to build an aircraft carrier, and so on), the best way to manage information is with a database. Whether you decide to operate within a document management program, or use a tool to build your own set of document controls, when the number of files you must manage exceeds 100, you'll appreciate getting some mechanical help and organization. Plus, the ability to search files on keywords or specific text makes finding things easier. (We won't even mention the other nice things a good database can do, like search and replace, automatic updates, and so on.)

This added level of structure and control costs you, to be sure, but it's worth considering because of the time and effort that it can save you and your users. If you don't believe us, try managing a huge, intertwined collection of files without computer assistance for even a brief time. You'll sing a different tune after dealing with changes galore by hand.

Stay Away from Diminishing Returns

On the other hand, you can go overboard when organizing your materials. The temptation may be nearly overwhelming to break your documents into perfectly formatted single screens of beautifully laid-out information for your user's enjoyment. Before you succumb to this impulse, remember the following "home truths" about the Web:

- ✔ All those beautiful graphics and on-screen controls aren't visible with character-mode browsers.

- ✔ What looks wonderful to you through your Super-Geewhiz 3-D VR Metaverse goggles looks pretty drab to the guy down the hall running the third version back of Cello or Mosaic on a plain VGA monitor.

> ✔ When aiming for perfection, the "last 10 percent" usually costs as much — and takes as much time to achieve — as the first 90 percent. Don't waste your time making the excellent look sublime; you have better ways of filling your days (we hope)! Concentrate on content if you really want to better your site.

As thrilling as the quest for a perfect page may be, it's usually not worth the effort. And, if the people who pay the bills (and your salary) find out about your costly quest for the "Holy Web Grail," even being penitent may not help you escape their wrath. Remember the words of the mystic sage upon seeing the infinite majesty of the Universe: "Enough already!"

Virtual Compass

One revolutionary addition to your Web site that you (and everyone else) should include in your Web navigation arsenal is called a *Wayfinding Toolkit*. This little gem is a tutorial, a help file, and a set of navigation instructions all rolled into one handy set of pages on a site. Of course, we think highly of the Wayfinding Toolkit because we pioneered the concept. Even so, we think you and your users will find this a worthwhile addition to most Web sites. And we cheerfully admit we stole the concept from the folks who build airports, amusement parks, and other venues where lots of people pass through and, therefore, need help finding their way around.

To see a Wayfinding Toolkit in action, visit our LANWrights Web site at

```
www.lanw.com/
```

Click on the world icon labeled "Site Overview" for more details.

As you can see, we include a list of the major sections for our site and describe what each one contains. Furthermore, we display and explain every navigational control used in the site. You needn't limit yourself to these two topics: Go ahead and include any relevant information or instructions that may help people find their way around your site. Anything you can do to simplify access or speed a user toward "the good stuff" will be rewarded.

You can view other Wayfinding Toolkits we created by checking the pages we included on the CD that accompanies this book — just follow the Wayfinding Toolkit link on one of the main pages.

You can also visit one of these other sites for more examples of this genre:

```
www.lanw.com/training/myw/
www.lanw.com/training/ht96/
www.lanw.com/training/beh/
www.lanw.com/training/wpd/
```

To access any of these collections of pages, you need a frame-compatible browser. Once you load the home page, click the compass icon to visit the Wayfinding Toolkit.

Rack-and-Pinion Steering in Your Site

There's nothing worse than driving a car with a broken steering wheel — you don't have much control over where the vehicle goes; worse, you can't get around quickly, for fear of crashing. The same is true of Web sites that fail to offer reasonable navigation. Every site need not work the same way — that's the beauty of the Web. But every site should be easy to get around. Don't force users to guess where links are — make them obvious!

We don't care if you use text, icons, or image maps (or even Java or scripting, if you're so inclined and have spare time on your hands). Just make sure you use something to help visitors navigate your site. Here are a few rules about effective navigation:

✔ Be consistent.

✔ Use navigation controls to enhance your content.

✔ Let the content dictate the controls.

✔ Make things as simple as possible to maintain.

✔ If controls are complicated, explain them in detail.

If you need some examples, check out the Web site we included on the CD; it has a nice set of controls.

Also, check out some of these Web sites to see a few other possibilities:

```
www.lanw.com/
www.holodeck3.com/
www.unitedmedia.com/comics/dilbert/
```

Where's the Search Lead?

As the Web becomes more commonplace and its publishing model better understood, expect to see more tools to help add structure to your creations. Today, proper decorum suggests indexing larger, more complex documents with a linked table of contents or a searchable index.

In the not-too-distant future, you'll be able to orient users with animated tutorials and other amazing feats of technology. The trend is clear, though: more and better communications based on a shared model of what Web pages can deliver, along with shared toolsets to help realize those models.

With this metaphorical view through the cyberportal of tomorrow, however, we leave the tools and advanced capabilities of HTML and search engines behind. The next chapter dives back into the reality of Web publishing, moving on to tackle the nitty-gritty details of going live, online, with a Web site. Allez!

Chapter 16

Going Live with Your Web Site

In This Chapter

▶ Getting your creation ready for prime time

▶ Understanding the problems of relativity

▶ Getting spaced

▶ Doing the FTP thing from local to remote

▶ Performing a déjà vu investigation

*N*ow that you've spent countless hours creating the ultimate Web site, you must get onto a public Internet Web server so the world can benefit from your genius. This activity is both simple and complex, so you need to thoroughly understand it. In this chapter, we walk you through the arduous process from final refinement to public scrutiny.

Prelaunch Checklist

Before you even think about posting to a public site, you've got a bit of work to do. First and foremost, you must make absolutely sure that you are not distributing federally protected documentation or instructions on how to build the ultimate weapon. The tall guys with the gray suits, dark hats, and earphones really hate when you do that. Actually, long before you review your content one final time, you need to investigate a few other important aspects of your site, such as whether it really functions.

If you're reading this book and following the material sequentially, then you may want to check out Extra 3 on the CD-ROM, which covers the process of testing your Web pages. However, in the interest of public safety and to prevent the cyber-equivalent of running with scissors, we walk you through the major points again.

First, double-check your tags. Many issues related to markup are absolutely essential to the proper operation of your site. These include

- ✔ Spelling the tag and its attributes correctly.
- ✔ Using quotation marks when required.
- ✔ Using a closing tag for all tag pairs that require one.
- ✔ Using the proper order when nesting tags.
- ✔ Using the correct tag for the job.

Instead of abusing you by requiring you to recite this 12 times while riding a hippopotamus, we assume that you've got this tag stuff down pat.

Second, double-check your navigation. This check should inspect the existence and proper sequencing of your navigation and prove, beyond all shadow of doubt, that users can drill down deep into your site and still get back out. Here are a few things to look into:

- ✔ Does every page have navigation capabilities?
- ✔ Do the navigation controls get users to the proper locations?
- ✔ Does navigation actually work?
- ✔ Is it clear and obvious how to use the navigation controls?
- ✔ Can you reach every document using only the navigation controls?
- ✔ Have you provided a site map to orient visitors?

Great, now you and your visitors can travel in style with only minimal possibilities of getting lost in cyberspace. We've been lost before, and you wouldn't believe where you can end up — sometimes it's not pretty.

Third, you must have your ticket validated. If you didn't pick up on it before, you need to validate all your Web documents. Validation is the process of running an HTML syntax checker against your markup to determine if you followed all those construction and use rules that the latest HTML DTD defines. This ensures that your site is compatible with the widest range of browsers.

Finally, check your content for polyps. If we've said it a hundred times, we've said it a thousand: Focus on your content. After you solve all the problems of construction, syntax, and navigation, you've only cleared the way to deal with the most important part of your Web site — its content. Before you even consider placing your Web site in the public eye, you must reexamine your content and consider these questions carefully:

- ✔ Is it relevant?
- ✔ Does anyone other than you care about this material?

✔ Is it arranged in bite-sized pieces?

✔ Does the multimedia (graphics, sound, video, and animation) draw attention to or distract from the primary content?

✔ Does your site add any real value to the global collection of knowledge?

We don't aim to burst anyone's bubble, but why should someone waste valuable Internet bandwidth distributing worthless gibberish if someone else can use that same bandwidth to distribute information about the plight of the endangered red horny-toed lizard? Make your content count!

All in the Family

Now we come to something good! Did you read the discussion about absolute and relative URLs in Chapter 15? If not, go back and read it. Anyway, we repeat the important bits here if you stick around, but if you want to go flipping pages or scrutinizing the index, go ahead — we'll wait for you right here when you return.

You have two schools of thought on how to name URLs in Web sites. The first claims that using absolute URLs is most reliable, and the second claims that relative URLs are the only way to go. We lean toward the relative side, but we sympathize with those on the wrong . . . er, we mean *other* . . . side.

The use of absolute URLs in a Web site offers you the solid and reassuring knowledge that every link points directly and only to the intended document or resource. Even if a user downloads one of your HTML documents, whenever they click a link, it will bring them back to your site. But using only absolute URLs also has its problems. If you host your site on multiple Web servers or move it from one directory to another, you must recode every URL to match the new system or path names. This recoding is a long, tedious, and easily messed-up task. If your site is stationary on a single server, however, absolute URLs may work perfectly for you.

If you use relative URLs in your Web site, you have similar, but nearly opposite, benefits and drawbacks. Relative URLs give you the freedom to move your site from one server to another or from one directory to another without significant recoding. However, if users download a document to their hard drives, they can't link back to your Web site when they attempt to activate a link — instead, they get an error.

Ultimately, whatever type of URLs you use within your documents doesn't matter as long as they function properly after you get your site situated on a Web server. But here's the kicker: If you tuned and tested your site on a local or test Web server and you use absolute URLs, you must change all of them to match the new location before transferring them to the new server.

In our opinion, doing this is too much work. So we always use relative URLs in our sites when linking to our own documents and only use absolute URLs for linking to resources or other sites outside our own. We find this method the easiest to manage and troubleshoot. But if you have a different opinion, you're welcome to it (as long as you remember that you're wrong, we'll get along just fine).

Here's the bottom line for this section: If you use absolute URLs, edit your URLs to match the new Web server location. If you use relative URLs, you don't have to do much of anything.

If you use CGI programs and other multimedia enhancements, you may be using absolute URLs in the call and response parameters for these items. In some cases, you won't have any choice but to use absolute URLs. Please, maintain a list of such "must be absolute" URLs so you can remember to update and change them when you post your pages to a public Web server!

Elbow Room

If this section isn't obvious, then maybe Web site hosting is a bit outside your experience. To post a Web site so that the public can access it, you must have space (that's hard drive space) on a Web server somewhere. Usually, an Internet Service Provider (ISP) gives or offers its users space to post their Web sites, but you must contact your ISP to uncover all the details of their Web hosting configurations and requirements.

If you don't already have an ISP, you must establish a business relationship with one right away. You can find more details on that process in Chapter 19 of our companion book *MORE HTML For Dummies* (also from IDG Books Worldwide, Inc.). Or if you are really brave, you can try to wing it yourself.

Many Web-server, storage-space, and ISP configurations exist — way too many to even attempt to describe them all here. Even if we did chronicle them, only one or two would be of any use to you. So instead of getting long-winded (which we *never* do), we just talk about a few common setups and let you get the specifics from your own ISP.

You must inquire about three aspects of personal Web page server configuration: your personal URL, your storage space location (and how to access it), and the Web server's default document name.

Most of the common configurations result in a personal Web page URL of

```
www.isp.com/~username
www.isp.com/username
www.isp.com/user/username
```

The Web server and the particular configuration of the ISP determine the actual syntax for your personal or business Web page's URL. Also, you need to ask your ISP what URL to use to access your Web site.

The storage space that an ISP grants to its users to post Web pages can be situated and arranged in a variety of ways. You need to ask your ISP for the specifics. Usually, you find one of two setups for this — storage beneath a home directory or storage on some dedicated Web server.

If your pages will be stored beneath your home directory, you must create a sub-directory with a specific name, such as "public-web" or "wwwhome." This name is programmed into the ISP's Web server so that when your URL is requested, the server knows it must extract your Web documents from that location. This directory essentially defines your Web site's root directory, which means that users can't access any data located outside it.

If your Web site resides on a dedicated Web server, this puts you in a situation where your ISP creates a directory for you on a remote hard drive. That directory defines your Web site's root. When your URL is requested, the Web server goes to that directory to extract your Web documents.

There are at least two more hosting configurations, but they do involve quite a bit more cost and work. One method is to acquire your own unique domain name. We discuss this process in more depth in Part IV of the companion book *MORE HTML For Dummies*. But if you just can't wait, call your ISP and ask them to give you a hand in obtaining your own domain name. You could be the proud owner of www.myoldbackporch.com where cyber-rednecks from across the world can gather to spit and yap on about getting drunk and pinching waitresses.

The second hosting configuration is to "co-locate" your own machine at an ISP's offices and obtain a domain name. This option is beyond the scope of this book *and* the companion book. However, we wrote another excellent book on the subject that covers these topics at length: *Building Windows NT Web Servers,* by Ed Tittel, Mary Madden, and David B. Smith (IDG Books Worldwide, Inc., 1996. ISBN: 0-7645-8004-3).

Finally, you must know the Web server's default document name. All Web servers include a configuration option that defines a name for an HTML document to load if one is not specified in a URL. The default name can be anything, but the most common names are index.html and default.html. Be sure to check with your ISP to find out exactly which name they use.

Why is this important? If users access your site but fail to include a filename and you don't provide a default document, they may get an error or a listing of your Web root's directory listing. Both responses are unacceptable. Instead, set up your site so a document is always loaded into a user's browser whether or not they name a specific document. You can accomplish this in one of two ways:

✔ Name your front page, home page, or main document using the default document name.

✔ Create a symbolic link between the default document name and the real front page, home page, or main document. This requires shell access into a Web directory, which many ISPs do not permit. But if you do have such access, the UNIX command to establish a symbolic link is

```
ln -s yourdocumentname.html default.html
```

Throwing Caution to the Wind

If you're ready to read this section, then you've prepared your site as much as you can (that is, if you've done as we state in the other sections of this chapter). Now you must transfer your Web site's files from a local drive to your Web server (wherever it might be). This may be difficult, but you won't get confused.

To move files from a local hard drive to a storage area at your ISP's site, you must use an *FTP* utility. FTP stands for *File Transfer Protocol* and is the primary method for transporting files across the Internet. FTP is like copying files to a floppy from your hard drive, but you use FTP to move files from your hard drive, over your Internet connection, to a storage area at the ISP.

Therefore, you must obtain and install one of these two types of FTP utilities on your computer: command-line and GUI utilities. It doesn't matter what kind you get as long as you can use it. Command-line versions require you to learn ugly and obtuse commands to perform file transfers, while GUI versions make the process much easier. If you want to learn a command-line version, get yourself a good UNIX book, read an FTP FAQ (see URL below), or read the program's help file.

```
ftp://rtfm.mit.edu/pub/usenet/news.answers/ftp-list/faq
```

We suggest you skip the pain and get a GUI FTP utility. Here are some great recommendations:

✔ For Windows: ipswitch's WS_FTP Pro: www.ipswitch.com/

✔ For Macintosh: Dartmouth's Fetch: www.dartmouth.edu/pages/softdev/fetch.html

Sorry, UNIX users, you have so many variants of the OS that we can't make a general recommendation for a GUI FTP. Unless you can find one, you are probably stuck with command-line FTP (but if you were really afraid of command-line utilities, you wouldn't be using UNIX in the first place).

Both of the previously mentioned GUI FTP utilities are easy to use, and their Web sites (and the utilities themselves) include extensive documentation about their use. Please take some time to read it.

No matter what type of FTP utility you use, you must know some important pieces of information. You must ask your ISP about many of these tidbits, but since you've no doubt already developed great rapport with them, asking a few more questions shouldn't be a big deal.

You must obtain the following information:

- ✔ The domain name or IP address for the FTP server that will receive your file uploads — this may be a Web server, a user host, or some other machine on their network. It will often have its own domain name, such as ftp.isp.com, but not always.

- ✔ A username and password to gain access — most often this will be your account name and password, but sometimes a unique name and/or password is required for FTP access to improve overall security. Remember, you probably (and most likely) will only have full control access (the ability to write and delete files) in your home directory, as opposed to root access.

- ✔ The name and path for a Web root directory into which you must place your files. This could be a subdirectory beneath your home directory with a name like "public-web" or a directory that takes your username on a dedicated Web server. Either way, you must know the exact name and path to deposit your files in the right place.

Here are the general steps involved in uploading your Web files to your ISP Web directory (we assume you've already established a PPP link to the Internet, otherwise the following steps will not work):

1. **Launch your FTP utility.**

2. **Contact the FTP server by providing its domain name or IP address to the FTP utility.**

3. **When prompted, input the username and password needed to gain access.**

   Depending on your FTP utility, you either enter this information at the same time as the domain name or you enter it when prompted.

4. **After you acquire access, traverse the directory structure to locate the path and assigned Web root directory.**

5. **If the Web root directory does not yet exist, create it by using the proper naming convention that your ISP mandates.**

6. **If you are unable to create the directory or the directory does not already exist, contact your ISP for help.**

7. **Locate the Web files on your local hard drive.**

8. **Initiate transfer of the files.**

   If you did not use subdirectories in your site, no additional transfer configuration is needed.

   If you used subdirectories and an FTP utility that supports directory tree transfer, be sure to command the utility to transfer and maintain the directory tree structure.

   If you used subdirectories and an FTP utility that does not support directory tree transfer, you must manually create each subdirectory and transfer the contents of these directories one at a time.

9. **Close the FTP connection.**

10. **Close the FTP utility.**

As we discussed earlier in this chapter about the default document name, if you need to create a symbolic link to the main document on your site, do so at this time by Telnetting to the site and by using the "`ln`" command. (Telnet is a terminal emulation program that enables you to perform functions on a computer remotely.)

You may also need to perform similar steps to upload CGI or special multi-media files that do not reside beneath the standard Web root. Contact your ISP to learn exactly how and where to post such files.

Final Exam

After you transfer your Web files to the ISP's Web server, or whatever location you must use, it's time to start testing all over again. The first thing you must do is launch your Web browser and attempt to access your newly situated Web site using your new URL.

If you can't access your documents or your site acts strangely, double-check that you transferred all the files and that you assigned the proper default document name. If the problem still persists, contact your ISP for help. The problem is probably some little configuration setting on their end that they forgot to tell you about.

After you are satisfied that your site is functioning properly and ready for worldwide access, you should inform the world about its existence (and location). A "build it and they will come" mentality doesn't really work on the Internet because no one goes anywhere unless they know the address (or can use a search utility that finds addresses for them). The only way around this is to post "press releases" of your own and to contact search engine sites to request the addition of a link to your new paradise. We detail this process in Chapter 20 of our companion book *MORE HTML For Dummies*.

That's it for the formal content of our book. If you haven't yet, please read on to find the *...For Dummies* famous "Part of Tens," wherein we do our best to summarize the key points of this book in the most side-splitting fashion possible.

 Also, don't forget to check out the Extras on the CD-ROM, where you find information about HTML frames, CGI, testing, feedback-solicitation techniques, and information about more HTML-related tools and techniques than you can shake a stick at! Enjoy. . . .

Part IV
The Part of Tens

The 5th Wave   By Rich Tennant

Andy soon began to think he shouldn't have opted for the cut-rate Web hookup after all.

In this part . . .

Here, we cover the do's and don'ts for HTML markup, help you rethink your views on document design, and help you catch potential bugs and errors in your pages. Enjoy!

Chapter 17

HTML's Top Ten Do's and Don'ts

*B*y itself, HTML is neither excessively complex nor overwhelmingly difficult. As better wags than we have put it: "This ain't rocket science!" Nevertheless, it's good to have a set of guidelines to help you make the most of HTML without stepping away from your need to communicate effectively with your users.

This chapter attempts to underscore the fundamental points that we made throughout this book regarding proper and improper use of HTML. We hope that you adhere to the prescriptions and avoid the maledictions. But hey, they're your pages and you can do what you want with them. The users will decide the ultimate outcome! (Just don't make us say, "We *told* you so!")

Remembering Your Content!

Darrell Royal, the legendary coach of the University of Texas Longhorn football team in the '60s and '70s, is rumored to have said to his players, "Dance with who brung ya." In normal English, we think this means that you should stick to the people who've supported you all along and give your loyalty to those who've given it to you.

We're not sure what this means for football, but for Web pages it means keeping the content paramount. If you don't have strong, solid, informative content, users quickly realize that your Web pages are relatively content-free. Then they'll be off elsewhere on the Web looking for the content your pages may have lacked.

Above all, this means placing your most important content on the site's major pages, and frills and supplementary materials on secondary pages. The short statement of this principle for HTML is, "Tags are important, but what's between the tags — the content — is what really counts." Make your content the very best it can possibly be!

Structuring Your Documents

Providing users with a clear road map and guiding them through your content is as important for a home page as it is for an online encyclopedia. But the longer or more complex a document grows, the more important a road map becomes. This map ideally takes the form of a flow chart that shows page organization and links, or it could even appear in graphic form on an orientation page for your site.

We're strong advocates of top-down page design. You should start the construction of any HTML document or collection of documents with a paper and pencil (or whatever modeling tool you like best). Sketch out the relationships within the content and the relationships among your pages. Don't start writing content or placing tags until you understand what you want to say and how you want to organize your materials.

Good content flows from good organization. It helps you stay on track during page design, testing, delivery, and maintenance. And organization helps your users find their way through your site. Need we say more? Yes! Don't forget that organization changes over time: Revisit and critique your organization and structure on a regular basis, and don't be afraid to change either to keep up with changes in your content or focus.

Keeping Track of Tags

While you're building documents, it's often easy to forget to use closing tags when required (for example, the </A> that closes the opening anchor tag <A>). Even when you're testing your pages, some browsers can be so forgiving that they compensate for your lack of correctness, leading you into possible problems from other browsers that aren't quite so understanding (or lax, as the case may be).

Also, despite the claims from the vendors of HTML authoring tools that "you don't even have to know any HTML," the HTML is still a big part of what makes Web pages work. Ensuring that things are correct and complete is something only you can ensure for your documents, whether you build them yourself, or a program builds them for you.

We can say lots of things about this, but we'll stick to the ones that count:

✔ Keep track yourself while you write or edit HTML by hand. If you open an anchor, or text area, or whatever, go back through and find the closing tag for each opening one. Most tools do this for you.

✔ Use a syntax-checker to validate your work as part of the testing process. These are mindless, automatic tools that find missing tags for you and also find other ways to drive you crazy along the way! Use these whether you build pages by hand or with software assistance.

✔ Here's a URL that's a jump page for HTML validation tools: www.charm.net/~web/Vlib/Providers/Validation.html.

✔ Try to obtain and use as many browsers as you possibly can when testing your pages. This not only alerts you to missing tags; it can also point out potential design flaws or browser dependencies (covered in a section later in this chapter). This exercise also emphasizes the importance of ALTernate text information. That's why we always check our pages with Lynx (a totally character-mode browser).

✔ Always follow HTML document syntax and layout rules. Just because most browsers don't require tags like <HTML>, <HEAD>, and <BODY> doesn't mean you can omit them; it just means they don't care if you do. Your users may, the spiders will, and we don't want you writing any improperly structured HTML, either!

Although HTML isn't exactly a programming language, it still makes sense to treat it like one. Therefore, following formats and syntax helps avoid trouble, and careful testing and rechecking of your work ensures a high degree of quality and standards compliance.

Making the Most from the Least

More is not always better, especially when it comes to Web pages. Try to design and build your pages using minimal ornaments and simple layouts. Don't overload pages with lots of graphics, add as many levels of headings as you can cram in, and create oodles of links of every possible description.

Remember that structure exists to highlight content. The more structure dominates, the more it takes away from content. Therefore, use structure sparingly, wisely, and as carefully as possible. Anything more becomes an obstacle to delivering content. This means: Stay away from excessive use of graphics, links, and layout tags!

Building Attractive Pages

Working within a consistent framework teaches users how to view and navigate within your pages. Making them easy to navigate only adds to their appeal. If you need inspiration, cruise the Web and look for layouts and graphics that work for you. If you take the time to analyze what you like about them, you can work from other people's design principles without having to steal details from their layouts and looks.

When designing Web documents, start with a fundamental page layout. Pick a small but interesting set of graphical symbols or icons and adopt a consistent navigation style. Use graphics sparingly and make them as small as possible (by reducing size, number of colors, shading, and so on), while still retaining their eye appeal. Use simple, consistent navigation tools throughout. You can make your pages both appealing and informative, if you're willing to invest sufficient time and effort.

Avoiding Browser Dependencies

When building Web pages, the temptation to view the Web in terms of your favorite browser is hard to avoid. That's why you should always remember that users view the Web in general and your pages in particular, from many different perspectives, through many different browsers.

During the design and writing phases, it's common to ping-pong between HTML and a browser's eye-view of your work. At this early point in the process, we recommend switching among a group of browsers, including at least one character-mode browser. This helps balance how you view your pages and helps keep your focus on content.

During testing and maintenance, you must browse your pages through many different points of view. Make sure to work from multiple platforms; try both graphical and character-mode browsers on each page. Such testing takes time but repays itself with pages that are easy for everyone to read and follow. It also helps viewers who come at your materials from a different platform than your own, and helps your pages achieve true platform (as well as browser) independence.

Evolution, Not Revolution

Over time Web pages change and grow. Keep a fresh eye on your work, and keep recruiting fresh eyes from the ranks of those who haven't seen your work before, to avoid the process of what we call "organic acceptance."

This concept is best explained by the analogy of your face and the mirror: You see it every day, you know it intimately, so you won't be as sensitive as someone else to the impact of changes over time. Then you see yourself on video, or a photograph, or through the eyes of an old friend. At that point, changes obvious to the world become obvious to you as you exclaim, "I'm bald!" or "I've gone completely gray" or "My spare tire could mount on a semi!"

Just as with the rest of life, changes to Web pages are evolutionary, not revolutionary. They usually proceed with small daily steps, not big radical ones. Nevertheless, you must remain sensitive to the supporting infrastructure and readability of your content as your pages evolve. Maybe the lack of on-screen links to each section of the Product Catalog didn't matter when you only had three products; now that you have 25, it's a different story. Over time, structure needs to adapt to follow the content. If you regularly reevaluate your site's effectiveness at communicating its contents, you'll know when it's time to make changes, both large and small.

This is where user feedback is absolutely crucial. If you don't get feedback through forms or other means of communication, you should go out and aggressively solicit from your users. "If you don't ask," goes the old saying, "you can't tell how you're doing!"

Navigating Your Wild and Woolly Web

Aids to navigation are key ingredients when building quality Web. In Chapter 14, we introduce the concept of a *navigation bar* to provide users with a method to avoid or minimize scrolling. By judicious use of links and careful observation of what constitutes a "screenful" of text, text anchors can make it easy to move to "previous" or "next" screens, as well as to "top," "index," and "bottom" in any document.

We believe pretty strongly in the *low scroll* rule: That is, users should have to scroll *no more than one* screenful in either direction from a point of focus or entry without encountering a navigation aid to let them jump (not scroll) to the next point of interest.

We don't believe that navigation bars are required or that the names for controls should always be the same. We do believe that the more control you give users over their reading, the better they like it. The longer any particular document gets, the more important such controls become. We find that controls work best if they occur about every twenty lines in longer documents (or in a separate, always visible frame, if you use HTML frames).

Beat the Two-Dimensional Text Trap

Conditioned by centuries of printed material and the linear nature of books, our mindsets can always use adjustment. When building documents, remember that hypermedia should add interest, expand on the content, or make a serious impact on the user. Within these constraints, this kind of material can vastly improve any user's experience of your site.

If you avoid old-fashioned linear thinking, you may not only succeed in improving your users' experience, you may even make your information more readily available to your audience. That's why we encourage careful use of document indexes, cross-references, links to related documents, and other tools to help users navigate within your site. Keep thinking about the impact of links and looking at other people's materials, and you may yet shake free of the linear trap imposed by Gutenberg's legacy (the printing press)! If you're looking for a model for your site's behavior, don't think about your great new trifold four-color brochure; think about how your customer service people interact with new customers on the telephone ("What can I do to help you today?").

Overcoming Inertia Takes Constant Vigilance

Finally, when dealing with your Web materials post-publication, remember that your tendency is to goof off. Maintenance is nowhere near as heroic, inspiring, or remarkable as creation, yet it represents the bulk of the activity that's needed to keep a living document alive and well.

Make maintenance a positive term and look for ways to improve its perception. Start with something valuable and keep adding value, and a site appreciates over time. Start with something valuable and leave it alone, and a site soon becomes stale and loses value.

Keeping up with constant change translates into creating (and adhering to) a regular maintenance schedule. Make it somebody's job to spend time on the Web site regularly and check to make sure the job's getting done. If someone is set to handle regular site updates, changes, and improvements, they start flogging other participants to give them things to do when scheduled site maintenance rolls around. The next thing you know, everybody's involved in keeping information fresh, just like they should be. This keeps your visitors coming back for more!

Chapter 18
Ten Design Desiderata

*W*hen building a Web site, you must know what you want to communicate. The content must always remain king. Nevertheless, we'd like to suggest a bevy of design desiderata to consider when laying out your pages. As long as you remember that these things play a supporting, not a starring, role, you won't get yourself into too much trouble.

Creating Page Layouts

When building or renovating a site, your first design efforts should focus on a common layout for your pages. Layout involves deciding whether to use text links or graphical controls, and also involves setting styles for page headings and footers. For ambitious designers, it may even mean building a Cascading Style Sheet to govern layout and typography for your site's pages. It may even involve establishing a set of *framing rules* to lay out common page areas and elements, if you choose to use HTML frames.

Headings can incorporate text navigation or other information that you want to make consistent on all pages. Footers should include contact information and an original URL for reference, preceded by a horizontal rule (or packaged in their own compact frames).

Some organizations go so far as to lay down a border for each page, with the area above the frame used as a header and the area below as a footer. Whatever layout you choose, make it as attractive as you can (without making it distracting) and use it consistently. Doing this helps create a welcome feeling of familiarity across your pages that, in turn, helps users find their way around your site. The CNET site (at `www.cnet.com`) is a good example of a good-looking, consistent site layout.

Building a Graphical Vocabulary

If you use graphics for navigation, keep icons or buttons as small and simple as possible. Using such graphics reduces transfer time and makes them display faster.

Building a small, consistent set of graphical symbols (what we call a *vocabulary*) also improves browser efficiency: Most browsers cache graphics so that they don't have to be downloaded after they first appear (for that session). It's much faster to reuse an existing graphic than to download a new one. That's why we advocate a fairly limited graphics vocabulary.

Supply ALT text definitions for graphical elements when you reference them. This keeps users with character-mode browsers from being left in the lurch. Such graphical elements should be simple enough that a single word or short phrase can substitute for, yet still deliver, the same meaning and impact.

Using White Space

While content may be king in Web pages, you can have too much of a good thing. Don't try to limit the amount of scrolling by eliminating headings and paragraph breaks.

White space is the term used by page designers to describe the space on a page that's unoccupied by things like graphics and type. A certain amount of white space is critical for the human eye to function well. In general, the more complex or convoluted the images or content, the more positive the effect of white space on a page.

Be sure to give your content and images room to breathe by leaving at least 20 percent of any screen unoccupied. You can build white space into your documents by using alignment attributes on graphics, by using headings to separate regions of text and graphics, or by building a style sheet that controls line spacing and white space for all kinds of tags. Whatever method you use, give readers plenty of room to follow your lead through your pages!

Formatting for Impact

HTML includes a variety of descriptive (<EM>, <STRONG>, <CITE>, and so on) and physical (<I>, <B>, <TT>, and so on) character tags. It also employs larger fonts and text styles to set headings off from ordinary text. When you use these controls, remember that emphasis and impact are relative terms: In fact, the less often you use such tags, the more impact they have. In the wake of Cascading Style Sheets, we think working with STYLE attributes may often make more sense than using such tags.

Overuse of character-handling, whether descriptive, stylistic, or physical, can blunt any document's overall impact. Be sure to use such controls only where impact is critical.

When deciding how to place emphasis on text elements, be aware that certain browsers provide wider options for descriptive tags than physical tags, and that style definitions have the widest latitude of all. Physical tags are often associated with certain fonts (for example, monospaced Courier is typical for <TT>). Descriptive tags are often associated with identical characteristics, but can also be represented by other fonts or text colors, especially for graphical browsers. Style tags give designers complete control over text appearance and layout, but can be overridden by savvy users. Thus, you must consider which — appearance or emphasis — is more important: If it's appearance, use a physical style; if it's emphasis, use a logical one or a style definition.

Enhancing Content

If a picture is worth a thousand words, are a thousand words worth a picture? When combining text and graphics in Web pages, emphasize the relationship between the two in the content. Graphics can be especially useful when diagramming complex ideas, when representing physical objects or other tangible phenomena, and when compressing large amounts of content into a small space.

But surrounding text needs to play off graphics, to use them as a point of reference, and to refer back to key elements or components as they're discussed. This makes labels, captions, and other methods for identifying graphical elements almost as important as the graphic itself. Careful integration of text and graphics enhances the content.

The same is true for other hypermedia within Web pages. Beyond the novelty of including sounds or music, animation, or video, the content that these media can deliver must be carefully integrated with the text to create the greatest impact.

Instead of explaining a leitmotif purely with text, the Web makes its possible to define, and then discuss, a leitmotif around a musical phrase from a symphony or string quartet. Likewise, discussion of film-editing techniques, like dissolves, can be amplified with examples taken from the work of classic directors.

Whatever materials appear in or through your Web pages, they should be solidly integrated and share a common focus. This applies as strongly to hypermedia as it does to text, but all the Web's possibilities to enhance content should be fully exploited.

Making Effective Use of Hypermedia

Strong integration of hypermedia with other content is the most important ingredient for its effective use. But Web designers must also understand the potential bottlenecks that some users face, when users must interact with hypermedia to fully appreciate a page.

Effective use of hypermedia, therefore, implies asking your users for *informed consent* before inflicting such materials on them. For graphics, this means preparing thumbnails of large images, labeling them with file sizes, and using them as hyperlinks to let users request a download of a full-sized image. In other words, users who decide to pull down a full-color image of *The Last Supper* cannot complain when they already know it's a 1.2MB file that may take several minutes to download. By the same token, including such an image on a Web page without asking permission irritates those who merely wanted information.

This principle applies equally to sounds, video, and other kinds of hypermedia. Remember to ask for informed consent from your users, and you can be sure that only those individuals who can stand the wait will be subjected to delivery delays.

Aiding Navigation

Including outlines, tables of contents, indexes, or search engines in your Web documents makes it easier for users to find their way around your materials. So why not use them?

Forming Good Opinions

We think no Web site is complete without an interactive HTML form to ask users for their feedback. Feedback not only gives you a chance to see your work from somebody else's perspective, but also serves as a valuable source of input and ideas to enhance and improve your content. Remember, "If you don't ask, they won't tell you!"

Knowing When to Split

As pages get larger, or as your content grows oversized, you may come to a point where a single, long document would function better as a collection of smaller documents.

How can you decide when it's time to split things up? By trading off convenience against impatience. A single, long document takes longer to download and read than any individual smaller one, but each time a user requests an individual document, it may have to be downloaded on the spot. The question then becomes "One long wait, or several short ones?"

The answer lies in the content. If your document is something that's touched quickly and then exited immediately, delivering information in small chunks makes sense. The only people who suffer delays are those who choose to read many pages; in-and-outers don't have to wait much. If your document is something that's downloaded and perused in detail, it may make sense to keep large amounts of information within a single document.

By using your materials frequently yourself (make sure to use them over a slow link as well as a fast one) and by asking users for feedback, you should be able to strike a happy medium between these extremes, as soon as one wanders by!

Adding Value for Value

Obtaining feedback from users is incredibly valuable and makes HTML forms all the more worthwhile. But responding to that feedback in a visible, obvious way can make the experience as good for the respondents as it should be for you.

Publicly acknowledging feedback that causes change is a good idea, whether for reasons good or ill. The "What's New" page that links to many home pages (and maybe on yours, too) is a good place to make such acknowledgments. We also believe in acknowledging strong opinions by e-mail or letter to let respondents know that you heard what they said and to thank them for their input.

If you cultivate your users as allies and confederates, they help you improve and enhance your content. These improvements, in turn, could lead to improved business or maybe just to improved communications. Either way, by giving valuable information and acknowledging the value of other people's contributions, you add to the total value of the Web itself!

Chapter 19

Nearly Ten Ways to Exterminate Web Bugs

● ●

In This Chapter

▶ Making a list and checking it twice

▶ Mastering the mechanics of text

▶ Lacking live links leaves loathsome legacies

▶ Looking for trouble in all the right places

▶ Covering all the bases

▶ Tools of the testing trade

▶ Fostering feedback

▶ Making the most of your audience

● ●

*W*hen you put the finishing touches on a set of pages, it's time to put them through their paces. Testing is a key ingredient that helps control your content's quality. Testing should include a thorough content review, a complete analysis of HTML syntax and semantics, checks on every possible link, and a series of sanity checks to make doubly sure that what you built is what you really wanted. Read on for some gems of testing wisdom to rid your Web pages of bugs, errors, and other undesirable elements.

Make a List Then Check It — Twice

Your design should include a road map for all individual HTML documents in your site, and the relationships among them. If you're smart, you kept this up-to-date as you moved from design to implementation (and in our experience, things always change when you go down this path). If you're not smart, don't berate yourself — go out and update the map now. Be sure to include all intra- and interdocument links.

A road map can serve as the foundation for a test plan, wherein you systematically investigate and check every page and every link. You want to make sure that everything works as you think it does and that what you built has some relationship, however surprising, to what you designed. This road map defines your list of things to check, and as you go through the testing process, you'll check it (at least) twice.

Mastering the Mechanics of Text

By the time any collection of Web pages comes together, you're typically looking at thousands of words, if not more. Yet the number of Web pages that are published without even a cursory spelling check is astonishing. That's why we suggest — no, demand — that you include a spelling check as a step in testing and checking your materials.

You can use your favorite word processor to spell-check your pages. Before you check them, add HTML markup to your custom dictionary, and pretty soon, the program pukes only on URLs and other strange strings that occur from time to time in HTML files.

Or, if you'd prefer, you can try out one of the several HTML-based spell-checking services now available on the Web. We like the one you can find at

`www2.imagiware.com/RxHTML/`

If Dr. HTML's spell-checker doesn't work for you, visit one of the search engines available at `www.search.com`, and use *spell-check* as a search string. For us, a recent visit to Yahoo! turned up over half-a-dozen likely looking candidates. Nevertheless, you must persist and root out all real typos and misspellings. Your users may not thank you, but they'll have a higher opinion of your pages if they don't find them full of errors!

Lacking Live Links Leaves Loathsome Legacies

Nothing is more irritating to users than when a link to some Web resource on a page that they're dying to read produces the dreaded `404 Server not found` error, instead of "the good stuff." Our unscientific and random sampling of users shows us that users' impressions of a set of pages is strongly proportional to the number of working links they contain.

The moral of this survey: Always check your links. This is as true after you publish your pages as it is before they're subjected to public scrutiny. Checking links is as important for page maintenance as it is when testing initial pages for release. If you're smart, you'll hire a robot to do the job for you: They work incredibly long hours, don't charge much, and faithfully check every last link in your site (or beyond, if you let them loose).

We're rather fond of a robot named MOMspider, created by Roy Fielding of the W3C. Visit MOMspider's home page at

```
www.ics.uci.edu/WebSoft/MOMspider
```

This spider takes a bit of work to use, but you can set it to check only local links, and it does a bang-up job of catching stale links before users do. If you don't like this tool, try a search engine with "robot" or "spider" as your search term. You'll find lots to choose from! The best thing about robots is that you can schedule them to do their jobs at regular intervals: They always show up on time, always do a thorough job, and never complain.

Another hint: If a URL points to one page that immediately points to another, that doesn't mean you should leave that link alone. If your link-checking shows a pointer to a pointer, do yourself and your users a favor by updating the URL to point directly to the content's real location. You save users time and reduce bogus traffic on the Internet, too.

If you must leave a URL active even after it's become passé, you can instruct newer browsers to jump straight from the old page to the new one by including the following HTML in the old document's <HEAD> section:

```
<META HTTP-EQUIV="REFRESH" CONTENT="0; URL=http://
www.lanw.com/html4dum">
```

This tells a sufficiently new enough browser that it should refresh the page, where the delay before switching to the new page is specified by the number to the left of the semicolon in the CONTENT string, and the destination URL by the string to the right of URL= in the same string. If you must build such a page, be sure to include a plain vanilla link in its <BODY> section, too, so that users with older browsers can follow the link manually, instead of automatically.

Looking for Trouble in All the Right Places

You and a limited group of users should test your site before you let the rest of the world know about it; this process is called *beta-testing*. When it comes to beta-testing your site, bring in as rowdy and refractory a crowd as you can possibly find. If you have customers or colleagues who are picky, opinionated, pushy, or argumentative, be comforted to know that such people make ideal beta-testers.

They use your pages in ways you never imagined possible. They interpret your content to mean things that you never intended in a million years. They drive you crazy and crawl all over your most cherished beliefs and principles.

These colleagues also find gotchas, big and small, that you never knew were there. They catch typos that the word processors couldn't. They tell you things you left out and things that you should have omitted. They give you a whole new perspective on your Web pages, and they help you to see them from extreme points of view.

The results of all this suffering, believe it or not, are positive. Your pages emerge clearer, more direct, and more correct than they would have if you'd tried to do all the testing yourself. If you don't believe us, try skipping this step, and see what happens when the real users start banging on your site! Beta-testing is a must for a well-rounded Web site, especially one intended for business use.

Covering All the Bases

If you're an individual user with a simple home page or a collection of facts and figures on your private obsession, this step may not apply. But go ahead and read along anyway — you just might learn something.

If your pages represent the views and content of an organization, chances are 100 percent that you want to subject your pages to some kind of peer and management review before publishing them to the world. In fact, we'd recommend that you build reviews into each step along the way toward building your site — starting with overall design, to writing copy for each page, to reviewing the final assembly of pages. These reviews help you avoid potential stumbling blocks. If you have any doubts about copyright matters, references, logo usage, or other important details, you may want to get the legal department involved (if you have one, that is).

It may even be a good idea to build a sign-off process into reviews so that you can prove that responsible parties reviewed and approved your materials. We hope you don't have to be that formal about publishing your Web pages, but it's far, far better to be safe than sorry. Is this covering the bases, or covering something else? You decide. . . .

Tools of the Testing Trade

When you grind through your Web pages, checking your links and your HTML, remember that automated help is available. If you check the validation tools in Chapter 16 and those that are mentioned on the CD-ROM, you'll be well on your way to finding computerized assistance to make sure your HTML is as clean and standards compliant as the freshly driven snow. (Do we know how to mix a metaphor, or what?)

Likewise, it's a good idea to investigate the Web spiders covered in Chapter 15 and use them regularly to check the links in your pages. These spiders will get back to you if something isn't current, so you know where to start looking for links that you need to fix. And while you're at it, remember to make link-checking part of your maintenance routine. In other words, schedule and use a spider at regular intervals! Arachnophobia — what's that?

Fostering Feedback

You might not think of user feedback as a form (or consequence) of testing, but it represents the best reality check that your Web pages are ever likely to get. That's why it's a good idea to do everything you can — including prizes or other tangible inducements — to get users to fill out HTML forms on your Web site.

That's also why it's even better to read all the feedback that you do get. Go out and solicit as much as you can handle (or more). But the best idea of all is to carefully consider the feedback that you read and then implement those ideas that improve your Web offerings.

Making the Most of Your Audience

Asking for feedback is an important step toward developing a relationship with your users. Even the most finicky and picky of users can be an incredible asset: Who better to pick over your newest pages and to point out those small, subtle errors or flaws that they revel in finding? Working with your users can mean that some become more involved in your work and in helping guide the content of your Web pages (if not the rest of your professional or obsessional life). Who could ask for more?

Part V

Appendix

In this part . . .

The Appendix in this part details all the neat programs and examples that we include on the CD-ROM that comes with this book. The following pages are kind of like the instructions for a Christmas bicycle: You don't always have to read them, but they're handy to keep around for when you need 'em!

Appendix

About the CD

$\bullet \bullet$

*I*n this section of the book, we explain what you find on the *HTML 4 For Dummies* CD-ROM. In a nutshell, it contains the following goodies:

- ✔ A collection of Web documents built just to help you find your way around the book's materials.

- ✔ A hotlist of all the URLs mentioned in the book to make it easy for you to access any of the Web resources we mention.

- ✔ An online version of the book's glossary, to help you look up all the strange and bizarre terminology that Webheads use from time to time.

- ✔ Copies of all the HTML examples, easily accessible by chapter.

- ✔ A hyperlinked table of contents for the book to help you find your way around its many topics and treasures.

- ✔ Extra information on cool technologies like frames, CGI programs, Webmaster tools, and more.

- ✔ A collection of Common Gateway Interface (GGI) programs, built especially for you, to help add functionality to your own Web server (and to provide what we hope are sterling examples of the art of CGI programming).

How to Use the Web Pages and Examples

Regardless of what platform and operating system you run, you can view all of the material straight from the CD. To do so, you must have a Web browser installed on your system. We did not include browser software on the CD, but you can download evaluation versions of Netscape Navigator at www.netscape.com/ or Internet Explorer at www.microsoft.com/ie/. To browse the CD contents, just do the following:

1. **Launch your Web browser.**

2. **Using the Open File command in your browser's File menu, open the file \h4d4e\html4dum.htm from the CD.**

This page, shown in Figure A-1, serves as the home page for the CD and connects you to all other files.

Bonus Chapters ▶ Book URLs
FTP Resources ▶ Book Examples
Site Overview ▶ Wayfinding Toolkit
Book Contents ▶ Contact Info

Welcome to HTML for Dummies!

You have reached the *HTML for Dummies* Web Pages, a charming, and hopefully helpful, addition to the WWW universe. These pages are designed to aid you in three key areas:

● To help you find current information about HTML on the Web

● To provide working examples and code for all the Web tricks in the book

Figure A-1:
The
CD-ROM's
home page.

You won't be able to edit any of the files on the CD. To make changes and save them, you need to move the examples and templates to your local drive. To do so, simply copy the h4d4e folder to your hard drive. This transfers the entire directory structure from the CD to your computer. You'll need about 2MB of hard drive space.

The HTML 4 For Dummies Files

The top level of the *HTML 4 For Dummies* CD directory includes the following items:

- The h4d4e folder
- Folders containing installers for shareware, freeware, and trial programs
- A License Agreement text file
- A Read Me file

The h4d4e folder contains all of the Dummies HTML files, while the software folders are chock-full of trial versions of some of the best HTML editors available. License.txt includes some important end-user information and Readme.txt is a text-only version of this appendix in case you lose your book somewhere down the line.

To give you an idea of what's in each of the folders, we cover the files within them according to their home directory — and subdirectory when necessary.

The h4d4e directory contains the majority of the *HTML 4 For Dummies* files. Nearly every file in this directory ends with the extension .htm, indicating that it is an HTML document.

All in all, the best way to explore the *HTML 4 For Dummies* Web pages is to fire up your browser and point it at the file named html4dum.htm. This is the home page for the whole collection. For a complete, linked, and graphical overview of all the files on the CD, open menu.htm. Table A-1 lists the remaining top-level HTML files and a brief description of each.

Table A-1	The H4D4E Directory File Listing
File	*Description*
contact.htm	List of e-mail, home-page, and biography-page links for the authors and Webmaster
copy.htm	Important copyright information
etbio.htm	Ed Tittel's biography page
html4dum.htm	The *HTML 4 For Dummies* home page
menu.htm	A bird's-eye view of the entire page collection
npbio.htm	Natanya Pitts-Moultis' biography page
sjbio.htm	Steve James' biography page
wayfind.htm	HTML navigation information

The h4d4e directory has eight subdirectories whose names are a good indication of what you find within them.

- ✔ **contents:** contains files listing the book contents by chapter
- ✔ **examples:** contains files listing the book examples by chapter
- ✔ **extras:** contains eleven bonus chapters that cover topics including frames, CGI, and Web tools
- ✔ **graphics:** contains all the graphics used with the *HTML 4 For Dummies* Web pages
- ✔ **h4dftp:** contains compressed versions of all the Dummies files
- ✔ **cgi-bin:** contains Applescript, C, and Perl CGI scripts
- ✔ **templates:** contains a collection of templates to get you started
- ✔ **urls:** contains files listing the book URLs by chapter

The following list describes the files within these subdirectories in greater detail.

✔ **h4d4e/contents:** The file default.htm within the contents subdirectory includes a hyperlinked listing of all the chapter titles. Click on a chapter title to view a listing of its contents. The other files in the subdirectory are named ch*nn*cont.htm, where *n* is a two-digit number between 00 and 09, and are keyed to the chapters of the book. ch01cont.htm contains the table of contents listing for Chapter 1. The easiest way to navigate through these pages is to choose a chapter from default.htm to view a chapter's contents. To return to the list of chapter titles, choose "Book Contents" from the bottom image map or text navigation.

✔ **h4d4e/examples:** The file default.htm within the examples subdirectory includes a hyperlinked list of all the chapter titles. The examples folder is further broken down into subfolders that contain the individual HTML example documents for each chapter. Click on a chapter title to view a listing of the examples included from the chapter. To view a specific example, click on the example name. Each example includes the code listing from the book and shows the final rendering of the example by a Web browser. Table A-2 shows the folder name and corresponding chapter number followed by a list of the files in the folder and a description of the HTML demonstrated in each example.

Table A-2		HTML Examples	
Folder Name (Chapter Number)	**Example**	**File Name**	**Description**
ch04 (Chapter 4)	ch04ex01.	My First HTML Page	
	ch04ex02.htm	The ISR Home Page	
ch06 (Chapter 6)	comment.htm	`<!-- ... -->`	The comment tag
	doctype.htm	`<!DOCTYPE>`	The document type tag
	a.htm	`<A> ... </A>`	The anchor tag
	abbr.htm	`<ABBR> ... </ABBR>`	The abbreviation tag
	address.htm	`<ADDRESS> ... </ADDRESS>`	The address tag
	applet.htm	`<APPLET> ... </APPLET>`	The Java applet tag
	area.htm	`<AREA>`	The image map area tag
	b.htm	`<B> ... </B>`	The boldface text tag
	base.htm	`<BASE>`	The document base tag
	basefont.htm	`<BASEFONT>`	The base font tag
	bdo.htm	`<BDO> ... </BDO>`	The bi-directional algorithm tag

Folder Name (Chapter Number)	Example	File Name	Description
ch06 *(cont.)*	big.htm	`<BIG> ... </BIG>`	The bigger text tag
	blockquo.htm	`<BLOCKQUOTE> ... </BLOCKQUOTE>`	The blockquote style tag
	body.htm	`<BODY> ... </BODY>`	The document body tag
	br.htm	` `	The line break tag
	button.htm	`<BUTTON> ... </BUTTON>`	The form button tag
	caption.htm	`<CAPTION> ... </CAPTION>`	The table and form caption tag
	center.htm	`<CENTER> ... </CENTER>`	The center text tag
	cite.htm	`<CITE> ... </CITE>`	The citation text tag
	code.htm	`<CODE> ... </CODE>`	The code text tag
	col.htm	`<COL>`	The table column tag
	colgroup.htm	`<COLGROUP>`	The table column group tag
	dd.htm	`<DD>`	The definition list data tag
	del.htm	`<DEL> ... </DEL>`	The deleted text tag
	dfn.htm	`<DFN> ... </DFN>`	The definition text tag
	dir.htm	`<DIR> ... </DIR>`	The directory tag list
	div.htm	`<DIV> ... </DIV>`	The document division tag
	dl.htm	`<DL> ... </DL>`	The definition list tag
	dt.htm	`<DT>`	The definition list data term tag
	em.htm	`<EM> ... </EM>`	The emphasis text tag
	fieldset.html	`<FIELDSET> ... </FIELDSET>`	The form field set tag
	font.htm	`<FONT> ... </FONT>`	The font style tag

(continued)

Table A-2 *(continued)*

Folder Name (Chapter Number)	Example	File Name	Description
ch06 *(cont.)*	form.htm	`<FORM> ... </FORM>`	The form tag
	frame.htm	`<FRAME>`	The frame tag
	frameset.htm	`<FRAMESET> ... </FRAMESET>`	The frame set tag
	h.htm	`<H*> ... </H*>`	The heading tags
	head.htm	`<HEAD> ... </HEAD>`	The body heading tag
	hr.htm	`<HR>`	The hard rule tag
	html.htm	`<HTML> ... </HTML>`	The HTML document tag
	i.htm	`<I> ... </I>`	The italics text tag
	iframe.htm	`<IFRAME> ... </IFRAME>`	The inline frame tag
	img.htm	`<IMG>`	The insert image tag
	input.htm	`<INPUT>`	The form input tag
	ins.htm	`<INS> ... </INS>`	The inserted text tag
	isindex.htm	`<ISINDEX>`	The document index tag
	kbd.htm	`<KBD> ... </KBD>`	The keyboard text tag
	label.htm	`<LABEL> ... </LABEL>`	The form element label tag
	legend.htm	`<LEGEND> ... </LEGEND>`	The form field set caption tag
	li.htm	`<LI>`	The list item tag
	link.htm	`<LINK>`	The document link tag
	map.htm	`<MAP> ... </MAP>`	The image map coordinates tag
	menu.htm	`<MENU> ... </MENU>`	The menu list tag
	meta.htm	`<META>`	The meta-data tag
	noframes.htm	`<NOFRAMES> ... </NOFRAMES>`	The frames alternative tag

Folder Name (Chapter Number)	Example	File Name	Description
ch06 *(cont.)*	noscript.htm	`<NOSCRIPT> ... </NOSCRIPT>`	The no script tag
	object.htm	`<OBJECT> ... </OBJECT>`	The object tag
	ol.htm	`<OL> ... </OL>`	The ordered list tag
	option.htm	`<OPTION>`	The form option tag
	p.htm	`<P> ... </P>`	The paragraph tag
	param.htm	`<PARAM>`	The object or applet parameter tag
	pre.htm	`<PRE> ... </PRE>`	The preformatted text tag
	q.htm	`<Q> ... </Q>`	The quoted text tag
	s.htm	`<S> ... </S>`	The strikethrough text tag
	samp.htm	`<SAMP> ... </SAMP>`	The sample text tag
	script.htm	`<SCRIPT> ... </SCRIPT>`	The inline script tag
	select.htm	`<SELECT> ... </SELECT>`	The form selection tag
	small.htm	`<SMALL> ... </SMALL>`	The small text tag
	span.htm	`<SPAN> ... </SPAN>`	The style span tag
	strike.htm	`<STRIKE> ... </STRIKE>`	The strikethrough text tag
	strong.htm	`<STRONG> ... </STRONG>`	The strong text tag
	style.htm	`<STYLE> ... </STYLE>`	The inline style tag
	sub.htm	`<SUB> ... </SUB>`	The subscript text tag
	sup.htm	`<SUP> ... </SUP>`	The superscript text tag
	table.htm	`<TABLE> ... </TABLE>`	The table tag
	tbody.htm	`<TBODY> ... </TBODY>`	The table body tag

(continued)

Table A-2 *(continued)*

Folder Name (Chapter Number)	Example	File Name	Description
ch06 *(cont.)*	td.htm	`<TD> ... </TD>`	The table cell data tag
	textarea.htm	`<TEXTAREA> ... </TEXTAREA>`	The form text area tag
	tfoot.htm	`<TFOOT> ... </TFOOT>`	The table footer tag
	th.htm	`<TH> ... </TH>`	The table column header tag
	thead.htm	`<THEAD> ... </THEAD>`	The table header tag
	tr.htm	`<TR> ... </TR>`	The table row tag
	tt.htm	`<TT> ... </TT>`	The teletype text tag
	u.htm	`<U> ... </U>`	The underlined text tag
	ul.htm	`<UL> ... </UL>`	The unordered list tag
	var.htm	`<VAR> ... </VAR>`	The variable text tag
ch08 (Chapter 8)	ch08ex01.htm	Basic Document Template	
	ch08ex02.htm	An Unordered List	
	ch08ex03.htm	The Dummies Unordered List	
	ch08ex04.htm	Adding Hyperlinks	
	ch08ex05.htm	Footer Information	
	ch08ex06.htm	The `mailto` Link	
ch09 (Chapter 9)	ch09ex01.htm	Basic HTML Table	
	ch09ex01.htm	A Rowspan	
ch10 (Chapter 10)	ch10ex01.htm	Adding Images	
	ch10ex02.htm	Graphics within a Table	
ch11 (Chapter 11)	ch11ex01.htm	TOC Links within a Page	
	ch11ex02.htm	Links to External Resources	
	ch11ex03.htm	Naming Your Web Pages with `<LINK>`	
	ch11ex04.htm	Nesting Lists within Lists	
	ch11ex05.htm	IDG Books' *...For Dummies* Page	
ch12 (Chapter 12)	ch12ex01.htm	Reader Feedback Form	
	ch12ex02.htm	Spicy Form	
	ch12ex03.htm	The Widget Waffle Iron Survey	

Folder Name (Chapter Number)	Example	File Name	Description
ch13 (Chapter 13)	ch13ex01.htm	Linking Style Rules to Web Pages
	ch13ex02.htm	Using Classes to Specify Style
	ch13ex03.htm	The W3C's Style Sheet
ch14 (Chapter 14)	ch14ex01.htm	CERN Map File
	ch14ex02.htm	NCSA Map File
	ch14ex03.htm	Alternative Text Navigation for an Image Map
	ch14ex04.htm	A Client Side Image Map

Note: The easiest way to navigate through these pages is to choose a chapter from default.htm to view a listing of the chapters examples and select the example you would like to view. When you finish with a particular example, press the Back button in your browser window to return to the list of examples by chapter, and then select Book Examples from the bottom image map or text navigation to return to the listing of chapter titles.

✔ **h4d4e/extras:** This folder contains information on several HTML-related topics that we think you may find interesting and useful. The file default.htm serves as a table of contents for these pages. The topics and theory-related first pages are shown in Table A-3.

Table A-3	The Extras
File	**Topic**
ex01/default.htm	HTML Frames
ex02/default.htm	Extending Your Web: CGI and Other Alternatives
ex03/default.htm	Dynamic HTML
ex04/default.htm	Testing, Testing 1-2-3
ex05/default.htm	What Do the Users Think?
ex06/default.htm	Tools of the Trade: HTML and Web Publishing Tools
ex07/default.htm	Using UNIX Uniformly
ex08/default.htm	More Macintosh Madness
ex09/default.htm	Webbing Up Windows
ex10/default.htm	Webmaster's Toolbox: A Case Study
ex11/default.htm	Top Ten Build or Buy Tips
glossary/default.htm	Glossary

✔ **h4d4e/graphics:** This is the graphics subdirectory for the graphics used in the HTML documents for the *HTML 4 For Dummies* pages themselves. As its name implies, this folder houses all the .GIF (Graphics Information Files) image files in our Web pages. If we used an image in on a Web page (except the templates pages), you can find it here. All we can say further is "Help yourself!"

✔ **h4d4e/h4dftp:** To make transferring our file collections easier, we included a Web page where you'll find links to download compressed versions of the CGI, H4D4e, and template folders. Each one is available as a .zip (PC), .sea.hqx (Macintosh), and .tar (UNIX) archive to make them accessible regardless of what operating system you use. Table A-4 shows the annotated list of CGI files in each compressed archive, categorized by operating system.

Table A-4	CGI Files by Archive CGI.zip Archive (Written in C)
Script/File	*Description*
COUNTER-CGI.C	counter script
TIME_NOW	compiled current time script
ISMAPPER.C	ismapper script
ISMAPPER	compiled ismapper script
TIME-CGI.C	current time script

	CGI.sea.hqx Archive (Written in Applescript)
Script/File	*Description*
COUNTCGI.TXT	read me file for counter script
RIGHT.HTML	text page for ismapper script
MAP_DEFAULT.HTML	test page for ismaper script
MAP.GIF	test image for ismapper script
LEFT.GIF	test image for ismapper script
ISMAP-TEST.HTML	test page for ismapper script
ISMAPPER-AS.CGI.HQX	ismapper script
COUNTER.ACGI.HQX	counter script
TIME-AS.CGI.HQX	current time script

	CGI.tar Archive (Written in Perl)
Script/File	*Description*
COUNTER.FORM.HTML	test page for counter script
RIGHT.HTML	text page for ismapper script
MAP_DEFAULT.HTML	test page for ismapper script
MAP.GIF	test image for ismapper script
LEFT.HTML	test image for ismapper script
ISMAP-TEST.HTML	test page for ismapper script
ISMAPPER-CGI.PL	ismapper script
ISMAPPER.LOG	ismapper log file
ISMAPPER.CONF	ismapper conf file
COUNTER-CGI.PL	counter script
COUNTER.LOG	counter log file
TIME-CGI.PL	current time script

✔ **h4d4e/cgi-bin:** This folder contains three subfolders (Applescript, C, and Perl), each of which holds unarchived versions of the appropriate CGI files listed in Table A-4.

✔ **h4d4e/templates:** For your pleasure and convenience, we include a few simple templates to get you started on your HTML authoring adventures. The folders main page, default.htm, gives you a complete rundown on each template. The graphics subdirectory within the templates folder contains all of the graphics we used in creating the templates. As we said before, "Help yourself!"

✔ **h4d4e/urls:** The file default.htm within the urls subdirectory includes a hyperlinked listing of all the chapter titles. Click on a chapter title to view a listing of all the URLs we include in it. The other files in the subdirectory are named ch*nn*urls.htm, where *nn* is a two-digit number between 00 and 09, and are keyed to the chapters of the book. The easiest way to navigate through these pages is to choose a chapter from default.htm to view a chapter's URLs. To return to the listing of chapter titles, choose Book URLs from the bottom image map or text navigation.

The Software

In addition to the nifty files, examples, and scripts described in the previous section, we also include a small software collection to the CD as well. We hope that you find among these evaluation and shareware versions of products a set of webmaster tools that fits your needs. Because the CD is a multiplatform hybrid format, you only have access to those packages that can run on the platform you currently use. To see the other tools, you must load the CD in a computer that uses a different OS. Table A-5 details the packages and their OS information.

Table A-5	The *HTML 4 For Dummies* Software List	
Package	*Vendor*	*Platform*
Visual Page	Symantec	Win/Mac
SiteCheck	Pacific Coast Software	Win/Mac
PageMill 2.0	Adobe	Win/Mac
HomeSite 3.0	Allaire Corporation	95/NT 4.0
BBEdit Demo	Bare Bones Software, Inc.	Mac
BBEdit Lite 4.0	Bare Bones Software, Inc.	Mac
NetObjects Fusion 2.02	NetObjects, Inc.	Win/Mac

Index

● ●

Note: **References to chapters on the CD-ROM are in the following format: Extra *n*. (For example, the entry on *acceptable use* refers you to Extra 12 on the CD.)**

IDG Books Worldwide, Inc., End-User License Agreement

READ THIS. You should carefully read these terms and conditions before opening the software packet(s) included with this book ("Book"). This is a license agreement ("Agreement") between you and IDG Books Worldwide, Inc. ("IDGB"). By opening the accompanying software packet(s), you acknowledge that you have read and accept the following terms and conditions. If you do not agree and do not want to be bound by such terms and conditions, promptly return the Book and the unopened software packet(s) to the place you obtained them for a full refund.

1. **License Grant.** IDGB grants to you (either an individual or entity) a nonexclusive license to use one copy of the enclosed software program(s) (collectively, the "Software") solely for your own personal or business purposes on a single computer (whether a standard computer or a workstation component of a multiuser network). The Software is in use on a computer when it is loaded into temporary memory (RAM) or installed into permanent memory (hard disk, CD-ROM, or other storage device). IDGB reserves all rights not expressly granted herein.

2. **Ownership.** IDGB is the owner of all right, title, and interest, including copyright, in and to the compilation of the Software recorded on the disk(s) or CD-ROM ("Software Media"). Copyright to the individual programs recorded on the Software Media is owned by the author or other authorized copyright owner of each program. Ownership of the Software and all proprietary rights relating thereto remain with IDGB and its licensers.

3. **Restrictions on Use and Transfer.**

    (a) You may only (i) make one copy of the Software for backup or archival purposes, or (ii) transfer the Software to a single hard disk, provided that you keep the original for backup or archival purposes. You may not (i) rent or lease the Software, (ii) copy or reproduce the Software through a LAN or other network system or through any computer subscriber system or bulletin-board system, or (iii) modify, adapt, or create derivative works based on the Software.

    (b) You may not reverse engineer, decompile, or disassemble the Software. You may transfer the Software and user documentation on a permanent basis, provided that the transferee agrees to accept the terms and conditions of this Agreement and you retain no copies. If the Software is an update or has been updated, any transfer must include the most recent update and all prior versions.

4. **Restrictions on Use of Individual Programs.** You must follow the individual requirements and restrictions detailed for each individual program in the "About the CD" appendix of this Book. These limitations are also contained in the individual license agreements recorded on the Software Media. These limitations may include a requirement that after using the program for a specified period of time, the user must pay a registration fee or discontinue use. By opening the Software packet(s), you will be agreeing to abide by the licenses and restrictions for these individual programs that are detailed in the "About the CD" appendix and on the Software Media. None of the material on this Software Media or listed in this Book may ever be redistributed, in original or modified form, for commercial purposes.

5. Limited Warranty.

(a) IDGB warrants that the Software and Software Media are free from defects in materials and workmanship under normal use for a period of sixty (60) days from the date of purchase of this Book. If IDGB receives notification within the warranty period of defects in materials or workmanship, IDGB will replace the defective Software Media.

(b) IDGB AND THE AUTHORS OF THE BOOK DISCLAIM ALL OTHER WARRANTIES, EX-PRESS OR IMPLIED, INCLUDING WITHOUT LIMITATION IMPLIED WARRANTIES OF MERCHANTABILITY AND FITNESS FOR A PARTICULAR PURPOSE, WITH RESPECT TO THE SOFTWARE, THE PROGRAMS, THE SOURCE CODE CONTAINED THEREIN, AND/OR THE TECHNIQUES DESCRIBED IN THIS BOOK. IDGB DOES NOT WARRANT THAT THE FUNCTIONS CONTAINED IN THE SOFTWARE WILL MEET YOUR REQUIREMENTS OR THAT THE OPERATION OF THE SOFTWARE WILL BE ERROR FREE.

(c) This limited warranty gives you specific legal rights, and you may have other rights that vary from jurisdiction to jurisdiction.

6. Remedies.

(a) IDGB's entire liability and your exclusive remedy for defects in materials and workmanship shall be limited to replacement of the Software Media, which may be returned to IDGB with a copy of your receipt at the following address: Software Media Fulfillment Department, Attn.: *HTML 4 For Dummies,* IDG Books Worldwide, Inc., 7260 Shadeland Station, Ste. 100, Indianapolis, IN 46256, or call 800-762-2974. Please allow three to four weeks for delivery. This Limited Warranty is void if failure of the Software Media has resulted from accident, abuse, or misapplication. Any replacement Software Media will be warranted for the remainder of the original warranty period or thirty (30) days, whichever is longer.

(b) In no event shall IDGB or the authors be liable for any damages whatsoever (including without limitation damages for loss of business profits, business interruption, loss of business information, or any other pecuniary loss) arising from the use of or inability to use the Book or the Software, even if IDGB has been advised of the possibility of such damages.

(c) Because some jurisdictions do not allow the exclusion or limitation of liability for consequential or incidental damages, the above limitation or exclusion may not apply to you.

7. U.S. Government Restricted Rights. Use, duplication, or disclosure of the Software by the U.S. Government is subject to restrictions stated in paragraph (c)(1)(ii) of the Rights in Technical Data and Computer Software clause of DFARS 252.227-7013, and in subparagraphs (a) through (d) of the Commercial Computer–Restricted Rights clause at FAR 52.227-19, and in similar clauses in the NASA FAR supplement, when applicable.

8. General. This Agreement constitutes the entire understanding of the parties and revokes and supersedes all prior agreements, oral or written, between them and may not be modified or amended except in a writing signed by both parties hereto that specifically refers to this Agreement. This Agreement shall take precedence over any other documents that may be in conflict herewith. If any one or more provisions contained in this Agreement are held by any court or tribunal to be invalid, illegal, or otherwise unenforceable, each and every other provision shall remain in full force and effect.

Installation Instructions

For Mac OS users

1. **Insert the CD into your CD-ROM drive.**

   The *HTML 4 For Dummies CD* icon appears on your desktop.

2. **Double-click the *HTML 4 For Dummies CD* icon.**

   A window that reveals the contents of the CD opens.

3. **Read the Read Me First file and the License Agreement file by double-clicking their icons.**

To view the examples and templates on the CD, including the *HTML 4 For Dummies* Web page, open your Web browser and, with its Open or Open File command, open this file on the CD: HTML4DUM.HTM. This file is in the H4D4E folder at the root level of the CD (H4D4E/HTML4DUM.HTM).

To install any of the software included on the CD, double-click the folder for the program you want, and then run the program's setup or installation file.

For Windows 95 users

1. **Insert the CD in your CD-ROM drive.**

   Wait a few seconds while your CD-ROM drive reads the CD.

2. **Double-click the My Computer icon on your desktop and then double-click the icon for your CD-ROM drive.**

   A window that reveals the contents of the CD opens.

3. **Please read the ReadMe file (readme.txt) and End User License file (license.txt) by double-clicking their icons.**

To view the examples and templates on the CD, including the *HTML 4 For Dummies* Web page, follow the instructions listed for the Mac in the previous section, "For Mac OS users." To install any of the programs included on the CD, double-click the folder for the program you want, and then run the program's setup or installation file.

For more information about the CD, check out the "About the CD" appendix.

WWW.DUMMIES.COM

Discover Dummies Online!

The Dummies Web Site is your fun and friendly online resource for the latest information about ...*For Dummies*® books and your favorite topics. The Web site is the place to communicate with us, exchange ideas with other ...*For Dummies* readers, chat with authors, and have fun!

Ten Fun and Useful Things You Can Do at www.dummies.com

1. Win free ...*For Dummies* books and more!
2. Register your book and be entered in a prize drawing.
3. Meet your favorite authors through the IDG Books Author Chat Series.
4. Exchange helpful information with other ...*For Dummies* readers.
5. Discover other great ...*For Dummies* books you must have!
6. Purchase Dummieswear™ exclusively from our Web site.
7. Buy ...*For Dummies* books online.
8. Talk to us. Make comments, ask questions, get answers!
9. Download free software.
10. Find additional useful resources from authors.

Link directly to these ten fun and useful things at
http://www.dummies.com/10useful

WWW.DUMMIES.COM

For other technology titles from IDG Books Worldwide, go to
www.idgbooks.com

Not on the Web yet? It's easy to get started with *Dummies 101*®: *The Internet For Windows*® *95* or *The Internet For Dummies*®, *4th Edition*, at local retailers everywhere.

IDG BOOKS WORLDWIDE

Find other ...*For Dummies* books on these topics:

Business • Career • Databases • Food & Beverage • Games • Gardening • Graphics • Hardware
Health & Fitness • Internet and the World Wide Web • Networking • Office Suites
Operating Systems • Personal Finance • Pets • Programming • Recreation • Sports
Spreadsheets • Teacher Resources • Test Prep • Word Processing

IDG BOOKS WORLDWIDE BOOK REGISTRATION

We want to hear from you!

Register This Book and Win!

Visit **http://my2cents.dummies.com** to register this book and tell us how you liked it!

- Get entered in our monthly prize giveaway.

- Give us feedback about this book — tell us what you like best, what you like least, or maybe what you'd like to ask the author and us to change!

- Let us know any other *...For Dummies*® topics that interest you.

Your feedback helps us determine what books to publish, tells us what coverage to add as we revise our books, and lets us know whether we're meeting your needs as a *...For Dummies* reader. You're our most valuable resource, and what you have to say is important to us!

Not on the Web yet? It's easy to get started with *Dummies 101*®: *The Internet For Windows*® *95* or *The Internet For Dummies*®, 4th Edition, at local retailers everywhere.

Or let us know what you think by sending us a letter at the following address:

...For Dummies Book Registration
Dummies Press
7260 Shadeland Station, Suite 100
Indianapolis, IN 46256-3945
Fax 317-596-5498

BUSINESS AND GENERAL REFERENCE BOOK SERIES FROM IDG

COMPUTER BOOK SERIES FROM IDG